How to Raise Kids You Want to Keep

The Proven Discipline Program Your Kids Will Love (And That Really Works!)

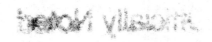

How to Raise Kids You Want to Keep

The Proven Discipline Program Your Kids
Will Love (And That Really Works!)

Jerry R. Day, Ed.D.

SOURCEBOOKS, INC.
NAPERVILLE, ILLINOIS

Published by Sourcebooks, Inc.
P.O. Box 4410, Naperville, Illinois 60567-4410
(630) 961-3900
Fax: (630) 961-2168
www.sourcebooks.com

Library of Congress Cataloging-in-Publication Data

Day, Jerry R.
  How to raise kids you want to keep : the proven discipline program your kids will love (and that really works!) / Jerry R. Day.
      p. cm.
  Includes index.
  ISBN-13: 978-1-4022-0745-7
  ISBN-10: 1-4022-0745-X
  1. Discipline of children. 2. Parenting. 3. Parent and child. I. Title.

HQ770.4.D30 2007
649'.64—dc22

                                                          2006024100

Printed and bound in the United States of America
DR 10 9 8 7 6 5 4 3

Dedication

Roena, the greatest mother ever!
Amanda and Mark, thanks for turning out to be keepable kids and wonderful adults.

Contents

Preface: Hints on How to Read This Book for Best Results. ix

Acknowledgments xiii

Chapter 1: The Secret. 1

Chapter 2: How to Create a Willingness to Live
    under Parental Authority. 25

Chapter 3: How to Build a Lasting Relationship with Your Child . . . 43

Chapter 4: The 30-Second Technique 69

Chapter 5: Pillow Talk 85

Chapter 6: The Now or Later Technique. 115

Chapter 7: How to Be a Good Dad in a Mom's World. 131

Chapter 8: The More Not Less Technique 165

Chapter 9: How to Get Your Parents to Give You
    Anything You Want (Within Reason) 183

Chapter 10: The Marks Method 195

Chapter 11: The Tell a Story Technique. 213

Chapter 12: The Scarlett O'Hara Technique 239

Chapter 13: The Poisoning the Well Technique. 251

Chapter 14: Raising the ADHD Child 263

Chapter 15: Final Thoughts 291

Index. 299

About the Author. 301

Preface

Hints on How to Read This Book for Best Results

My theoretical background was highly influenced by cognitive behavioral therapists and Milton Erickson, MD. I studied with Dr. Erickson for eleven years, and I was indelibly imprinted by his unique and nontraditional ways of interacting with children. Dr. Erickson was a genius at communicating very important life lessons in fun and irresistible ways. He was a great storyteller. If his listener was not ready for the main message of the story, the story remained just a story. However, if the child and parent listeners were ready for the lesson, the story became a powerful teaching tool that was almost impossible to resist. Direct advice can be ignored or resisted because the point is obvious. A story may have many points imbedded into it that are learned at the subliminal or subconscious level of awareness. As you read the stories in this book, enjoy them, but don't worry about teasing out all the various points of the story. The main point will always be clear, and the other lessons will come as you continue to read. One day I was commenting on Dr. Erickson's excellent storytelling methods, and he looked at me and said, "So, you think therapy is storytelling! Dr. Day, you have much to learn." I soon learned that good therapy is storytelling and more.

I do not spend much time delving into the background of parents or children. It isn't that I think history has no relevance, but my approach is to be a more action-oriented, teacher-counselor type of therapist.

I love to solve problems, and I like action. I like for my children and parents to leave my office with homework to do. I have developed a variety of techniques that have proven effective many times over the course of my long career. I won't spend a lot of time on *why* you should do the suggested techniques, but instead will focus on how best to do the techniques. I want you to trust that what I write about has been tested over and over with uniformly good results. You and your family will benefit from practical application, not from expanding your childrearing knowledge or philosophical background regarding various aspects of child development. This is a read-and-do book. You will learn and come to embrace the extraordinary benefits of teaching one theme to children: learn to willingly live under authority, and the joy of life is greatly enhanced.

Learning anything is accomplished either through negative reinforcement, positive reinforcement, or a combination of both. Let's look at negative reinforcement first because it is definitely the most common way to teach children to willingly live under authority. Sometimes negative reinforcement is called punishment learning, escape learning, or ordeal therapy. Most parents were raised in a home by a parent or parents who punished bad behavior in hopes of teaching the child to behave. The parent may have taken privileges away, put you in time-out, or administered a spanking. These are common punishments and are frequently sufficient to accomplish the positive goal of teaching a child to live under control. Punishment learning is a time-honored way of teaching a child; however, there are some common problems associated with punishment learning.

For punishment learning or negative reinforcement to really work, there must be three things available. First, a parent must be able to consistently catch a child doing wrong. This component is usually available to a parent. The second factor needed is the ability to deliver punishment swiftly. Parents can do this one as well. Unlike in our slow court system, in a family, a child can be caught, convicted, and punished within the same hour. There is no appeal process in the average family. What we may not have available is the third requirement: an effective method of punishment. Children have an uncanny ability to neutralize a parent's punishers. What works for one child will not necessarily work for another child. My daughter Amanda could not stand to be isolated in her room. It was truly a great punisher for her. On the other hand, my son Mark loved to be sent to his room because he could turn it into a pirate ship and sword fight the enemy. He hated to be scolded, but Amanda didn't care if we scolded her as long as she wasn't isolated. Children learn to take away their parent's punishers by saying, "I don't care." If you take away a toy they may say or think, "I don't care." If you use time-out, they may say, "I don't care." When they get to their teen years they may shorten, "I don't care" to one word—"so." By the time parents arrive in my office, their punishers may annoy the child, but they definitely do not punish the child.

Punishment works only if the punishers truly punish. If a parent applies an effective punisher and offers the child an escape into cooperative behavior, a child almost always chooses the cooperative behavior to escape the unpleasantness of the punishment. (I like to refer to negative reinforcement as escape learning.) This is how the child learns to behave in the manner his or her parents are seeking. If traditional punishers are effective for a parent, I encourage their use. I do not interfere with methods that are typically used if they are working. However, if a parent's methods have been rendered ineffective, I have developed a variety of effective methods that create an uncomfortable ordeal from which a child may escape into comfortable, cooperative behavior. The methods suggested in this book are strong methods, but all are ethical, moral, legal, and effective.

Another successful method of teaching children to live under authority is the technique of positive reinforcement. Adults and children tend to repeat any behavior that brings reward and pleasure. When a child responds to punishment by escaping the ordeal into a designated positive cooperative behavior, the new cooperative behavior must be rewarded. As you read, you will find a number of suggestions to help you to use effective positive reinforcement. Rewards programs are sensitive, and they must be applied correctly or they will not work. If the new behavior or attitude is properly reinforced, it is internalized and becomes an intrinsic part of the child's decision to live willingly under parental authority. Cooperation with parental authority results in a pleasant experience, and the child will want to repeat the behaviors that bring reward and pleasure. Chapters two and three are devoted to teaching a child to willingly live under parental authority through the application of positive reinforcement.

As you read and prepare to take action based upon what you read, keep in mind that the theory that underpins this book is that if children learn to willingly live under authority, they will grow up to be adults who can live under self-control. There are many rewards associated with the ability to live within a system of authority. The suggestions presented entail learning and understanding a wide variety of psychological tools and methods that will help a parent to teach a child to live under authority.

The best way to approach this book is to enjoy reading the teaching stories and look for the obvious meaning embedded in the story. Your subconscious will work on the more deeply embedded meanings. Enjoy the story and enjoy the meaning at various levels of understanding. Names, identifying features, and circumstances have been changed to disguise the identity of the children and their parents in all case-history presentations.

This is a read-and-do book. Apply the concepts and techniques proposed and enjoy the wonderful results. Raising children you want to keep can be a lot of fun.

Acknowledgments

I am indebted to Roena for supporting me with countless hours of patience while I wrote, edited, wrote, edited, etc. I am forever grateful to the late Dr. Milton Erickson who introduced me to escape learning. My thanks to Patsy and Tom Riley for generously letting me write in the peace and quiet of their mountain cabin. I will always be grateful to my agent, Pamela Brodowsky, who took a chance on an unknown author and made things happen. I extend my appreciation to the copy editors at Sourcebooks, Inc., for making me a better writer. Many thanks to Dorothyanne Pelte who gave me good advice and put up with my scribble writing without too many complaints. Lastly, thank you Henry Webb for being my best friend and greatest encourager.

Chapter 1

The Secret

It seems like a secret. At least I rarely hear or read about the one thing that is essential to raising kids you want to keep. This book is about the one thing parents must support, teach, and do to raise children that they will be proud to keep. The secret is teaching your child to *willingly* live under parental authority. Until your child learns to live under your authority, there is little hope that he can, as an adult, effectively live under self-control in a society of laws and rules. If he doesn't learn to willingly submit to the authority of his parents, there will be unbearable strain and tension in the home, and likely in the classroom as well. However, children who do learn to live under their parents' authority can grow up to be adults who know how to live under self-control in a complex and demanding society. The adult reward is nothing short of marvelous!

Fighting Freddie

Fighting Freddie was a young boy who was off to a poor start in life. His parents would have gladly considered a low offer from anyone willing to buy him from their family. He was loud, demanding, and very resistant to any attempts to put limits on what he wanted. Freddie didn't want to be bothered with brushing his teeth, bathing, coming in from play, eating his peas, dressing for school, cleaning his room, or going to bed. You get the idea.

Freddie was an unprincipled fighter. If his mother told him it was time to turn off the TV and get ready for bed, Freddie would start his act. In scene one, he ignored his mother's first thirty calls. In scene two, he argued loudly, using abusive put-down words like, "I hate you," "Stupid," and, "You're mean." He concluded his play with screaming, throwing anything within reach, and finally falling on the floor, immobile, like a crying boulder. His mom or dad would pick him up and take him to his room where he started his defiant act again with scene one. Freddie's clear message was, "I will do what you tell me to do, but you will have to make me do it."

Freddie was out of control. From the moment of his birth, Freddie was a tightly wound, high-energy child who sought constant stimulation. He grew increasingly more difficult for his parents to control. It was just easier to give into Freddie's ceaseless tantrums than to correct him. Fighting Freddie systematically took away the normal punishment methods parents typically use, like time-outs, restrictions, spanking, and loss of privileges. Nothing worked.

Freddie's parents were middle-class parents who held the values of hard work and family in high esteem. They did not abuse or neglect Freddie. Unfortunately, his mom was a nagger and a screamer, and his dad was short tempered, scolding, and pouty. They loved Freddie, but didn't know what to do about his attitude toward unwanted parental directives. Freddie was an equal opportunity abuser of parental authority. He would cooperate neither with his father nor his mother.

Freddie was not always bad. In fact, he was bright, curious, active, and a lot of fun until crossed. I met with the entire family and, of course, Freddie was a little angel in my office. I discovered that his dad was an easygoing, fair, and consistent man. His mom was energetic, creative, caring, and emotionally high-strung.

I chose to start with the 30-Second Technique, which is a negative reinforcement method that immediately confronts the "who's boss" issue and is over within thirty seconds. His dad liked my suggestions because they made sense to him, but when he tried to carry them out, World War III broke out. As usual, Freddie refused to comply with his dad's directives. His father became so frustrated with Freddie and me that he refused to attend any further counseling sessions.

Fortunately, Freddie's mom did not hold the same opinions, and she continued to attend counseling with Freddie. She used two of my authority control methods, the 30-Second Technique and the More Not Less Technique, and it made almost an immediate difference with little Freddie. Freddie and his mom resolved the issue of who was in charge in the family rather quickly. Freddie's behavior was so dramatically changed for the better that his dad became encouraged again and decided to employ the same techniques that were so effective for his mom. They worked equally well for Freddie's dad. For his father, we added the Now or Later Technique to help Freddie comply with chore assignments without anger. Soon Fighting Freddie became willingly compliant with his mom and dad's directives without excessive anger. His dad became less tense when around Freddie and as his son's behavior improved, he started seeing the good in Freddie. When Freddie used appropriate, cooperative replacement behavior, both his mom and dad used the rewards program they had been taught. Their relationship with Fighting Freddie markedly improved. Freddie internalized his father and mother's concepts of authority, and after a month or two he began to want to control his negative, demanding, bossy need for control. Freddie was learning to willingly live under his parents' authority and he liked it. They decided to keep Freddie!

This case history illustrates several points:

1. Success occurs when the methods and techniques discussed in the following chapters are appropriately implemented. Any parent who is ready and wants to apply the philosophy and techniques can accomplish similar results. Freddie was not a bad child or a "sick" child, but he did need direction and firm boundaries from his parents. Fortunately, Freddie's parents were equal to the task.
2. The sooner the intervention into a disruptive, failing interaction between parent and child takes place, the more quickly one can see positive results. Freddie was tough to correct at seven years old, but consider how much more difficult it would have been if Freddie had been fourteen years old. Although it is never too late, intervention is much more effective at earlier ages.
3. Either parent can effect behavioral change in the child/parent destructive cycle. Once the child begins to express a willingness to live under parental authority, it allows the parent to intervene with positive support for the child. The remarkable point to this story is that in only two months Freddie was well on his way to becoming a child his parents wanted to keep forever.

Reasons That Children Fail to Live under Authority

There are many reasons that prevent children from learning to live under their parents' authority. For example, if a child is not securely attached or bonded to one or both parents, the child learns to trust only himself and will not submit to authority. In some children, an insecure attachment is the result of difficult or traumatic experiences suffered under the care of one or both parents. Neglectful or inconsistent parent care may also produce an un-bonded child. A child under the care of a rigid, harsh, or abusive parent can-not safely submit to the authority of his parent, so he learns a system of elaborate avoidance or rebellion.

Children living with abusive or excessively harsh parents learn that they cannot depend on a present, loving, caring parent to take care of them. However, there are other, less traumatic experiences in the life of a child that can create a rebellious, selfish, or loosely attached child. Children who are given everything they want and more cannot easily submit to a parent's authority. These children learn to believe that they are royalty and that it is their birthright to get everything they desire. Parents who can't say no to their child and cannot stand to see their child experience even the slightest form of discomfort usually raise a child who cannot submit to parental authority. Children who are indulged and raised without rules, limits, or boundaries are often selfish and demanding, and may not develop an effective conscience or high moral values. Indulged, spoiled children often become adults who have dissatisfying marriages and interpersonal relationships.

The absence of bonding with and lack of trust in adults can also occur when a child has an infant or childhood physical disorder. For example, chil-dren who have chronic earaches often cannot be comforted when their ear hurts. Bonding is a system that involves a child experiencing a need, like hunger, and a caretaker meeting the need of the child. When a child cannot be comforted by having their hurt reduced by a parent, they may grow up with a distrust of adults. Authority problems are not necessarily a product of family trauma, neglect, or abuse; they may simply be a result of a chronic infantile physical illness.

Over the course of my thirty-seven years as a counseling psychologist, I have seen parents experience a great deal of shame and guilt about how their children turn out. My profession has been known to have increased that guilt by placing blame on parents when things go wrong with their child. Parents often claim that they can't explain why their child is so oppositional and rebellious.

There is a good reason for parents' confusion. One of the fundamental reasons that many children live out of control and strongly resist parental authority is found in genetics. Some children are high-energy, tightly wound kids who want constant stimulation. They always push limits. As science advances and understanding of genetics and biochemistry improves, it seems probable that we could find that the majority of our personality is genetically generated. Even if this proves to be true, much of a child's personality will still be influenced. So, even if the majority of our personality is genetically influenced, there is still a rich and fertile ground for parental influence in a child's personality development. Some children are a challenge to raise, and some are not. Many parents should not be quick to criticize themselves when a child does not cooperate with them because much of the problem may be genetically determined. The good news is that all children can learn to live under parental authority and develop a set of effective controls. Some children are more difficult than others to train, but with the right kind of techniques, every parent can make a huge difference in the way a child responds to authority.

My children were very different at birth. I watched both births and was astonished at how each child reacted differently to his/her own birth. Amanda, my firstborn, was cold. The lights were too bright and she didn't like being jostled around by doctors and nurses. She cried, kicked, wiggled, and objected for an hour or so. Mark's birth, two years later, was similar to Amanda's birth, but his reaction was very different. He looked around, cried and kicked for four or five minutes, and then went to sleep. Mark began life being more accepting of what reality brought. Amanda was strong-willed in her early years. She had an opinion about everything and wanted to have a say in everything that affected her. She loved to be in control. Mark was more compliant and was willing to more quickly agree with my directives. Mark was not a passive child but he was more accepting of authority. Each child required different parenting techniques. Amanda thrived under firm boundaries and limits; Mark was sensitive to criticism and became intimidated if I was too firm with him. Both children grew up to be exceedingly responsible and successful adults. Amanda harnessed and directed her strength and has used it productively through her work to help thousands of teenage girls. Mark is a fireman, paramedic, and captain in one of our local fire departments. He is charged with the responsibility to train and lead his firemen to save lives and help others. Both are good citizens, service-oriented, highly responsible, and extremely successful in their chosen areas of work. Each of them gives to others more than they take and both easily live under self-control and work authority, and within the rules of society. My parental goals were the same for both children—teach them to first live under the authority of their parents and second to live under self-control.

The psychological tools suggested in this book are designed to liberate and empower children, not to suppress their initiative and creativity. I do not advocate or support "breaking a child's will" and creating a timid, robot-like compliant child. In fact, children should mature with a reasonably controlled wild streak in them. I want to help a child grow into a mature adult who will stand firm for what he or she believes, take the harder but higher road, and be willing to take responsible risks. I do not want to contribute to raising a child who is "wild and irresponsible," which is what happens when a child emerges from childhood without first developing the desire and ability to live under parental authority.

My heartfelt goal for the reader is to use these tested techniques and raise children you'll want to keep. In the broader sense, my desire is to help parents raise children whom they will be proud of and, ultimately, whom society will want to keep.

Seven Benefits of Living under Authority

When a parent sets limits and teaches a child to live comfortably under his or her authority, there are at least seven remarkable benefits the child typically experiences. The benefits accrued from learning to cooperate with authority cannot be overstated; it is a very powerful concept. The following teaching stories illustrate the seven benefits that typically follow a child into adulthood.

Benefit Number One: The ability to accept wise counsel

Children who successfully learn to live under authority will not be condemned, relegated, or sentenced to learn from personal experience only. They do not have to make painful and dangerous mistakes again and again in order to learn valuable life lessons. The child who willingly lives under authority can accept counsel and advice from more experienced, wiser persons. By listening to mature adults, a child can learn to avoid poor decisions and bad judgments. In contrast, the child who only trusts herself and only listens to her own counsel is doomed to make painful, perhaps irreversible judgment errors that may negatively impact her for the entirety of her adult life. This child cannot take wise counsel from an adult because she sees advice as an attempt to control her. The child who has never learned to willingly live under authority cannot tolerate anything that sounds like, or appears to be, any form of control. This child only believes her own counsel, her own advice, her own control. She is so strongly competitive with authority figures that she turns benevolent suggestions into a win-lose competition. She will make many mistakes and judgment errors. Ideally, she will learn from her negative experiences, but frequently a child learns nothing of importance from her mistakes and is doomed to repeat them over and over. The same pattern will be repeated as an adult. Wise counsel and life experience will be of little help in the adult years. Now let's turn to Sarah's story.

Know-It-All Sarah

Fourteen-year-old Sarah did not know how to willingly live under the authority of her parents or within the rules of society. Sarah's parents had recently divorced, and Sarah had experienced anger and hurt as a result. Her unresolved anger and hurt contributed significantly to her rebellious and criminal behavior. While under house arrest for shoplifting, Sarah decided that it would be a good idea to go to a party where drugs and alcohol would be available. She was sure that the stupid police would never catch her and that her father would not turn her in, although he had fully warned her about leaving the house without permission. To Sarah's shock, her dad reported her missing from home. She was apprehended, and the results of her judgment error were disastrous for her. Sarah's sentence was more than tripled for her mistake.

Sarah's parents loved her but put few boundaries on her as a child. In her early years, she was willful, but not impossible to control. As she grew older, she became more defiant, and since she trusted only her decisions, she would not listen to the advice of her parents. She made many poor choices that resulted in bad outcomes, but her judgment did not improve despite the shabby results of her bad decisions. Counseling did not help Sarah very much. She continued to swim upstream against a swift current. Had Sarah learned to willingly live under her parents' authority as a child, she might have been capable of submitting to the rules of society.

As an adult, Sarah could not consistently hold a job for very long. She always thought she could run things better than the boss. Her interpersonal relationships were a long series of disasters. She had three more charges of shoplifting. Sarah was unable to learn from her past mistakes. As a young adult, she could not live under self-control.

Benefit Number Two: The ability to do the hard thing first

If children do not learn to live comfortably under their parents' authority, they usually find it difficult to postpone getting an immediate reward so they can get something even better later. It is difficult as an adult to get promotions at work, go to college, or serve in the military if immediate gratification cannot be postponed for something more important later on.

Don't–Bother–Me Roger

Roger is thirty-six years old and he works for the security division of a very large company. Roger walks around the perimeter of the company buildings and through the company hallways rattling door knobs on the night shift. At twenty-five years of age, he demonstrated high potential at his job with the company, and his future looked bright. His supervisors suggested that regional promotions could be obtained with good effort on his part, but Roger could never get himself organized or motivated to do what was expected by the company to qualify for promotion within the security division. He knew that he needed to take two emergency medical technical courses within the next two years to qualify for a promotion to the next level in the security promotion chain, but he never got around to taking those requisite courses. Roger did take the test for lieutenant, but he didn't pass. It never seemed to have occurred to him that in order to pass the complicated test, disciplined study would be required.

Roger would rather play softball, go to a movie, and participate in the bowling league than study for a test or take training courses. He could never discipline himself to do the hard things first so he could have something better later. Roger never learned to live under self-control. Roger has been passed over so frequently that he no longer has a bright and promising future with the company. Roger will probably never lose his job, but he is buried in mediocrity at the company.

As a child, Roger found it extremely difficult to postpone immediate reward for something much better later. Children who will not willingly submit to their parents' authority grow up to find it equally difficult to submit to their own authority. Roger knew it was in his best interest to take the required courses and pass the qualifying test, but he could not submit to his own personal directions to prepare for future promotions.

The interesting thing about Roger's situation is that he had loving, kind, and generous parents. He came from an intact home where both mother and father were family centered. His parents were not well-off, but Roger never suffered any physical deprivations. Life was good for Roger. Although well-intentioned, Roger's parents required very little from Roger. They were indulgent and could not say no to him. Roger did what he wanted to do with few, if any, consequences resulting. His parents learned to give in to Roger's demands to avoid his angry, attacking fits. Roger was a happy tyrant as a child. Although Roger had a mediocre job, he did have a steady income. He also had a social life. So what's the problem? The problem lies within Rogers's outlook on adult life. Most children who did not learn to willingly live under parental authority are not happy with their lives as adults because they know that they had the potential to live a much more exciting, productive life. Roger felt slighted and cheated as he saw others promoted ahead of him. He was frequently grumpy, irritated, and unhappy. He blamed the system, management, his wife, and children for his lack of professional progress. He was often glum, blue, discouraged, and depressed. Because of his "attitude" he lost many of his old, long-time friends. They just didn't want to be around a person who was so negative. Roger didn't think adult life was very good to him. Roger lived life convinced that he was just unlucky.

All children are naturally selfish and self-centered. Selfishness is necessary for the survival of the child. A child wants what he needs, and he wants what he wants. A child does not care if his parent is inconvenienced or put in harm's way. The child knows what he wants, and he is determined to get it. The child will take the short-term gain every time if the parent will permit it.

Roger's parents were heavy on the love side of things but just could not bear to install any brakes on Roger. To raise a child you want to keep, both love and discipline are required. As a child, Roger was never willing to live under his parents' authority. As a result, he never acquired the self-control and self-discipline that would help him succeed as an adult.

Benefit Number Three: The ability to survive and thrive under criticism

Sensitive Susan

Susan is forty-two years old and is starting her fourth teaching job in seven years. She is an excellent teacher and receives high praise for her teaching from the principal and school board. She works long hours and puts her students first.

Susan is very creative and prepares thoroughly for her class. The problem that Susan has is that she cannot accept criticism. When Susan is told to do something with which she disagrees and is required to comply with an authoritative directive, she is prone to go to the principal's office and complain bitterly about how unfair and unwelcome his directives are. Parents who take issue with her teaching methods aren't well-received either. She is frequently reported to the principal for the aggressive methods she uses to defend herself against a parent's criticism. For Susan, forming a close relationship is difficult and progressing at a professional level has been hard.

The fascinating aspect of Susan's story is that both of her parents made her submit to their authority, but their strictness often bordered on abuse. Susan eagerly sought every opportunity to secretly rebel against her parents. She was secretive, manipulative, and often lied to her parents to keep them from discovering her secret life. She sneaked out of her bedroom window at night to meet boys, she got drunk regularly, and she often lied about her whereabouts. Susan also had minor problems in school. She was bright but did not achieve up to her level of potential. She ditched classes, and on occasion would get into verbal battles with her teachers. Susan was well-liked by other students, but tended to associate with the wild and rebellious kids.

I was not surprised when Susan told me that she had never felt loved by her parents. She was convinced, as a child, that she could never please them, so it wasn't worth trying. She did overtly obey her parents because of their harsh control methods, but she did not willingly live under their authority. People who grow up without learning to submit to parental authority find it almost impossible to accept or profit from constructive criticism given by any authority figure. Susan did not feel rewarded by her parents for cooperative behavior, so she lost the motivation and desire to cooperate. She knew that she had to obey her mom and dad because she could not take care of herself yet, but she longed to get away from them. She was exceedingly angry with her parents and, over time, lost respect for them.

The point of Sensitive Susan's story is that it takes both discipline and love to truly teach a child to willingly live under authority. It is not enough to simply dominate and intimidate a child into obeying a parent's directives. A child cannot develop the willingness to live under authority if she does not feel valued, respected, or rewarded for her cooperation. A sure sign that a parent has successfully applied the concept of firm boundary setting coupled with unconditional love and respect is that a child can cooperate with authority outside of the home. When a child can voluntarily comply with directives from teachers, older adults, and law enforcement, it is a good bet that her parents successfully taught the concept of living under authority. Susan overtly complied with her parents' orders but never learned to live under self-control. She always thought that she knew best, and she was unwilling to let someone else have a significant role in directing her life. This inability to live under self-control caused Susan to have a very difficult time staying employed. Susan was simply too sensitive to tolerate even the mildest type of criticism.

Benefit Number Four: The ability to accept and give love

Doreen the Drama Queen

Doreen is the ultimate paradox. Her husband, Joel, never knows who he will wake up with on any given morning. Doreen thrives on chaos. She may be grumpy, irritable, or angry one day, and the next, she can be sweetness and light. In the morning Doreen may be a model for cooperativeness, but by nightfall Doreen can be pushy, bossy, and fault-finding. She will push Joel to the point that he threatens to leave her; she then becomes tearful, insecure, and apologetic. She is absolutely terrified of being rejected or abandoned by Joel or anyone else. Doreen is the consummate drama queen. She tests everyone's loyalty and devotion by brassy, pushy dominance. Children who have not learned to willingly live under parental authority frequently grow up to be insecure adults who believe that selfish control is an acceptable method of obtaining loving acceptance.

Doreen was raised by a very abusive mother. Her father abandoned the family when Doreen was four years old, and she never saw him again. Doreen's mom used a belt, a wooden spoon, her hand, a fly swatter, or anything handy to hit Doreen when she was frustrated. Doreen's two aunts have told her that her mother severely neglected Doreen in her first two years of life. Her mom was too busy having fun and taking care of herself to attend to Doreen. Doreen was not only physically abused and neglected, but she was also emotionally abused. Doreen's mother was strict and frightened her child into consistent compliance with her directives. Doreen was not raised in a consistently safe environment and as a result, Doreen became an insecure, untrusting adult. Doreen desperately wants to be loved and valued, but she wants these values only on her terms. She has become a demanding, manipulative woman who confuses, intimidates, and controls her husband with her acts of drama. Doreen's self-image is so damaged that she feels she must put everyone's willingness to love her to the ultimate test through her dramatic actions. For example, she has attempted suicide three times in response to some perceived neglect from Joel. Doreen does not want to be dead—she wants to be in control and to feel loved. Unfortunately, she has no clear concept of how to obtain both through positive, cooperative behavior.

Doreen suffers from a deep-seated personality disorder as a result of neglect and abuse at the hands of her mother. She learned that she could not trust her mother's authority. She learned that lying and manipulation paid rich dividends in helping her escape her mother's wrath. Doreen learned from her mother to use power tactics to bully others into compliance to her wants and demands. In her growing years, Doreen did not learn to receive or give sincere love, and she was unable, for good reason, to willingly submit to her mother's tyrannical control.

Doreen the Drama Queen is a classic example of how a child who is raised by a harsh, neglectful parent can develop one of the common personality disorders. A personality disorder is usually developed young and is deep and enduring. Childhood abuse, neglect, or abandonment frequently plays a significant role in the development of a personality disorder. Some of the adult personality disorders that I have found consistent with parents who abuse and neglect are:

1. Paranoid Personality Disorder. This disorder is characterized by a pattern of looking for rejection or harm.
2. Narcissistic Personality Disorder. These individuals are utterly selfish and self-centered, and will do anything to be the center of attention.
3. Borderline Personality Disorder. Like Doreen, these people are extremely insecure, desperately want to be loved, and collapse when threatened by abandonment. Their life is characterized by chaos.
4. Antisocial Social Personality Disorder. Adults with this disorder have no respect for the rights of others. They are usually chronic liars and display little conscience or empathy toward others.

It is clear that the stakes are high, but the point is that teaching a child to willingly live under control is the antidote for the development of such a personality disorder. Love and care coupled with firm boundaries provide the best prevention for developing a personality like Doreen's.

Benefit Number Five: The ability to help the oppressed and downtrodden

Children who learn to live under the authority of their parents are much more capable of feeling empathy for others, rendering acts of kindness toward others, and showing mercy for the oppressed. Whatever the personal sacrifice to a parent, it is worth it to guide children into adulthood possessing these marvelous qualities.

Children who fight authority have a tendency to develop a callous attitude regarding the feelings of others. They are not reluctant to ask for sacrifice from others, but feel no compunction about refusing to inconvenience themselves for others. Here is an example.

Pete the Prince

Pete grew up to be utterly selfish and unable to express true and real empathy for others. One day, when Pete was nine, his mom suggested that he help his friend mow the lawn so that they could get off to the park sooner. Little rebellious Pete said, "Why should I? What's he ever done for me?" Children who resent living under the benevolent control of a parent find it difficult to postpone immediate pleasure and reward so that better things can be obtained later. Pete had difficulty seeing how it was to his advantage to put himself out by helping his friend so he could stay longer at the highly interesting, enjoyable park.

Children who are unwilling to live under the authority of their parents frequently feel like they are victims when asked to give to others. A child who hates authority may feel put upon, maligned, and disrespected when asked to pull weeds or set the table. The hard-to-handle child does not simply feel irritable and inconvenienced. They have the attitude of a victim and challenge the right of a parent to even ask for such excessive service from them.

I met Pete when he was nine years old. Pete was the child of a single mother who went through a bitter divorce with Pete's father. Pete's mom grew up in a family that spoiled her with things. His mom felt guilt about Pete's suffering during the divorce and decided that since she could not give Pete very many material things, she could make up for the loss of his father by doing everything for Pete and expecting little from him. Because of this excessive indulgence, Pete gradually became Pete the Prince. He had few rules to guide him, and he was exceedingly rude and disrespectful to his mother. His mom cooked, cleaned, washed, provided, protected, and played with Pete, but Pete had zero appreciation for her sacrifice and demanded more and more from her as he got older.

I tried to teach his mom how to get control of Pete by first using negative reinforcement to stop bad behavior, and then highly rewarding him for more cooperative replacement behavior. She just could not bring herself to upset her son. She could not bear his anger, hurt, whining, or rejection, so she dropped out of therapy. She called me after Pete left home at age eighteen. The nine years after she aborted therapy had been very difficult and disappointing for mom. Pete felt entitled to get from his mother anything he wanted. If she refused, he became the abused, whimpering victim, and she caved in. If that didn't work, Pete went to plan two. He became the rageful, demanding, threatening Pete until his mom caved. He had no insight into what he was doing and zero empathy for his mom's distress.

Pete did not help his mother around the house. He regularly stole money from her purse, and although intellectually capable, Pete was a poor student and always on the brink of failure. As he got into his teen years, he ran afoul of the law. He was caught shoplifting twice and spent a considerable amount of time on probation. He chose friends who were very much like himself—under-motivated and abusive of the generosity of their parents. Looking back on the last nine painful years, Pete's mother expressed a sadness that she had not set boundaries for Pete or taught him how to willingly live under her authority.

She never remarried because Pete never approved of her suitors. He was a genius regarding finding ways to drive mom's boyfriends away from her. Pete was the boss and he would tolerate no other. Now that Pete is grown, he refuses to communicate with his mom or even tell her where he lives or how he supports himself. She means nothing to him. Now she wishes she had required Pete to respect her but there is no longer an opportunity to do so. Pete has very little capacity to feel or express empathy. He is a selfish user and expects to be served. As an adult, Pete is out of control and incapable of living under self-control.

Pete's mother still loves him but he was a child who was hard to keep. His adult years will probably be very difficult for Pete. He may never successfully marry or develop a meaningful career.

Benefit Number Six: The ability to develop abundant self-esteem

A parent's job is to teach a child to become an adult. Parents are not required to flawlessly apply appropriate parenting skills in order to raise children who become functional adults. I have interviewed a thousand normal adults about their childhoods. Many were raised by parents who were not sticklers about enforcing home rules and parental directives. These children seemed to turn out to be pretty good adults. They were not very rebellious and their parents were lenient regarding the enforcement of family boundaries. Why did these children turn out to be good adults? I really don't know. Childrearing is a complex task and no one has the final authoritative word about how it should be done. However, I think the risk is too great for failure if parents just do their best and hope the kids will turn out okay. By accepting that the best adults are those who learned as children to live willingly under their parents' authority, and by applying the techniques discussed in the following chapters, you will remove the guesswork and like your kids ever more. Obviously, my philosophy and methods are going to be most needed with the child who is unwilling to live under a parent's authority. I submit to every parent that my methods work with every child and help every child grow into an adult who can live under self-control. They are practical childrearing methods for both the hard-to-handle child and the easy-to-raise child. Raising children you want to keep is markedly enhanced by employing the philosophy I propose and the techniques I teach. The damage done to the child who does not learn to willingly live under parental authority is pervasive. I assure you that failure to fully accomplish this essential task will result in some form of deficit that will manifest itself in the child's adult life.

Pushy Patricia

Patricia is an example of a child who didn't like to be controlled. She grew up to be a pushy adult who loves be in charge. Her home life was far from horrible, but she was never taught to live under control and has huge self-esteem issues.

Pushy Patricia was raised by a thrice-divorced mother. Patricia's mother was very moralistic. She applied some of the teaching of her faith very strictly when it came to her daughter. Moral lectures were constant, and criticism of behavior was never ending. Patricia usually complied with her mother's directives, but she hated doing so. She did not willingly live under her mother's authority. Pushy Patricia outwardly appeared to cooperate with her mother's authority. An outside observer would probably compliment Patricia for being such a nice girl. As Patricia grew into a teen, her disdain for her mother's excessively authoritarian control became more evident. Patricia began to select boys who were rebellious and noncooperative who led marginally moral lives. Patricia did not develop strong self-esteem under her mother's teaching, so she chose boys whose standards were minimal.

Patricia's school performance was marginally successful. Her grades were low and her satisfaction with school was minimal. Patricia hated control and found ways to avoid the control of her teachers. As an adult, she has gone through several job changes. She does well, gets promotions, but loses interest in the job and finds major fault with how the business is run and how she is treated. Patricia has had two marriages, and she is very critical of her present husband. She finds much fault with him and admits to very little responsibility for their marital unhappiness.

Patricia is obnoxiously pushy. She pushes her husband to give into her wishes. She is pushy with her friends and wants to control every aspect of their friendship. Patricia is pushy with her coworkers and, to their dismay, offers them a never-ending stream of advice. She is pushy with her clients and expects them to unquestionably comply with her suggestions. She is pushy with her boss and is willing to endlessly argue her points.

I have included the story of Pushy Patricia to illustrate that a parent does not have to be the epitome of bad parenting to raise a child who becomes a troubled adult. Patricia's mother was too controlling of Patricia's home life and too unrewarding of her positive behavior, so while Patricia was compliant at home, she sought every opportunity to resist all other forms of authority. Patricia became an adult who loved to be in control and pushed against authority of any sort. Patricia has a damaged ego and lacks adequate self-esteem. She uses pushy control methods to bolster her weak self-esteem.

Patricia's mother was able to make Patricia obey her through the use of harsh tactics, but mother never caught on to the "willing" part of the formula. Even if a child is not an openly rebellious, defiant child if she resists authority, she will, in some form, experience adult personality and performance damage as Patricia did. If you want to keep a child, it is imperative to teach the child to willingly submit to reasonable authority.

Benefit Number Seven: The ability to develop outstanding character traits

The teaching story that follows is quite different. The story is not about a client but about one of my contemporaries. It's the story of a teenager,

Albert the Angel, who clearly illustrates three positive outcomes of learning to live under authority.

1. Children like Albert who learn to live under parental authority are never hung up on proving themselves as worthy by acquiring things. They do not need to have more and more physical things to prove their worth and value to themselves or others. They develop a sense of self-security that is not defined by the acquisition of material possessions.

2. The second desirable quality found in these children is an overt ability to tell the honest truth. Albert could be counted on. What you saw was what you got with Albert. There was no secrecy or hidden agenda with him. What he promised, he did.

3. The third characteristic of Albert the Angel and kids like him, which I believe is a frequent outcome of raising children to willingly live under authority, is that the older they get, the happier they become. It may be a stretch for the reader to connect the concept of living under authority with present and future happiness, but I believe the connection is distinctly there. The key to this happiness connection is in decisions. The child who is given a choice between a good decision and a poor decision is highly rewarded by making the good choice. If a parent gives a child the choice between cleaning her room before supper and earning the privilege of watching television that evening, or not cleaning her room and losing her television privileges, and the child chooses to clean her room, then heaven opens up and happiness comes down. The child's parents are pleased, the burden of cleaning is removed, and supper tastes better than ever. In my long years of experience, I have seen this feeling of happiness occur over and over when a child decides to willingly submit to authority. When children decide to give in and comply, they almost feel euphoric happiness. They know it is the right thing to do. Rather than being grumpy or angry, they instead feel relief and happiness that they made the right decision. This happens over and over when a caring parent is teaching a young child to live under authority. One good decision leads to three good decisions and happiness abounds. Children are happier when they make the healthy decision to cooperate with the reasonable directives of a caring parent.

Albert the Angel

Albert was a happy teenager. He lived under self-control and made consistently good decisions. I spent hundreds of hours with Albert and I am a living witness that Albert definitely learned to live under self-control. He could live under self-control because he learned to willingly live under the authority of his parents as a young boy. He not only learned to submit to the authority of his parents, he also learned how to willingly submit to reasonable authority through his school experiences. We attended the same school, and in the "olden" days teachers were like substitute parents. Mr. E. L. Hunter, the principal of our school, was a kind, loving man who set firm boundaries and saw to it that they were strictly enforced. No one crossed Mr. Hunter and got away with it.

He also learned to willingly live under authority from the examples of other mothers and fathers, who not only required their children to show respect and compliance to their authority, but also expected and required it from their children's friends. I am talking about a neighborhood society that existed a long time ago, but is not as commonly found today. Parents back then felt welcomed to discipline other parents' children when necessary. Parents felt comfortable telling a visiting child what to do, and equally as comfortable telling the child's parents what the child did wrong and what was done about it. The school, our community, and his parents probably all played a significant role in raising Albert. Albert was a natural leader.

Albert the Angel was never envious of what others had. Most of my friends were like me, and grew up with very modest means, but Albert had even less. His self-esteem never seemed to be attached to having as much or more things than his friends. He was very serene within himself and didn't seem to need better clothes or the latest baseball glove. We all knew that Albert was willing to live within the rules of the school and society, but he was not seen as a "Goody Two-shoes." To put it bluntly, Albert was just fun to be with. He was not the class clown, but when we were around Albert, there was lots of laughter.

When we were young teenagers, Albert and I played on a very good summer baseball team. Albert was the catcher and I was the third baseman. Our team was tied for first place with the team from the rich part of town. They had uniforms and we wore blue jeans and white tee shirts with the name of the team stamped in black letters across the front. There was no love lost between us and them! We had identical records and each team had defeated the other team once. We met once again on the field of battle. This contest was for the league championship. The winner would advance to the state tournament.

It was a hard-fought contest and in the last inning, the score was tied 1–1 in the bottom of the ninth inning. If we could just hold them scoreless in this inning, the strongest part of our batting order would be coming to bat in the tenth. They had worked a man to third base with one out. If at all possible, the best play for an out would be to go to home plate if it was hit on the ground. The ball was hit on the ground, and it was a screamer directly to me. I fielded it cleanly and the runner broke for home plate. I threw a perfect strike over the left shoulder of the runner to Albert, who waited at home base. To avoid a head-on collision, Albert stepped to the side of the base path to tag the runner. He was going to be dead out. Albert reached out to touch the runner on the shoulder, and the umpire called him out. The runner shouted, "He missed me!" Albert the Angel turned to the umpire and said, "I missed him. I never touched him." The umpire reversed his decision and called him safe. The run scored and we lost the game. Perhaps we would have lost anyway, but we will never know because of those four words uttered by Albert, "I never touched him!" Fifteen teenaged boys were stunned. The amazing thing to me was that, to the best of my knowledge, not one boy scolded Albert or criticized him. We hated that we lost the game but we admired Albert. Albert just took it in his stride and said that the best team won that day, but that we would "get 'em" next year. Next year didn't come for us and I lost contact with Albert, but I never forgot him. Albert is an example of a young man who lived under self-control. Albert went on to become the mayor of a modest-sized town, and he served his community in numerous public offices and capacities.

Albert just didn't need a first place trophy to feel good about himself. The material possession and the honor that would come to the league champion weren't more important to Albert than integrity and honesty. Albert didn't mope around after the loss; instead, he suggested we get together the next day, practice for awhile, and then go to Floe's Café for a Coke.

I really admire Albert. He represents an excellent example of typical personal benefits a young person derives from learning to willingly liver under authority. When this is accomplished young people, like Albert, will not need to prove their worth by acquiring things, will tell the honest truth even when doing so is at a personal cost, and will live a life replete with fun, joy, and pleasure.

Summary of Concepts

The secret to raising children you want to keep is to teach them to willingly live under the authority of their parents. When children learn to willingly submit to the reasonable authority of their parents, they grow up to be adults who can live under self-control. This principle is not just about parental control. Harsh, abusive, punitive parents can control their children, but they do not raise children who are willing to live under self-control and cooperate within a society of rules. What the techniques found in this book teach is the benefits of a child willingly living under control. The willing part of control is crucial to get a child to internalize the desire to live under parental authority. This requires a good balance between setting firm boundaries and limits and the intrinsic reward of cooperating with parents who are generous with gentle actions of love and care. A child's cooperation and willingness to submit to parental authority must be richly rewarded with praise, love, and care. The result is a child who willingly lives under parental authority, and grows up to be an adult who lives under self-control. These are children that you will want to keep and that society will be proud to have as members.

The following benefits are commonly associated with adults who learned to willingly live under parental authority as children:

1. They can learn from experience and can accept the advice of older, more mature, and more experienced persons. The adult who never trusts the advice from others cannot profit or learn from others' mistakes.
2. They are able, as adults, to postpone immediate short term rewards in order to get something better later. When children who have not willingly learned to live under authority grow into adulthood, they find it difficult to achieve distant but important goals.
3. They are capable of listening to corrective criticism as adults. The child who resisted or fought against his parents' authority finds it difficult, as an adult, to listen to corrective criticism without anger or hurt. He simply cannot benefit from constructive criticism. Instead, his first response to corrective criticism will be defensive.
4. They do not believe that they must control every person and situation around them. Trouble follows the dedicated adult controller. Those whom they attempt to control through dramatic, intimidating, manipulative behavior usually give in return great amounts of hostile resistance.

5. They will grow up to be adults who can feel empathy for others. The more a child is willing to submit to reasonable authority, the more clearly they understand how others feel and perform caring acts of kindness.

6. They are provided, by their parent(s), an environment in which self-esteem, self worth, and self-confidence are encouraged and nurtured. Children who live under control receive many rewards, compliments, and praises from appreciative parents, grandparents, aunts, uncles, teachers, and friends. The expressions of respect and admiration from others gradually shape the personal feeling of self-worth and self-confidence.

7. There are three interrelated characteristics that are frequently observed in the adult who learned as a child to willingly live under parental authority. First, they are not often controlled by things. Morals, values, ethics, relationships, and honesty are more valued than cars, boats, tools, clothes, houses, yards, fishing supplies, or cosmetics. The paradox is that people who live cooperatively with society are given almost unlimited freedom (authority). Society rewards the person who voluntarily lives under self-control and values the rules of society. The hard-to-handle, rebellious child, more frequently than not, grows into an utterly self-centered and selfish adult who must have more than others to attain any noticeable security or self-esteem.

The second characteristic commonly found in adults who grew up living under parental authority is the high value attributed to honesty and truth telling. Adults who, as children, willingly submitted to the authority of their parents as well as other authority figures are not intimidated or fearful of telling others the truth. Adults like this were required by their parents to tell the honest truth; they learned that lying and dishonesty would get them into more trouble with their parents than if they told the simple truth. Children who defy their parents or do not trust their parents to provide consistent care for them grow into adults who believe they must minimize the truth or lie to survive and avoid failure. Their self-esteem is in shambles. These children believe they have a fatal flaw and that this flaw must never be discovered by others. Lying comes easily to them because they feel that their personal survival is at stake. Children who cannot accept authority soon discover an effective way of avoiding authority through lying and cheating.

Children who are comfortable with authority are simply happier than children who avoid their parents' authority. Life goes better for the child who is not constantly resentful when told no or given a direct order. Children who learn to willingly comply with reasonable authority grow up to be adults who see the positive before the negative. They are more optimistic. Being happy has become an adult way of life because the question of authority was settled early in childhood. Look around and observe children. I think you will find that children who are cooperative with parental directives have a good relationship with their parents and are observably happier than those who cannot willingly live under parental authority.

The effort, time, and sweat equity a parent expends to raise a child is heavy, but it is also a wise investment. Not all parents are willing to expend the effort it takes to raise a child they would want to keep. I explained one of my techniques to a mother of a thirteen-year-old daughter, and she said she didn't want to do the assignment because she would be more punished than her child. She told me that my method would greatly inconvenience her, so she was not sure she would do it. I looked at her with my most serious look and said, "It will greatly inconvenience you, but it is your job to be inconvenienced as her mother. It is what you signed up for when you became her mother." The mom complied with my suggestions, and she is finally seeing the child she always wanted. The stakes are high when children come into the lives of parents, but the rewards are also high. Helping your child learn to live under authority is an excellent investment that pays rich dividends now and forever.

Conclusion

Writing a self-help book reminds me of the story about several blindfolded men who were given the task of examining an elephant and describing what the elephant looked like. They had never seen an elephant before. The one who examined the elephant's trunk described the animal as long, pliable, and wiggly. The one who examined one of the legs described the elephant as round and sturdy like a tree with a flat bottom. The one who felt the elephant's side thought the elephant was a flat textured wall. They all described accurately the part they examined, but none got the whole picture of an elephant. Advice on how to effectively raise children is something like the blindfolded men's report on what an elephant looks like. There are many effective and useful childrearing methods and techniques that are helpful in raising children. All are useful, but few provide an adequate answer to the question, "How do parents raise a child they would want to keep?" Looking back on a thirty-seven-year career of treating children and families, I have discovered that the one unifying concept that makes it possible to raise a child whom parents want to keep and whom society is proud to have depends upon teaching him or her to willingly live under parental authority. When this is successfully accomplished, this child will grow into an adult who can live under self-control. Children will respond positively to all the techniques I teach if parents will invest quality time and effort in applying the numerous methods found here. The earlier a child learns these essential concepts, the easier it is to enjoy his presence in your family. Remember though, that it is never too late to help a child to learn to live under authority.

I would be remiss if I did not conclude with a few thoughts about therapy. What I have written is designed to help the average parent create an environment in which a child can thrive. The book is useful for all parents who have children at home. The techniques apply equally well to children who are easy to raise and to those children who are very hard to handle. However, some families need extra help. If you are one of these families, I suggest that you seek professional counseling. It is my opinion that none of the techniques I recommend would adversely affect the process of family counseling. My bias is toward family counseling versus individual counseling for the child or the parents. There is something powerful associated with the cooperative involvement of both the parents and the child in the therapeutic process. The methods suggested should fit reasonably well with any therapists' theoretical training and application of behavioral techniques. My recommendation is that you choose a cognitive/behavioral therapist who does family counseling.

Lastly, I would like to re-emphasize that the success of teaching children to willing live under your authority depends on the equal and fair application of two psychological teaching tools. Tool number one is to stop noncompliant behaviors that undermine a parent's reasonable authority. Note the word "reasonable." I do not advocate harsh control of a child's acting-out behavior. Parental authority must not be applied harshly.

The second tool covers how to teach a child to enjoy living under parental authority. The reader is reminded that the term "willingly" is used every time I tell a story about a child learning to live under parental authority. If your heartfelt desire is to teach a child to cooperate with your authority, the child must be rewarded for their compliance with your authority. Tons of love and truckloads of caring must accompany the use of the techniques offered in the book. Parents are often much better at catching children doing wrong than they are at catching children doing right. Some children are not easily loved and cared for when they routinely defy authority, but the unlovely child definitely becomes easier to live with and care about when his bad behavior is stopped by using one of the techniques described in this book. As new and more cooperative behavior is added, your child is definitely more easily reinforced with "atta boy" and "atta girl'" compliments. It gets easier to love them. Trust me and read the chapter on "willingness" (chapter 2).

Read on. I think you will enjoy what you read and find the techniques offered useful in everyday family life.

Go forth. Do good.

How to Create a Willingness to Live under Parental Authority

The premise supporting all of the techniques that I recommend is that children who willingly learn to live under parental authority are the children parents want to keep. Not only are they pleasant, reliable companions to parents, but they also become adults who do very well in our society. The first authority children encounter is their parents. Children are not born with a hardwired, built-in program that allows and values submission to authority. In fact, children are born utterly selfish and have no respect at all for their parents' position of authority. They do not understand that it is definitely in their long-term best interest to give in to their parents' control. The child is wired to survive. She must eat, drink, and be protected from harm. She will scream, kick, bawl, wiggle, and whine until a good parent solves her discomfort problem and takes care of her needs. She wants what she wants and will spare no effort to obtain it.

Some children are genetically built to demand more loudly and persistently than other children, and as children get older, they get more cunning and creative at being selfishly demanding. Parents often grow weary of dealing with the natural demands of their children's needs and wants. Parents can become discouraged and may feel helpless to teach their child to consistently mind their reasonable requests because little that they do successfully puts limits on the child's devouring demands for service. All parents agree that children should be taught to live under control, but many find that the methods that they know to use such as scolding, take-a-ways, time-outs, and spankings are ineffective or unworkable. Parents know that using harsh methods would damage the child's ego and self-esteem and would be too great of a price to pay for compliance, so they hesitate to employ these methods. What's a good parent to do? This chapter presents effective ways to teach children how to want to live under a parent's authority. It is not enough to dominate and subjugate a child into compliance if there is no willingness to live under authority.

If a child hates his parents' authority, his oppositional attitude will emerge in several ways. He may find many ways to sneak his way around complying with his parents' rules and directives. He may comply with their authority, but oppose the authority of teachers, principals, and police. Until he is willing to live under his parents' authority, he will find many ways to oppose the authority of his parents as well as the authority of other caregivers.

The most challenging problem facing a parent is to find a way to teach a child to internalize the desire to submit to authority. Compliance to parental authority must be rewarding so that submission will occur again and again. Living under parental authority must bring pleasure before it will be repeated. As a child matures, it is necessary for him to decide to comply with parental authority and then self-reward. This means he must learn to take pleasure in the decision to submit to authority. This is not an easily accomplished goal. Remember, children are naturally selfish and do not come to us programmed to submit to authority. It is even harder to get them to want to submit to authority. The good news is that even the most naturally resistant child can be taught to willingly submit to the authority of his parents.

Disciplining with Your Child's Temperament in Mind

Children come to parents with a built-in, genetic, core personality. Their core personality will determine what parental discipline and control methods will be most effective to teach them to abandon selfishness and embrace cooperative family teamwork.

Let's take a brief look at the four core personalities children are born with.

1. Some children start life with a social, fun-loving, energetic personality. They love to be spontaneous, and they seek lots of stimulation. These children hate boredom and resist routine. I like to use Pillow Talk and the More Not Less Technique for this temperament.
2. About 25 percent of all children appear on the scene with a focused, practical, and driven personality. They are extremely competitive and love to win. They set personal goals and then go for them with strength and

dedication. They love to be the boss and exercise personal control over everything and everyone. The Now or Later Technique is very good to use for this temperament. The 30-Second Technique also works well.

3. Another 25 percent come to us with a precision personality. They like evenness and predictability. They are picky, critical worriers. They control by micromanaging everything. This temperament responds well to the Marks Method and the More Not Less Techniques.

4. Finally, there are those children who have the easy-going, laid-back, and cool personality. They are low maintenance, generally cooperative rule followers. They are quiet, but socially comfortable. They are not pushy, but they can be a bit selfish. Any method works for this temperament.

Every method I recommend will work regardless of temperament. For some children the methods I recommend will be very easy to apply, and the results will be quickly and pleasantly effective. For other children, like those who are very social and those who are goal-directed controllers, it will be a struggle to make any technique work. They will work, but a parent must be persistent and dedicated to obtain the positive results I suggest. You might want to start with the discipline methods recommended above.

Children are worth whatever is required from parents to teach the most important thing children will ever learn: how to willingly live under parental authority. Parents have about eighteen years to get the job done. This life theme is very important to the long-term welfare of a child. There is no price too great to pay.

Children not only come to us with different personalities, they also come with basic needs. At a minimum there are five basic needs of all children. When a parent meets the five basic needs of a child—safety, food and shelter, love and standing with parents, acceptance, and relationship—the child will thrive under parental care.

1. Safety

Children want to feel safe. When parents cannot or will not put firm boundaries around their children, they feel unsafe. A child intuitively understands that he is incapable of running the affairs of a complex family. If a child is the boss in the family, it is very frightening for him. Children want their parents to make rules, place firm but reasonable boundaries around them, and consistently enforce the family rules. Children who have parents who do not require their children to live under authority feel insecure and unsafe. These children constantly push their parents further and harder, hoping that their mom and dad will say, "Stop! Far enough! No!" Strong disciplinary tools help parents establish boundaries and control. Children will hate them but love them.

2. Food and shelter

The child's need for both of these is obvious. Children rely entirely on their parents for both.

3. Love and standing with parents

Children need to know that they are loved by their parents. They also feel secure if they are sure that they have good standing with their parents. Children need to know that parents care enough about them to put firm controls on out-of-control behavior. In my practice I have seen this happen over and over. Children calm down and become more tender and loving to their parents when parents take control again. In their heart of hearts children intuitively know that it is in their own best interest for their parents to be in charge. When children submit to their parents' authority, they are free to love.

When children are willing to live under their parents' authority, it creates an environment in which parents can freely express their love. Parents feel more comfortable and inclined to compliment and praise their child's cooperative behavior. As long as guerrilla warfare is occurring between parents and children, parents cannot readily see the good in their children. When good cannot be identified because of uncooperative behavior, it is difficult for parents to express their emotional love for their children.

The discipline techniques in this book help parents to establish reasonable authority with their children, and a natural outcome is a stress-free, loving relationship between parent and child.

4. Acceptance

Children thrive if they believe their parents accept them without a pressing need to change them. Children who live out of control cannot experience that kind of acceptance. If parents are willing to set firm boundaries on their children and enforce them, children and parents are free to express acts of acceptance. When applied appropriately, my methods will help create a favorable environment for acceptance to occur.

5. Relationship

Children who live out of control desperately need to experience a bonded, connected relationship with their parents. It is my opinion that a child's private opinion is, "Please, please control me because I know I can't do it." Parents are human too, and they ordinarily find it very difficult to have a comfortable, stress-free relationship with a child who cannot control himself. Teaching your child to live willingly under your authority creates an environment in which acceptance can flourish.

The benefits resulting from meeting the needs of children are greatly enhanced when children are taught how to willingly live under parental authority. When children are taught to live under self-control, they quickly become children their parents want to keep.

Megan the Morning-Killer

Megan is thirteen years old, tall, pretty, bright, athletic, the oldest of two girls, and very defiant to both her mother and her father. Neither can control her. Her mother is nurturing, but busy and impatient. She lets Megan "get away with murder." Megan is verbally harsh and disrespectful toward her mother, and her mom is either like water or frozen ice with her punishments. Often she is just too busy to follow through with her directives. Sometimes she punishes, but gets sidetracked because of work and forgets the punishment she imposed. At times, she is impatient and screams Megan into compliance. Megan's mom sometimes threatens Megan with sending her away to an "all-girls school." She tells Megan that she is impossible to deal with and that she will be glad when she leaves home. At other times, she can be very loving, fun, and friendly with Megan.

Megan's dad is Mr. Black-or-White. There is no middle ground for him. He is rigid, critical, and extremely strict. He scolds without mercy. Once he begins to "preach," he just won't stop for forty-five minutes. Megan tunes him out. Megan argues with her dad, complains to her mother or anyone who will listen to her about her dad, and seeks every opportunity to defy him. Megan is out of control.

When all is well, Megan is fun, creative, resourceful, mature, and just a joy to be around. Usually the stars, moon, sun, and Venus must be in alignment for this to happen, so it is not a frequent occurrence.

Through family therapy and the brave and consistent application of several of my suggested techniques, Megan's evening behavior was improved. Her parents were becoming more positive, relaxed, and rewarding when around Megan, so we agreed to intervene in Megan's morning misbehavior.

Mornings are still a nightmare in Megan's home. Her dad leaves for work earlier than her mom (lucky guy) and misses Megan's best performances. Her mom is usually busy getting ready for work when Megan "goes off." Here are some things that drive Megan's mother crazy. Megan dominates the bathroom she shares with her nine-year-old sister, Sarah, and won't let her in to get ready for school. Typically, Megan torments her sister until both are screaming, and Sarah runs to her mother crying and complaining. Megan shouts from the upstairs bathroom to her mother, who is frantically trying to put herself together, that she can't find something. Megan demands, in the most unkind manner, that her mother help her find some needed article of clothing. Her mom finally gets herself dressed and ready and hurriedly fixes breakfast. She calls both children to come down to eat. Sarah comes promptly, but Megan goes into her stubborn delay tactics. Her mom scolds and demands but to no avail. Megan is on her own time schedule and responds to nothing. At last Megan comes down to eat and continues to torment Sarah. She complains relentlessly about the quality of the food. Breakfast is frenetic and unpleasant. Afterwards, Megan can't find her homework, books, coat, and backpack. Now, her mother is frantic. It is almost time to leave for school and work, and she and Megan are in a frenzy to get the last-minute stuff done. Megan's mom is in a foul mood, and Megan is in a rage. Megan has just killed another morning.

You may ask, "So why doesn't her mother help Megan pack up and lay her clothes out the night before?" Well, she has tried that repeatedly, but Megan always finds one or two things to forget or cause a drama over the next morning. Megan's mom is in a bind. Although she is tempted to do so, she can't leave Megan at home all day, and she has no child care resources readily available to her. She is stuck with Megan, the Morning-Killer.

We decided, in a family therapy session, to not use a negative escape learning method in this case. Megan's mother just does not have the morning time available to her to apply one of the negative reinforcement techniques that has worked so well in the evenings. Remember there are two ways to teach children to willingly submit to parental authority. We can use negative reinforcement to teach a child to cooperate or we can use positive reinforcement to accomplish the same purpose. The whole family agreed to the following positive reinforcement program.

Everyone, including children, tends to repeat any behavior that brings reward and pleasure. We chose only one of the many misbehaviors—not sharing the bathroom—to work on and decided the others would be addressed after we got control of that one issue. It was carefully explained to Megan what sharing meant and what her mom was going to look for. Sarah and Megan were involved in the design of the program for both children. It was mutually decided that for Megan, the reward for cooperation would be money. She was a teen and very interested in buying "foo-foo" items to look and smell nice. Sarah had other rewards for doing her part. Megan would get one dollar for every day she shared the bathroom with Sarah, and fifty cents for every morning that Sarah did not come down crying and complaining about Megan hogging the bathroom. Megan could earn a total of seven dollars and fifty cents every week. She received the money each morning that she complied with her mother's directive. She put her money in a clear Mason jar on her dresser so she could visibly see the rewards grow. In addition to the money, Megan's mother agreed to do two things. She promised to take Megan shopping every Saturday so she could spend her money on pretty things, and she agreed to refrain from screaming, punishing, and threatening Megan with death if she didn't improve her other morning terrorist tactics. She agreed to these rules knowing that we would attend to Megan's other bad habits one at a time. Sarah was not ignored. She was also rewarded for not yelling, screaming, or tattling.

Megan began to respond to the program. The first week she managed to share the bathroom with Sarah twice. Three dollars wasn't much, but Megan enjoyed shopping with her mother (without Sarah), and she bought two inexpensive hair pieces. Megan the Morning-Killer began to change, and so did mother. This relationship took a decided turn for the better. We added the next criteria for getting $1.50 when she was able to consistently share the bathroom with Sarah. Megan was hooked. She looked forward to her spending spree with her mother, and her mom enjoyed it too. Seven dollars and fifty cents plus some time was well worth it to Megan's mother for some peace of mind every workday morning. Soon, we thinned the rewards, and Megan enjoyed the praise, love, and care that came with cooperating with mother. Megan's morning name changed. She is now called Megan the Morning Star!

Some parents might take issue with the idea of paying a child to cooperate with the parents' reasonable requests and expectations. I will discuss this question in greater detail and provide a solution in the Average Alice story later in this chapter.

A Rule: Reward or Die!

Megan's story is a great example of how to teach a child to willingly comply with a parent's authority through positive reinforcement. When a child stops her uncooperative, negative behavior, the resulting cooperative, compliant behavior must be amply rewarded to get a child to repeat again and again the desired positive behavior. It doesn't matter if the cause of change in a child's behavior is a result of negative reinforcement or positive reinforcement, the cooperative behavior must, in some meaningful way, be rewarded. This is a rule that must never be violated. For Megan, her changed behavior was rewarded with both a tangible reward, and the reward of her mother's approval. If positive changes in the behavior of children are not rewarded in some meaningful manner, these changes will simply quietly die a slow, agonizing death.

Most parents are aware of and agree that rewarding good behavior is a good idea. Most parents even try rewards once in a while. Unfortunately, most rewards programs fail and are abandoned as unworkable. Rewards programs are sensitive and tricky. There are definite rules that must be followed for a rewards program to work.

Parents, It Is All about You

Parents often feel a strong sense of failure when they try their best and still do not see the desired behavior in their children. Perish those feelings of failure! There is nothing wrong with your ability to parent. You have the God-given ability to be an effective parent. Personal criticism and feelings of guilt do not make you a more effective parent. What parents need is an effective rationale for good parenting and workable techniques to produce the desired changes in their children. Raising children you want to keep is a learnable skill.

Learning how to correct a child's destructive behavior is a skill that you can master if the following three factors are present.

1. The first factor needed is motivation. You must want to learn more effective child guidance methods. For example, if you want to learn how to play tennis, you must be motivated enough to buy a racquet and tennis balls. Next, you must be motivated enough to willingly go the tennis court where tennis is played. It is the same with learning how to teach

children to willingly live under parental authority. You must want it badly enough to learn how to do it. All is well so far. You have this one. You are patiently reading this book and have progressed to this page in your search for doable childrearing techniques.

2. The second factor is a willingness to listen to an expert teacher. That is my role. I have thirty-seven years of experience behind me, and I have tested these change methods thousands of times with good results. You can learn to play tennis by watching, but the chances are good that you will learn to play tennis poorly. You can also learn child discipline techniques by observing others, but not as well as you can if you have a good, experienced teacher. I will be your teacher throughout this book.

3. The third factor needed to learn a complex skill is practice. A tennis coach will eventually ask you to go hit balls at the practice court using an automatic serving machine. He will arrange for you to play a few practice games with other beginner tennis players. Similarly, you must, for best results, be willing to practice the techniques suggested in this book. You are not expected to perform the discipline techniques perfectly the first time you try them out. However, every time you practice one, you will get better and better. Soon, skill will develop and your learning will be complete. Practice is the key to success. When the techniques become a habit, you have really learned the method well.

I am sure you will soon notice that there is a strong emphasis on parental responsibility. I find that children wait for their parents to take the responsibility to make them cooperate. It is your responsibility to teach your children how to cooperate with you, yet the children must internalize a desire to cooperate. Much responsibility rests on your shoulders as the parent in navigating the fine balance between your child wanting to comply with parental directives and just feeling that he *has* to mind his parents. This chapter is about teaching children to want to mind.

Enjoy the learning experience and your reward will be so fantastically great that you will want to apply these discipline methods again and again. I guarantee it!

Average Alice

Alice is in the sixth grade, and although she is not failing, she is just barely passing. Alice will not seriously study. Her parents and Average Alice agreed to the following intervention program to help improve her study habits.

By means of several family interviews, it was determined that Alice actually enjoyed, at a subliminal level, the huge amount of negative attention she obtained from her parents, grandparents, and teacher. All she had to do for this negative attention was not study and barely pass. Sound familiar, parents? I asked her mom and dad to observe Alice for a week to determine what she really, really liked to do. We knew the negative things about Alice. She played after school and put off studying until she was tired and cranky from the day's activities. She was the best at procrastination and had, through careful personal research and study, developed a wide variety of study avoidance skills! Her teacher reported that Alice was the best twelve-year-old daydreamer she had in her class. Threats and punishment had not worked for Alice. Remember, she likes attention, even if it is negative. Near failures and relentless criticism had also eroded her school self-esteem and personal confidence. She simply assumed, based on her past experiences in school, that she was incapable of better school performance.

Her mom and dad's observation revealed two things that Alice really, really liked to do. Alice loved to ice skate and to eat lemon pie. That was it, according to her parents. Fortunately, her dad had a special relationship with Alice. Alice's dad talked to her, and they agreed that if she would work steadily, at a decent hour, on her homework for just ten minutes per day, then he would take her ice skating Friday evening. Alice thought she could do that, so a contract was successfully negotiated. Alice did her part and so did her dad. Alice had a great time. The next week, study time was extended to twelve minutes. Alice did it again, and so did her dad. So far, so good. Alice was gradually being hooked on working for a reward. Next, we added lemon pie for not daydreaming at all within the first hour of the school day. The teacher agreed to send a voucher home with Alice to verify that she fulfilled her assignment. Alice helped her mom bake the lemon pies that would be used to reward her for not daydreaming for one hour per school day. Alice had a few misses, but generally did quite well. She really did like lemon pie! Time was gradually extended until she was studying about thirty minutes per night without complaint. Daydreaming at school took a little longer, but over time, she progressed to a half-day of non-daydreaming at school. We froze operations at thirty minutes of useful home study and a half-day of no daydreaming at school.

We next set about to wean Alice from the habit of expecting a reward every time she studied thirty minutes at home and didn't daydream for a half-day at school. The goal was to teach Alice to study at home and not daydream at school because she wanted to do it, not because she was paid to. The way we accomplished this was to tell Alice that her dad would count the times she studied thirty minutes at home and when she had enough times, he would take her ice skating. For Alice, it was now a new and exciting game. When would she get to go skating? She didn't know. Isn't anticipation a great thing? Her dad was easy at first. He waited three days during week one of the new rules and took her ice skating after he got home from work. It was a little hard on her dad, but Alice was thrilled. Alice was getting very good at ice skating. All of her new friends at the ice rink noticed, too. They envied Alice and wished they had a dad like hers. The ice skating reward was varied considerably after that. Sometimes, it was after five nights of studying; sometimes, she was rewarded after two weeks of good study performance.

Alice's mom followed a similar program of lemon pie reward for non-daydreaming for one half of the school day. Not only did Alice learn to skate better, to the envy of her friends, but her grades gradually came up, and she enjoyed doing special things with her mother like learning to bake and leisurely talking over a nice piece of lemon pie. Life was good for Alice.

Eventually, her dad suggested that the game was over and that he and Alice's mom would be very proud of Alice for not daydreaming at school or home and studying a reasonable amount of time every night. Alice's parents substituted verbal praise for ice skating and lemon pie. Alice's new behavior also brought many new rewards she had never experienced before. Her self-esteem and personal confidence grew by leaps and bounds. This entire program took four months to complete. Too long? Not really, when one considers the alternative of continual scolding, disappointment, and near failure. It turned out to be a reasonable investment of her parents' time and money to obtain results like those Alice received. The only down side was that Alice gained a few pounds from the lemon pie reward, but long walks with her dad and a more controlled use of lemon pie took care of that problem. Alice continued to apply her newfound behavior and did reasonably good work (Cs to Bs) through high school. In Alice's case, positive reinforcement succeeded where punishment learning failed.

The Essentials of a Rewards Program

The story of Average Alice is an example of the power that positive reinforcement has to teach a child to want to cooperate with her parents and learn to willingly live under their authority. As stated earlier, the laws of learning are orderly and predictable. The following list represents the key elements in a reinforcement program.

1. Children tend to repeat that which brings them reward and pleasure. Alice was rewarded for better study habits and not daydreaming. The greater lesson, however, was learning the benefits of positive cooperation with her parents. She wanted to repeat this learned behavior because by doing so, she pleased her parents and made them very proud of her new efforts at family cooperation.

2. Specify exactly what behavior change you are looking for. Write it down. Alice needed to have a clear understanding of the requirements expected of her before she would be rewarded. To say something like, "Alice, you have to study harder and try harder in school" would not be specific enough. Be clear on what you want from your child.

3. At first, choose only a small part of the overall goal to reinforce. For Alice we wanted thirty minutes of study per night, but we started with ten minutes. It was important that Alice believe she could do the task and have a very good chance to get the reward. Make it easy to get the first rewards. We want to first hook the child on working for reward. In Alice's case, we were prepared to drop back to five minutes if she couldn't accomplish the ten-minute requirement.

4. Observe your child and identify potential rewards they will want to work for. For Alice it was only two rewards, but for most children, the list will be five to ten rewards long.

5. Develop a menu of rewards. Put five to six of the top rewards on the menu and let the child choose one from among the many. Children tend to change rewards on parents. The reward may lose its effectiveness, but having several to choose from will keep interest high. Fortunately for us, Alice never grew tired of lemon pie. Older kids can often postpone immediate reward, and that was the case for Alice. She could wait a week to go ice skating, but we gave her lemon pie every day she didn't daydream at school. Younger children, ages two to ten, usually need to be rewarded very soon after fulfilling their agreement. For younger children, it is best to reward them the same day they do the required task.

6. Determine who should administer rewards by letting the child decide. Sometimes it will be daddy and sometimes mommy. In Alice's case, it was clearly daddy. Don't be jealous!

7. Make a formal agreement with your child. If she will do her part, mom or dad will let her choose from the menu. Make a deal.

8. Consistently apply the rewards when criteria behavior is met. Take-away is not allowed if the child fulfilled her part of the deal. No matter how naughty she might have been during the day, give your child the reward if she meets the agreed-upon requirements.

9. Increase requirements to get rewards, but increase them modestly. For Alice, we increased her study time for the next week by only two minutes. She could get the same great reward for only two minutes more of effort. For Alice, it was definitely worth the increased effort and she was dead sure she could do it.

10. Thin the rewards schedule. When your child is consistently performing up to gold standards, go on a variable rewards schedule. This means that you will not tell your child when she will get the rewards menu. Vary your schedule of requirements. Sometimes, it will be easy to get the reward, and sometimes, harder. She will never know what to expect. It is during this phase that the child will begin to internalize the required behavior on her own. Alice started to decide to do the requirements because she wanted to. This is a very important concept to remember. Thin the rewards but do not abruptly terminate them.

The Sunday School Director Story

I think a teaching story would be helpful to reinforce the power and need for principle number ten, thinning the rewards. When organized positive reinforcement programs were new on the face of the earth a long time ago, the importance of thinning rewards to get children to internalize cooperative behavior was dramatically taught to me through a program I organized. I was a new psychologist having graduated from Oklahoma State University only the year before. I was also the new Sunday School Director for the children's program at the local church I attended. Keep in mind that this was thirty-seven years ago, and learning theory incorporating positive rewards system was relatively new and untried. I know it sounds incredible but we didn't know as much about these types of programs then as we do now.

There were two children's departments in my church. Attendance was poor and we had almost no new growth in these departments. I organized the following behavior rewards program. I observed the classes for a while and discovered that the children, aged seven to ten, rarely brought their Bibles, rarely gave any money to the church, and attended class irregularly. These were lower-middle-class kids for the most part so getting special things was important. They wanted things like pretty hair bows, fancy pencils, matchbox cars, colors, coloring books, squirt guns (parents hated this one), rings, whistles, and chocolate candy.

I told the children specifically what I wanted from them. They were to bring their Bible, come regularly, and give something (money) to the church every week. For doing that, they would get points they could redeem for good things from the prize wagon that would be wheeled into their classroom every Sunday. The prizes had a point value attached to each item. For example, the squirt gun cost more than the pencil. For attending they got five points; for bringing their Bible they got five points; and for giving to the church they got five points. If they brought a friend to church, they got fifteen points. I showed the children the array of wonderful prizes, and they eagerly agreed to participate.

All went very well. Both departments, as expected, significantly improved in all four categories, but that is not the point of my story. The program lasted six weeks. For department one, the program was terminated at the end of six weeks. For department two, we went on a variable schedule of rewards as described previously. The differences between departments one and two were dramatic. For the rest of the year, department two retained its gains with very little loss of performance. Department one, the one not intermittently reinforced, shortly returned to pre-program levels of attendance, Bibles brought, money given, and guests attending.

The story doesn't end there. In most churches, the children are all promoted to the next level together. The classes remain about the same from year to year. I followed the two departments' programs the next year. Using only the children who went through the reinforcement program, I found that department two kids retained their gains. One and three-quarter years later, the department two kids were still bringing their Bibles, giving to the church, and attending class significantly more regularly than the children in department one. Remember the two departments were approximately equal at the end of six weeks. Department two received the rewards wagon only six more weeks on a variable schedule before the program was terminated. That six week period of variable rewards made all the difference. Department two kids internalized the desire to carry out the identified tasks. I should also point out that the department two teachers were taught how to verbally praise their children's performance, so they continued to reinforce compliance to the agreed-upon behaviors long after the wagon stopped running. Department one teachers were only thanked for their six weeks of participation.

As I write about this remembered experience, the program seems a little cold and somewhat cruel for the department one children. I was fresh out of graduate school, full of new ideas, and eager to experiment with them. I hope department one has forgiven me by now. I moved the next year and lost contact with both departments. The point of the teaching story is that no positive reinforcement program should be abruptly terminated. The follow-up variable reinforcement phase should always be an integral part of a positive reinforcement program.

11. Keep good records. Children respond very well to charts and graphs. For example, make a chart with every day of the week listed. Put a mark or gold star for every successful performance. I did not mention it, but we used a weekly chart for Alice. It was attached to her bathroom mirror so she could see her progress every day. Everything is improved by charting. For example, if you want to increase your consistency for physical exercise, start keeping a chart. Every time you exercise during the week, chart it. You will see an improvement in your performance. For older children, please do not hang the chart on the refrigerator door. It embarrasses them!

Rageful Ray

This is the last teaching story for this section on positive reinforcement to get your child to willingly submit to your authority. After reading this case history, you should be able to construct a successful program of your own. It is tempting to tell you another teaching story using a young child as an example. Young children are much easier to work with in terms of applying the concepts of positive reinforcement. Instead I want to tell you about Rageful Ray. His was a difficult case, but does illustrate that the principles taught above are just as effective with the really challenging children.

Rageful Ray's History

At sixteen and one-half years old, Rageful Ray was a holy terror to his mom. He was the oldest of three children with two younger sisters, ages thirteen and ten. The girls got along pretty well with their mom. Ray was the rageful product of a bitter divorce. Ray's father and mother fought like cats and dogs until their divorce four years ago. Ray was mad at his father for leaving, at his mother for causing it, at his teachers for telling him what to do, and at the mosquitoes that had no right to annoy him, but did it anyway. He was mad, period. Although time was spent in session talking about the source of his rage, that is not the point of this story. Ray, when in a rage, punched holes through walls, slammed doors, and broke things. When he wasn't punching, slamming, and breaking, he was verbally abusing mother with vile language. He would not turn his hand to do any assigned chores, and his room and bathroom were pig pens. He was one unhappy boy. Ray was out of control. The first thing that had to be done was to flat-out stop his aggressive, destructive behaviors. I wanted to use an aggressive negative reinforcement method to stop his bad behavior, so I chose the Marks Method Assignment to start addressing his anger. This is a negative reinforcement method discussed in chapter 10. It worked pretty well. We next applied the Now or Later Technique to get more cooperation with chores, and that one worked very well. The next project was the obnoxious, abusive language Ray used against his mother when things didn't go his way. Because his anger was under better control, we used a positive rewards system for this one. Remember, children repeat anything that brings reward and pleasure. I should also mention that Ray did pretty well in school. His rage was mostly confined to home.

The Rewards Program

The first step was to tell Ray exactly what we wanted from him. In a family session, I listed all of the vile, threatening, and mean words that I didn't want him to say, and the things I didn't want him to do, so there was no misunderstanding about what we wanted him to change. Ray was often apologetic after one of his angry outbursts, and in the quiet of my office, he readily agreed that he shouldn't say or do the things on the list. So far, so good.

Identifying meaningful rewards was a challenge. For Ray, they had to be really good ones, or we would have no chance to get him to control his habitual verbal abuse. After considerable observation, his mother came up with the following things he really liked.

1. Driving the car. He had his learner's permit but was seldom out of trouble long enough to get to drive the car.
2. Staying up late at night. We made bed time 12:00 a.m. for this one.
3. Playing Xbox games all day Saturday with no chores.
4. Going to PG-13 movies.
5. Spending the night at a friend's house. Ray's mom was constantly worried that he would tear into someone other than her, so she seldom permitted overnighters. Ray didn't have a record of losing his temper away from home, but she worried anyway.

6. Go to bed without taking a shower or brushing his teeth. Ray liked this one!

Ask for Some of What Is Wanted

The deal was struck. Ray's mom and I asked him to hold his tongue for one hour every evening. If he did this successfully, he could choose one, two, or six on the menu each and every evening. Numbers three, four and five would require a civil tongue for three out of five evenings. If he succeeded in this, he could enjoy choosing one of the big three for the weekend.

Decide Who Will Administer the Rewards

Prior to our session, I called Ray's dad and asked for his help. He was happy to help and thought it would be fun. Ray chose to drive with his dad because his mom was too nervous when he drove. He chose his mom to go with him to the movies. She liked popcorn and so did he, and she didn't talk during the movie. The rest of the rewards did not require an adult's presence.

Be Consistent

Ray's mom faithfully applied the rewards even though it cost her a few bucks and considerable worry. It was at times tempting to take away the reward when he would tie into her upon reaching the sixty-first minute of the assignment. The rewards were so appealing to Ray he did not miss one night of the first week. He did not verbally assault his mom one time during his designated hour.

Increase the Requirement

We slowly upped the ante. The next week we required him to go one hour and twelve minutes to get the rewards. Ray was pretty sure he could meet that requirement, too, and he did.

The Results

Life got better for Ray and his mom. In four weeks, he had stopped using filthy language with his mom. He would still get plenty mad, but he learned to storm off to his room without violence or abusive language. His mom was so pleased with the results of the positive reward system that she eventually applied the concepts to doing a few household chores to help her out.

Thin the Rewards

After six weeks of the program, I told Ray that we were going to do it differently for the rest of the year. I explained variable reinforcement and why it was necessary. He was somewhat disappointed, but agreed to the intermittent reward system. As expected, his new habits became internalized, and he didn't really need the reward to watch his mouth. Over time, his mom applied the reward menu only occasionally. It sort of died a natural death.

Ray eventually became a regular late-teenage rascal. He didn't do everything perfectly right, but what teenage boy or girl does? He had improved a lot since I first began seeing him, and his mom was very pleased.

Now you are ready to try a rewards program out on your own kids.

Go forth. Do good.

Chapter 3

How to Build a Lasting Relationship with Your Child

Raising children you want to keep involves helping your children create and nurture deep, pleasant, rewarding relationships with the most important people in a their lives—their parents. Children will want to cooperate with parents *they* want to keep. An abiding, pleasant, bonded, deep relationship between you and your children is needed for reciprocal cooperative behaviors from your children. The most effective reward you can give your child for compliant, cooperative behavior is a good relationship with you. Parents often study books on cooking recipes and how to change spark plugs but do not as often put equal time and energy into learning how to build a loving, caring relationship with their children. Not only do children like this kind of relationship, but neglect and abuse are almost nonexistent between two people who respect one another. A good relationship between parent and child is absolutely necessary before a child will willingly live under parental authority.

You may have noticed that newborns don't come with a set of instructions or a lifetime warranty against problems. You just get them, as is, and like it or not, the teaching begins. Parents are teaching machines who run twenty-four hours a day. We teach by what we say and how we say it, as well as by our tone of voice and body language. Children are natural learners. They are experts at reading body language and between the lines of verbal communication. For example, a five-year-old girl who has spilled her milk and broken the glass knows her mother is mad at her. She understands her mother's verbal lesson about being more careful. She also knows, by way of body language and tone of voice, whether mother loves her, wants her, and thinks that she is worth keeping even if she spills milk and breaks a glass. Her self-confidence and self-esteem greatly depends on what the nonverbal cues—body language and tone of voice—say about her value in her mother's eyes. One of the most difficult tasks I face as a family therapist is teaching parents to monitor and eventually correct inappropriate nonverbal messages sent to children. Children know when a parent inwardly believes they are just a big burden to put up with. This section on how to build a lasting relationship will be vital for raising children you want to keep and who want to keep you.

I think nearly all parents start parenthood desiring a great relationship with their child. However, we had parents at one time and our relationship skills depend greatly on what we learned from our parents. If you had a miserable upbringing, don't despair. You do not have to repeat the mistakes of your parents. My great friend Henry grew up under the authority and teaching of a mother who had some of the worst parent-child relationship skills I personally know about. I have known Henry for forty-six years. I would gladly match him up with any husband or father and fully expect him to win the contest, hands down. He loves his wife, Patti, and is a great father to his two boys. How did he do it? He used mom's lack of relationship skills as a negative model and simply said that is not how he wanted to relate to his family. Henry also has learned a number of excellent life strategies through his faith and painful observations. This section can become a life strategy for you, like Henry, to outgrow the negative relationship building lessons your parents may have taught you. You will learn how to build new and productive relationship skills. Henry did it and you can too.

We can all change. I know I did. We are never stuck where we are. I had good parents and there was love between my father and mother. However, they were terrible models for physical intimacy. I rarely saw a kiss or snuggling activity between my mom and dad. I grew up not knowing how to express physical intimacy. After two years of marriage, my wife, Roena, announced that she wanted to start a family. I agreed, but there was a condition. I said to Roena, "OK, but here is the deal. I'll bring home the bacon and you raise the kids." She was shocked, but I was terrified of the intimacy having children implied. In about a year, Amanda arrived. Roena was willing to keep her part of "the deal," but there was a problem. Roena had Amanda by Caesarean operation. A country doctor slit her from her navel to her pubic bone. Her stomach muscles were sore and weak. She asked me if I would just go get Amanda and bring her to the bed for her night feeding and diaper change. After feeding Amanda and a diaper change, Roena would wake me up to deliver her back to the crib for the rest of the night. I carried Amanda, without a word said. I treated her as if she were an ancient Ming vase—very carefully. It wasn't too long before Amanda developed a little personality and cooed and smiled at me. I responded with a few grunting attempts at communication. That was the meager beginning of what would eventually become a warm, comfortable relationship. Amanda began to play more on the way back to the crib and so did I. In a couple of months I was keeping her up to play with me for awhile. I remember fondly many nights when I would rock her to sleep in the old, worn out, overstuffed rocker. The next morning I would still have her in my arms, and we were both wet (we used cloth diapers in those days). She was just what I needed to improve my inhibitions about physical affection. I learned to enjoy hugging and kissing my daughter, and Roena, too. I am far from perfect but I am now much more comfortable with expressing physical and emotional affection. We can all change and improve our past negative parental lessons. Henry and I did it, and so can you.

The Four Principles Necessary to Build a Great, Lasting Relationship

To develop a positive, rewarding, lasting relationship with your children based on the four principles in this chapter, you need to be willing to do three things.

1. Learn the four principles.
2. Make a plan to use them.
3. Tell, show, and reward.

You are the best teacher your children will ever have. Never abandon your teaching role no matter how old your children are. You are their lifetime mentor. You will need to make a conscious plan to develop a positive relationship with your child based upon the four principles outlined in this chapter. You will need to act upon your plan and practice the four principles. You will need to tell your child what you are doing, show them how to do it, and reward your child for her cooperation. An example is in order. When my granddaughter Kellie was five years old, I had an opportunity to teach Kellie mutual respect (principle two). Kellie said, "Would you get me a Coke?" I said I would and told her why (tell). I said, "Kellie I would be glad to get you a Coke because someday Papa will ask you to do something nice for me, and I will expect you to do it." I got her a Coke with ice and brought it in to her (show) and leaned down and kissed her on the forehead (reward). The Kellie illustration will be developed in a teaching story in the section on shaping behavior.

Principle One: Tolerance

The first principle to do and teach a child, in order to have a good relationship with you, is tolerance. I'm not talking about "putting-up-with." We can put up with anything. I am using the word tolerance to mean acceptance; that is, accepting children as they are, without a felt and pressing need to change or fix them. The more acceptance there is, the stronger the relationship. You will need to talk about this principle, over time, in a hundred different ways. For example, "Honey, Mom likes to have some quiet time and you like to play with me. I am going to set the timer for thirty minutes and when the timer dings, I will play a game with you. This is called accepting each other. I will do for you and you do for me." You have fulfilled your teaching responsibility. Mutual respect has been emphasized, a plan effected, and a reward given. Brothers and sisters provide countless opportunities to emphasize or highlight this relationship building principle. For example, "Sally, your brother is four years old and you are six. He likes to play with trucks and do things you have outgrown. If you will play with him for thirty minutes without complaining once, I will play a big girl game of hopscotch with you. This is called acceptance. You accept that he is four and likes to do things you are too big to really like anymore. By doing this, you will learn to love him more and he will love you back." You have just taught the principle of tolerance. I can hear it now, "Oh sure, and you think that will work. You don't know my kids." Well, I do know your kids. I know about all kids. It may not make much difference immediately, but I can assure you that it does make a long-term difference. Think of your children as banks. In these simple examples, you have made a positive deposit in your child's bank. Keep depositing, and after a hundred or so deposits of acceptance, you will start earning big interest returns. Young children are really skilled at accepting you, their mom and dad, just as you are. They are not very good at accepting the competition of a brother or sister. The concept needs to be taught, so look for opportunities. I also like the storytelling way of teaching siblings acceptance. Go to the storytelling chapter (chapter 11), and you will find some stories on acceptance. Learn how to tell a story that is appropriate for your child's needs. I like the story about the goose whose cooperator was busted.

I realize that there may be some behaviors that your child does that you are not willing to tolerate. That's fine. I didn't accept everything my kids did as okay either. If, for example, your child sasses you using rude or abusive language, I don't think you should accept it as fine. I would expect you to stop it and replace his sassy words with better ways to communicate his unhappiness with you. Choose one or two of the methods taught in later chapters and use them to correct the problem. Fix the intolerances and move on. The more acceptance you have, the stronger your relationship will be.

This is what I would suggest you do before moving on to principle two. Write out two lists. The first list is probably the easiest one to do. Make a list of all the behaviors your child does that you are not willing to tolerate. Put your list in the book and when you read of a behavioral change technique you would like to try out on one of these "intolerables," write the name of the technique beside the behavior you want to change. Use the change technique when you have time and are ready to get something done about that intolerable behavior. I strongly urge you to do this. This exercise will help you with your tolerance. Think of every other unpleasant thing your child does as simply annoying for the moment. Say to yourself, "This is not on my list of intolerances, so I accept his behavior as simply annoying; therefore, I'm not going to start World War III over it." Use the common correction tools like distraction, short time-outs, or parental "discussions" (a nice name for lecture) and be done with it. I will guarantee that your body language will alter for the better and your tone of voice will not sound like the grim reaper is talking. Your child will love this "new you," and your relationship will make nice progress.

Now for list two. This is the hard one. I want you to make a similar list but this time it is about you. This may sound harsh but here is what I want you do to. Make list of everything you are doing to destroy your relationship with your child. The page may remain blank, but I doubt it. You probably are aware of two or more things you do that do not enhance your parent-to-child relationship. Be brave and write them down. Magic will occur. Your subconscious mind will start working on your personal deficits. Read your personal list at least once per week.

You've Got the Same Pants to Get Glad in as You Got Mad In

Here is a teaching story to bring this point home. Marriage and parenthood have something in common. Kids don't come with instructions and neither do new marriages. I loved Roena, but I had no idea how to solve relationship differences. When we were courting and I got mad at Roena, I could get into my 1951 Mercury with the big motor, peel out and leave fifty feet of black rubber in front of her house. She knew I was mad, and so did the neighbors. In a day or two, I was all better, so I would go see her again. After we married, I had to go into the house with her. I had no idea about what to do, so I pouted. I was good at it, too. I could pout for days. I am ashamed to admit it, but I could pout so long that I would, at times, forget what it was I was originally mad about. Early in our marriage, a good thing happened. I was pouting, and Roena wanted to talk about what was bothering me. That's Roena's style. If it's wrong, talk it out and fix it. That wasn't my way. I pouted and didn't fix it. I'll never forget that fateful day. I was pouting and shaving. I didn't have my shirt on, which is important to the story, and Roena was standing in the bathroom doorway asking what was wrong. I said "nothing" in that male tone of voice that means everything is wrong. In exasperation, Roena said, "Jerry Day, look at me." So I turned and she hit me square in the solar plexus. Now I want to quickly say that Roena is not a violent woman. She had never hit me before, and in forty-five years of marriage, she has never hit me again in anger. I should also point out that Roena is 5 feet 1 inch tall and couldn't hurt me anyway. It was a lucky blow, and I lost my breath and couldn't speak. Roena "seized the moment," as the commercial says, and said the words I have never forgotten. They were, "Jerry Day, you have the same pants to get glad in as you got mad in and if you ever decide to talk to me, you look me up." She stormed out of the bedroom mad as a hornet. I distinctly remember saying in my mind, "I'm going to have to stop this pouting thing; it is destroying our relationship." I knew it was wrong, but I didn't want to really know it was wrong.

Now that you have made your list, I want you to use the Marks Technique to correct what you are doing to destroy your relationship with your child. The Marks Technique is discussed in chapter 10. Read it and apply the technique to your needs.

Principle Two: Respect and Admiration

For relationships to thrive there must be mutual respect, and lots of compliments (admiration). We live in a very negative world. It is not frequent that we get praised for what we do right. What happens when you go to work and it's break time? Does anyone praise the company and say things like, "You know I think I am overpaid for the work I do. This is a great company to work for, the vacations are generous, and the boss treats me with the respect I so richly deserve."? Most workers complain during lunch breaks about the low pay and the unbearable work conditions. Did any of your teachers put a red mark by any of the correct answers you got on a test? Probably not. They marked the wrong ones, though. It's rare that a teacher calls a child up to the desk and says, "Fred, you made sixty-five on your test. That's almost passing. You're close, so try a little harder and you will be passing." Most teachers warn about the danger of failing and remind the child about the excessive daydreaming and talking that no doubt led to this terrible grade. You most likely were raised in a negative household. Mistakes and failures were emphasized, and your successes were followed by silence.

Most children above the age of ten notice these things and complain to people like me that they "never" get credit for what they do right. For example, if a twelve-year-old boy's job is to pick up his clothes from the bedroom floor, he may remember to do it six out of ten times. What does he want to hear about? Yes, he wants credit for doing the pickup chores six times and only forgetting four. What do we do as parents though? We usually scold excessively about the four slipups. The point is that children like to be praised. They are bottomless pits and can't be overfilled with too much praise. Relationships are built on the consistent admiration of the things that are right and good. We cannot build a positive relationship upon an excessive focus on what we want to correct. Home is where we go to get our life battery charged. School is a negative place where kids criticize other kids and teachers correct mistakes. The important point of this discussion is to put as much effort and attention into catching your child doing right and good as you do at pointing out what's wrong. Relationships grow when there are more positive interactions than negative ones.

Respect is clearly associated with positive admiration of a child's accomplishments. Respect has to do with treating your child at least as well as you do a neighbor or a clerk in a store. That isn't always the case in the home.

Behind closed doors, parents frequently say and do things to their children that they would never do or say in public. The sad thing is that children are, more often than I like to know, treated with less respect and human dignity than a neighbor or a store clerk. If you are not one of those parents, then God bless you. Disrespect goes further than just parent-to-child disrespect. Parents may model a system of disrespect for one another to their child. Things are done and said between parents that are disrespectful to one another. It is a horrible model for children.

I hope you will tolerate my soap box speech for a moment longer. Sammy's father is an example of parental disrespect. Because Sammy did not like to play catch with him, his dad called Sammy his "little faggot boy girl." He may have intended to foster manliness in his child but the result was a disappointed and defeated child who thought his dad didn't want him. A mom in session with me said, in front of her teenage daughter Sue, "I worry about Sue. I am afraid she will be like one of those whores she hangs out with." These are extreme examples to be sure, but the principle of respect is violated in less dramatic fashion in many homes. It will be of immense help to think back on what you have said in frustration and anger to your child. One mom remembered, with shame, that she said to her daughter during one of her many fits, "You are possessed by a devil and will never be any good." If you would not say it to a store clerk or a neighbor, don't say it to your child. They hear and register everything.

Let's finish principle two with a few "Don'ts." Principle two is about being positive with your child. Relationships thrive in an atmosphere of positive exchanges of respect between parent and child. It is not appropriate to punish your child with your attitude so avoid the following seven negative attitudes:

1. **Don't pout.** When your child doesn't follow your directive, use one of the suggested methods, correct the problem, and be done with it. You have done what you can, so it is over. Pouting and the silent treatment negate the good you have done and create a negative relationship.
2. **Don't withdraw.** When discipline is over, play, talk, and interact. Avoidance, isolation, and withdrawal, whether physical or emotional, perpetuate a negative atmosphere for relationship-building.
3. **Don't continue scolding.** Do your corrective teaching in short bursts. Children usually don't listen when they are angry, hurt, or afraid. Keep

it short at the time of the infraction, and come back to the problem later if more needs to be said.

4. Don't shame your child. Relationships are never made better when shame or guilt tactics are used. For example, don't say, "Look what you've done, don't you know how bad that makes me feel?"

5. Don't personalize. When your rules are broken, it is not directed at you personally. Relationships are never enhanced when a parent takes an infraction of directives personally.

6. Don't posture or pretend to be mean. Just take care of business and move on. Making a child afraid for his life is a relationship-killer.

7. Don't threaten a punishment you won't actually do or stick to. To say to a child, "The next time you get lost at the store, I'm going to leave you there and you can get home on your own." There is no chance you will carry through with your threat. Don't ground a teenager for a year unless you are prepared to consistently carry out that punishment. Your credibility is undermined with your child if you don't follow through, and it weakens the quality of your relationship.

Take the high but harder road. Create an environment for positive exchanges and watch your relationship grow stronger and more fulfilling year after year.

Now it's time for an assignment. I call it the three-compliment-rule. Tell your son, for example, that for two weeks you are going to do something different. You will give three compliments about him, and he is to give you three compliments in return. The dinner table is a good place to do this assignment.

If practiced, saying compliments will become standard and a pleasant habit.

Here is the next assignment. It is similar to the first, but with a twist. Ask your child to tell you three things they liked about school today. Be prepared to hear negative things, but restate that you want to hear positive things. Here is what happened in session one day. I asked Jill to tell me three good things that happened in school today. Jill said, "Billy pulled my hair and made me cry," "I fell down and hurt my knee," and "I didn't like lunch." Again, I asked her to tell me three good things that happened in school. Jill took a breath and reflected a moment and said, "I failed spelling," "Sarah was mean to me, and she is not my friend anymore," and "I didn't like lunch." If you ask a child to tell you three bad things that happened today, they often can do it immediately without even taking another breath. Try it. I think you will be astonished with how easy it is for your child to tell you the bad of the day and how hard it is to tell you the good the day brought. To continue with Jill, she finally told me one good thing, "Pete did not push me down at recess." That was it. She couldn't think of one more good school happening. This assignment is forever. Keep asking until your child is married.

Principle two is about creating a habit of positive interactions and exchanges between a parent and child. Good happens when this principle is experienced in abundance. Go forth, be positive.

Principle Three: Fun

This is a short one. Have fun. Relationships that make it are able to put aside problems for a bit and frolic. We took into our home a foster daughter who was, to put it mildly, "Hell on wheels." She had been in eleven foster homes before coming to live with us. Her behavior was awful. She needed lots of corrective teaching, which involved some complex discipline. I used several of my favorite corrective techniques in the early stages of our relationship. One of those techniques is the three-level method of discipline. She was fully aware of the three levels of discipline, for I had discussed it with her on several occasions. She knew that level one was a warning with no penalty attached. She simply had an opportunity to cooperate with family rules. She could fix the problem with no punishment at all. Level two involved a mild punishment, which was, in her case, no television for one evening. Level three was the atomic bomb. She would be grounded, horror of horrors, from using the phone for one long, agonizing week. For a social fourteen-year-old girl, that is the hydrogen bomb. She wouldn't do what I told her to do, so she finally got to level three. Darcy was pouting in her room when I went to her door and knocked. With a sullen, mean tone she invited me in. I said I had to do an errand and if she liked, she could come and we would stop off at Baskin-Robbins for some ice cream. Darcy said, "I thought I was in trouble and grounded from the phone for a week. Am I ungrounded?" I said, "No, you are still grounded from the phone for the week, and if I catch you using the phone for any reason, I am going to banish you to your room for an entire year. Now get your shoes on and let's go." She went, and we had a good time, but she still couldn't use the phone!

Have fun with your children. It is one of the four necessary principles that are absolutely required for a positive, long-lasting, satisfying relationship.

Fun is not of less importance than tolerance or being positive. The earlier you start, the better. Starting at about age thirteen, children often seek fun with their friends rather than their family. Here is your assignment. Start doing family night weekly, bimonthly, or monthly. Don't schedule it less frequently than monthly. My family did this into the teen years. Mark and Amanda would invite a teen friend to family night. Most of their friends were a little reluctant to come when they heard what we did. However, by the end of the evening, they were sold on family night. We popped popcorn, had soft drinks, played a variety of board games, and of all things, talked.

Principle Four: Communication

Without good communication, healthy relationships are not possible. There are three requirements for healthy communication to occur between child and parent.

1. The key to healthy communication does not rest with the one who talks. The success of any communication falls on the listener. The wise parent listens first to understand. Parents are not prone to do this well. Typically parents want to talk and talk and talk. Parents usually talk to win the argument. The paradox is that until a child feels heard, they rarely want to change or be responsible for their actions. This is such an important concept it bears repeating. Children are unwilling to change their behavior or listen to wise parental advice until they feel they have been heard. Listening to understand is difficult for the average parent. Parents just don't want to hear a bunch of excuses from their child. Parents often believe that since they know best anyway, listening to their child's point of view is basically a waste of their time. Parental problem-solving action is usually initiated without any thought given to listening before corrective action is taken.

Non-defensive listening is required for healthy communication between parent and child. There are two important rules to follow when listening non-defensively. Don't interrupt your child, no matter what the age. He has something he wants to say. Interruptions communicate to the child that what he is saying is not important. The child comes to believe that it is only what his parent thinks that is important. Interruptions are self-esteem killers for the child. Remember, listening does not mean agreement. It does mean you value your child and what he has to say. Interruptions usually results in "rabbit chasing." A rabbit never runs a straight line. It darts here and there.

If a parent interrupts, a child will defend and respond to the content of the interruption and lose track of what he started off to communicate. Most children just give up, quit talking, and refuse to listen. The second rule of non-defensive listening is to set your emotional feelings aside and listen without defending or correcting. If you are angry or hurt by what your child is saying, then your feelings are placed in front of you, and everything is then heard through filters. It is my estimate that we miss approximately 15 percent of everything said when we are doing our best listening. The brain just won't hear it all. If anger is in front, that alone may drop your understanding to only 15 percent. This is not enough understanding to be an effective listener or problem solver. Non-defensive listening on the parent's part does wonders for the child, who feels validated and respected. Those are big pay offs for such a simple response. First, listen to understand. Second, listen non-defensively. Don't worry; your turn to talk is coming soon.

2. The second requirement for good communication between parent and child is to do feedback listening. Sometimes this is called reflective listening. I am sure you have experienced the question, "Do you know what I mean?" while listening intently to an adult speaker. What do you say? It's almost always, "sure," because you really think you've got it. When one hears that question, it's rare indeed that the response is, "No, I don't have a clue." The only sure way of knowing if you have "got it" is to say back, in brief form, what you think your child's point is. Start now practicing feedback listening. Tell your child what his point is. If he says, "Uh huh," then you are free to speak. You've got it.

There are other good reasons for giving feedback. If you missed something, your child has a chance to correct your misunderstanding before you respond. For example, if nine-year-old Jim tells you that he didn't bring home his homework assignment notebook because Fred borrowed it and didn't give it back and you say, "Jim, your point is you don't care about school and want to fail fourth grade," Jim can agree or disagree. Jim will probably disagree and tell you he just forgot to get it back from Fred. That's his point. If you say, "Let me see if I have this straight. You loaned your assignment notebook to Fred and you forgot to ask Fred to give it back. Is that right?" Jim will say, "Uh huh." Now you are free to talk about responsibility and suggest a fix for his forgetful ways. It keeps you on target, less emotional, and open to problem-solving action. Unless you get it, long lectures on the value of school and what passing means to his long-range future is pointless. If you listen non-defensively and give accurate feedback, Jim will feel respected and validated and be a lot more willing to abide by your corrective suggestions regarding how to prevent it from happening in the future. Non-defensive listening will vastly improve your relationship and help build a lasting bond between parent and child. Kids simply like to hang out with parents who are willing to listen.

3. The third requirement for good communication is solving the problem. When you have listened to understand, listened non-defensively, and engaged in feedback listening, you are free to say anything you want to say. It's your child's turn to listen. It is helpful to take a moment to tell him what you have just done. "Son, I have listened to you without getting hurt or angry, without interrupting you, and you said that I got it right, so now it's your turn to listen to me without interruption and without getting upset." A short—emphasis on the "short"—discussion of your point of view is in order. Next, you have to offer a solution before the conversation ends. The best way to solve a problem is through bargaining. Bargaining will, I believe, completely change 94 percent of all the problems that occur between a parent and a child. Remember, you are your child's best teacher, so teach him what a bargain entails. You might say, "Son, let's make a bargain and this is what I mean by bargain." Now you teach. A bargain is something for something. Each gives a little until it feels good for both sides. For example, in the story about Jim, you might say, "Now, to help you quit forgetting and remember to bring home your assignment notebook, here is what I propose. If you forget again, you are to forfeit your entire week's allowance of five dollars. What do you think?" Jim may think that's not fair so you will ask him what he thinks would be fair. Jim might say. "I think ten cents would be enough." Of course, you are not going to go for that solution, but neither is Jim going for the loss of his entire five-dollar weekly allowance. So, you might say, "I don't agree to a penalty of only ten cents. What if we say you forfeit one dollar and twenty-five cents. Does that sound like a better bargain?" For our example, Jim says, "Okay," so it's a done deal. Every time he forgets, he loses one dollar and twenty-five cents of his allowance. Teach the method of bargaining. Both you and your child will get enough that each will think it's a good deal and a wonderful life principle has been taught.

I can assure you that Jim will be pleased and you have taught some very important problem-solving skills as well as communication skills to him. He will feel really good about you, and the relationship will have advanced. If the rules of communication are applied consistently, Jim will be a lucky boy to have a mom and dad like you because he will grow to be a man who can communicate with a boss, a spouse, and best of all, his own children.

It is much easier to teach a child to willingly live under parental authority if quality time is devoted to developing a positive relationship between parent and child. It takes time but the effort pays excellent dividends. Always remember and never forget that when a child learns to willingly live under a parent's authority, heaven opens up and happiness comes down. The time and effort invested in teaching a child how to develop a lasting relationship is nothing compared to the rewards it brings the parent and child. Children simply want to cooperate with parents that they respect and like. The efforts invested in teaching a child how to form a positive, rewarding relationship with both parents is also an investment into his long-term future. Not only are you his first authority, you also represent his first opportunity to learn valuable lessons from his first quality relationships. If he can do it with his mom and dad, he can form relationships with other important people who come into his life.

I want to conclude this section on communication and how it relates to relationship with two teaching stories. These stories illustrate two points.

1. Start developing that strong, abiding relationship with your children when they are young. The younger they are, the greater the rewards; but remember, it is never too late to use the principles discussed in this chapter. There is no doubt that children who have been taught how to have a healthy relationship with their mothers and fathers are much more easily taught how to willingly live under parental authority.

2. Teaching a child how to effectively communicate is the supportive foundation for solving and resolving all misbehavior problems. Communication goes both ways. Children need to learn how to do it and so do parents. It's a fact that children do not learn how to communicate if parents can't do it right. A parent is the best teacher a child will ever have. Parents can communicate many positive lessons, but they are just as capable of teaching unwanted negative ones. Don't wait. Begin now by listening to understand, giving feedback, and using problem-solving bargaining.

Mark the Communication-Tester

This is a story about my son Mark and how he tested my willingness to listen and communicate. When Mark was young, I started doing something that I would recommend that you start doing. I noticed that when Mark and I were away from our house, he would talk more. Getting away from the familiar sights, sounds, smells, and distractions of the home encourages more meaningful communication. For Mark, it was long walks in the neighborhood. For Amanda, our talk-time was over two scoops of ice cream and a walk around the mall.

Usually on our walks, I listened first, and when he ran down, I would talk about the issues he had brought up during our walk. Mark was in the beginning months of his eighth-grade year. He had all the symptoms of a hormone-filled teenager. Mark said "Dad, I want to talk to you about something." I said, "Okay." He continued, "Dad I've thought it over and I have decided to smoke marijuana." Well, you know what I wanted to scream back. I wanted to get into his face and say, "No, you're not going to smoke marijuana! I'll kick you out of the house! I'll have you arrested! I won't stand for it. You're not going to do it, and that's that!" But instead I gulped, took a deep breath and said as calmly as I could, "Interesting, would you tell me more about it?" Open-ended questions are good for getting more talk, and talk he did. I learned things I didn't know like where he could buy it, the current cost, and the new teen drug language. He was a cornucopia of rich information that I would surely use with my future teenage clients. We had passed by our house three times by the time he finished. I gave him a short version feedback summary and asked him if I had gotten the point. He affirmed that I "got it." We walked in silence for a few minutes and I said, "Mark I have patiently listened to you talk, haven't I?" He agreed. Then I said, "I have a few things I would like to talk to you about and I would like for you to listen to me non-defensively like I listened to you." Mark said, "Okay, Dad." So far, so good.

I spent a good while talking about the potential damage marijuana can do to the brain. I went on to talk briefly about our family values and concluded with the illegality of marijuana and its legal punishments. Mark listened patiently and then said something that has stayed frozen in my brain since. Mark said, "Dad, don't worry about me. I'm not going to smoke marijuana. I just wanted to hear what you would say." I almost kissed him. What a relief. To my knowledge, he never did smoke marijuana, nor did he do any other drugs for that matter.

I have always wondered what might have happened if I had listened, not to understand, but defensively. What if I had let my temper explode, interrupted his story, and tore into him as my first inclinations had suggested? I might be telling a different story about Mark the Pothead. I just don't know, but I am glad I never had a chance to experience ending number two!

The principles of communication were employed by both of us and the results were ever so satisfying.

Amanda the First-Grade Drop-Out

This is a story about Amanda, my oldest child. It illustrates the same points as the Mark story, but there is an emphasis on poor communication. The story also highlights a special type of feedback listening that I want you to start practicing immediately. The rewards of this special type of communication are immediate and excellent. Listening for feelings is the special aspect of communication I want to illustrate in this story.

Amanda was an outspoken, opinionated, high energy little girl. I knew she would have trouble with the teacher in the first grade. I didn't know when she would be in trouble with her teacher; I just knew it was inevitable. I think it happened within the first twenty minutes of her first day at school. We lived just a little out of town, so Amanda rode the bus to and from school. Roena reported that Amanda hopped off the bus, flew into the house, ripped her backpack off, yanked her sweater off, threw it down on top of her backpack, and announced that she was quitting school because her teacher was mean to her. According to Amanda, her teacher hated her and she hated her teacher. Amanda's tirade went on for forty-five minutes or longer. She could not be calmed or soothed. Roena is really good with kids, and a former teacher, but she didn't have a lick of luck with Amanda that day. Amanda didn't drop out of first grade, but every two or three days, the same story repeated itself.

I was teaching in college in those days, so I had flexible hours that would allow me to be home when Amanda arrived from school. The great psychologist took over, and I told Roena not to worry, I would take care of it. Sure enough in a few days, Amanda came stomping into the house. It was the same routine that Roena had described. All of a sudden I was no longer the wise, controlled psychologist. Instead, I was a mad dad with no communication skills to be found anywhere. I used my gruffest daddy voice and said, "Alright, Amanda, that's enough of that. No kid of mine is going to act this way. Now, I'm going to get to the bottom of this. What did you do wrong, young lady?" Amanda said she didn't do anything wrong. It was her mean teacher that was wrong. She continued her tirade for forty-five minutes.

I felt pretty defeated and a little ashamed of my behavior, but I was determined to try it one more time. In a few days Amanda came stomping into the house. It must have been God who told me what to say because I sure didn't have it planned out. By the time she flung her backpack down I heard myself say in the most controlled voice I have ever used, "Well Amanda, I don't know who is right or who is wrong, but I know one thing for sure, you're plenty mad." Amanda looked up at me and said, "That's right, Daddy, I am plenty mad." And out she went to play. I just learned a valuable lesson. Again and again for forty-five minutes at a time, she had tried to tell us that she was "plenty mad," but no one had listened to her feelings.

The point of the story is that neither Roena nor I were able to hear her feelings. She didn't want us to solve her problem with facts and logic. I tried that. I even went to the school and talked to her first grade teacher. Instead, Amanda wanted someone to hear and respond to her feelings. Whether adult or child, it is very healing to have someone hear our feelings. Until her feelings were heard, nothing else we said or did counted.

Here is your assignment. For seven days, listen for your child's feelings. Use feedback listening and reflect back to your child the feeling you heard. Observe what happens. Here is a rule to follow: facts for facts and feelings for feelings. If your child talks facts, you talk facts back, but if she talks feelings, talk feelings back. Young children are usually short on facts and long on feelings. Frequently they do not want a factual lecture; they want a short response about what they are feeling.

Communication is the foundation for problem solving. Until a child is heard, he or she is not willing to change. They desire to be heard before they want to comply with parental authority. Amanda stopped threatening to quit school after the second time her feelings were heard and reflected back to her. She continued in school and graduated with a bachelor's degree. Although I didn't get it right the first time or two with Amanda's problem, I can report that I did learn my lesson from this early unpleasant experience. When Amanda was in her teens, she had boyfriend problems. Sometimes, she would cry and tell me that her boyfriend was mean to her. I had learned my lesson when she was six years old, so I would take her into my arms, pat her on the back, and say, "I don't know too much about boyfriend problems, but I know one thing for sure, he really hurt your feelings." Amanda would say, "Thanks, Dad," and her tears and pain faded quickly. Listening for feelings really works. Try it. Go forth, do good!

Behavior Shaping

A parent's job has two distinct parts. Unfortunately, many parents focus on part one of their job and grossly neglect part two. It is very easy to identify the rebellion, mistakes, bad habits, and naughtiness of a child, and make the correction of these undesirable behaviors the single mission of the parent. My book has a strong emphasis on unique, creative, and effective methods to correct uncooperative behavior, but the use of my negative reinforcement techniques does not constitute the entire purpose of my book. Good parenting is more than successfully correcting bad behavior.

Parents need to create good behavior. Create means to take something from nothing and make it exist. All parents want children to do things that they don't usually do. For example, parents may want their child to:

1. See things that need to be done and do them without being forced or reminded to, such as clearing the table and picking up papers and toys from the living room floor.
2. Be friendly to visiting adult guests by greeting them and staying in the room for a few minutes.
3. Share favorite toys with visiting children without being told to do so.
4. Help a younger brother or sister to dress without being scolded into it.
5. Scrub dirty elbows when taking a bath or shower.
6. Be less grumpy and more pleasant in the mornings.
7. Acknowledge that a parent has spoken directly to a child by making some form of verbal response.

These behaviors and many more probably don't happen nearly as often as a parent would like. I am about to share with you a way that can make them happen on a regular and consistent basis. The method I want to teach that makes this possible is called Behavior Shaping. It is a thoughtful, organized way of identifying a behavior that rarely or never happens and systematically shaping it into existence.

What I would like for you to do right now is to stop reading after this paragraph, and do something that will make this section on behavior shaping much more meaningful to you. First, find a clean piece of paper and a pencil. Next, write a list of things you would like to see your child do that would please you and be good for him. This will be your operational list. As you read the rest of the section on behavior shaping, think about how you can apply what you are learning to your specific goals for your own child.

The Professor

In a previous section, I fully discussed the value of rewards as a teaching tool. I discussed how to set up a rewards program in a way that makes it highly likely that a child will respond in a positive manner. Remember that the premise that all rewards programs depend upon is that children will repeat anything that brings to them reward and pleasure for the doing of a defined behavior. The following teaching story illustrates the techniques I want you to use and the tremendous power of behavior shaping.

Long ago, when I was in graduate school learning about how the brain works, something very interesting happened. At the time, the concept of behavior shaping was new, exciting, and mysterious. Graduate students tend to go through graduate school as a group, and there were about thirty new students who started at the same time, so we took many classes together. We also formed strong social bonds. At a party that most of the thirty attended, we began to talk about what we were learning. The subject of shaping behavior came up, and we decided we needed to practice what we were learning.

As a group, we decided to practice on our statistic professor. We were afraid to practice on any of our psychology professors. The statistics professor's habit was to sit on his desk and swing his legs while lecturing to us about the wonders of statistics. Occasionally, he would leave his desk to write something on the board, and then return to his desk and sit on it in his customary way. It is important to describe our classroom. It had a high ceiling and five very tall windows with an eight-inch window sill that struck him about mid-chest high. His desk was in the middle of the room and the windows were to his right. Our specific goal was to train him to lecture to us from the second window in the front of the room with his right elbow resting on the window sill. Remember, his long-standing habit was to lecture to us from his seat on top of his desk. He never lectured from the second window with his right elbow resting on the eight-inch window sill.

Our job was to shape his behavior to what we wanted without his awareness of what we were up to. We had developed a highly specific goal so the next step in our planning was to decide how we would reward the professor for movement toward the goal of lecturing from the second window with his right elbow on the window sill. After a lot of thought, we decided that we would reward the professor with our attention and interest. Professors love it when their students pay attention to what they say and write down copious notes about the points made. They are suckers for interest and attention. It's better than gold. Well, maybe not better, but the reward of attention is powerful. So, we now had a specific goal and a good reward.

The next step was to find opportunities to reward him. Here is what we did. On occasion, he would stand up to rest his rear. He would lecture for a few minutes while standing in front of his desk and then sit down again to finish his lecture. When he lectured from the top of his desk we would, one at a time, close our book and notebook and look out the window or at the floor. We didn't do this all at once or he would have caught on that our behavior was planned. When he got around to standing up, we would, one at a time, here and there across the room, unfold our arms, open up our books and notebooks, fetch our pencils, look at him with an expression of interest on our faces and start taking notes. We repeated this behavior at every class. In a few class sessions our professor was consistently lecturing in front of his desk while standing. So far, so good. Now we needed to move him toward the window side of the room.

We noticed that on occasion he would turn toward the window and look at something outside while continuing his lecture. We knew that we had a good reward that worked, so we had to find opportunities to use it. A rule in behavior shaping is to reward small movements or steps toward the specific goal. We stopped paying attention if he lectured, while standing in front of his desk. As soon as he turned toward the windows, we gave him our attention. When he turned back to the desk, we stopped taking notes and wouldn't give him eye contact. Soon he was lecturing a few feet to the right of the desk. We then stopped paying attention if he lectured from that position. His subconscious mind was beginning to catch on that we wanted him to move toward the window, and he was learning faster now. In a few months he was lecturing, every day, from the window side of the room. Now we had to move him to the second window from the front of the room. We applied the same methods and he slowly moved toward the second window.

To get him to put his right elbow on the window sill was quite a challenge. One of the rules of behavior shaping is to increase the requirements to get the reward. We had to sit for several weeks without giving him attention before he fulfilled the next level of requirements. He had to, in some manner, touch the window sill to get us to resume our attentiveness to his lecture. One day, for unknown reasons, he reached out and put his hand on the window sill. Don't forget his subconscious had begun to search for ways to get and keep our attention. We immediately, one at a time, here and there across the room, opened our notebooks, took notes and made eye contact with him. It took another three weeks but he finally put his elbow on the window sill. Before the year ended, he was lecturing from the second window from the front with his right elbow on the window sill. The statistics professor never caught on.

Shaping behavior takes time and patience, especially when you are trying to create a consistent behavior that has never before existed. It took us seven months to shape the professor's behavior. It was a great experience that taught me about the potential power of behavior shaping. Incidentally, we had to hire a private tutor to help us pass statistics. We hadn't paid enough attention to pass on our own!

The Short Version of the Rules

My manipulative graduate school class carefully followed the lawful rules of behavior shaping. Remember, the laws of learning are orderly and immutable. That is why they're referred to as laws. People will repeat anything that results in a rewarding and pleasant experience. The following are the rules that must be followed for best results. If you reread, "The Professor Story," you will recognize how each of these rules was applied.

1. The goal must be specific. For example, if a parent sets a goal that his child must behave better when children come for a visit, the goal is not specific enough. The goal might be restated like this. "I want my child to share three toys with Troy when he visits." "I want my son to share his Legos, his football, and his Candy Travel Game without bossing, crying, pushing, grabbing, hitting, spitting, or yelling."
2. Decide on the rewards you will use. Hugs, kisses, pats, high fives, and verbal praise are powerful rewards but so are ice cream, money, a game with a parent, and staying up late.
3. Look for opportunities to reward. Be generous, and quickly reward approximations toward the larger goal. Reward very small steps toward

the goal. My dad often said, "Even a blind hog will eventually find an acorn." Keeping with our sharing toys example, if you are alert, your child will eventually briefly share one of the three toys for a few minutes with Troy. Ultimately, the law of probabilities will take over and he will briefly share one of the three toys. A parent's job is to be vigilant and catch him sharing, then reward it. Be generous with your rewards and reward frequently.

4. Increase the requirements to get the reward. At first, the child is rewarded for sharing one toy for a few minutes. When he is sharing one toy for brief periods, consistently up the ante. Don't give him praise or ice cream until he has shared two toys for eight minutes. It's alright to share with your child what you want and expect. Your child doesn't have to be naive like the professor. Tell him what you expect and why you are praising him or giving him a dollar.

5. When your child is consistently doing what you want, then thin the rewards and eventually terminate the behavior shaping program for that goal. For example, reward him one out of every two or three times he shares his toys with Troy. Your child will internalize the desire to share without being rewarded. Eventually, he will do it because he wants to.

Mariah the Morning Grump

Mariah is my granddaughter. She is now twelve years old, but when she was four years old, she was the grumpiest girl in Tucson, Arizona, before 10:00 a.m. She frequently spent the night at our house. She usually was up watching cartoons when I came in to eat breakfast. I would say, "Good morning, Mariah," and she was stony silent. She would not acknowledge my presence in the room. I decided to shape her morning attitude and behavior. I wanted her to smile and say, "Good morning, Papa." One morning, I went over to Mariah and stood between her and the television and said, "Mariah, from now on I will come into the room and say, 'Good morning, Mariah,' and I want you to look at me, smile, and say, 'Good morning, Papa.'" She looked at me with a blank stare and said nothing.

The next morning I prepared her favorite breakfast, an apple Pop-Tart and juice. I went over to the couch and said, "Good morning, Mariah." She said nothing. I then coached her. I said, "Now it's your turn. I want you to say 'Good morning, Papa.'" She cooperated and I said, "Thank you." I then sat down beside her, put my arm around her, hugged her, and said, "I like that." I gave her the Pop-Tart and juice and she returned to watching television. In a few weeks, Mariah was saying, "Good morning, Papa," every time I greeted her in the morning. I next added the look-at-me-and-smile part. Every time she complied, I hugged her, kissed her, and praised her. I also told her how good her greeting made me feel. In a few months, an interesting thing happened. When I came into the kitchen in the morning, Mariah would get up from the couch, come into the kitchen, say, "Good morning, Papa," and give me a hug. I really liked that.

Mariah has always loved me, but she had the annoying habit of ignoring me before 10:00 a.m. She always treated me well after 10:00 a.m., but before then., she was very grumpy. Morning civility and cheerfulness just didn't exist. I identified a behavior I wanted to see and shaped it until Mariah consistently displayed it.

Kellie the Queen

Kellie came into our family at about age five when my son married a wonderful girl with three children. Kellie did not have a pleasant, bonded relationship with her biological father, and she was very distant and usually uncommunicative with me. I noticed that about the only time she acknowledged that I existed was when she wanted something. She was good at giving me orders like, "Hand me the TV remote," "Get me some more ice," "Hand me those crayons," and "Get me my shoes." She wasn't mean about it, but seemed almost indifferent, like a queen giving orders to her helpers.

My goal for her was to develop a warm relationship with me characterized by mutual sharing of tasks and needs. More specifically, I wanted her to express appreciation for what I did for her with hugs, smiles, and thank-yous. I also wanted her to return my favors by doing things for me that I specifically asked her to do. I chose praise, touch, kisses, and hugs as the reward for attachment and cooperative behavior.

One morning Kellie was sitting on the couch watching cartoons. As I walked by, she said, without looking up, "Get me a Coke." I was ready. I said, "I would be happy to get you a Coke because sometime, I will ask you to do something for me, and I will expect you to do it." She looked up at me with a slight smile on her lips, but said nothing more. I got her Coke, took it in to her, and said, "Here is your Coke. I love you, and I hope you enjoy it." I also stooped down and kissed her on the forehead. She didn't say a word. Later on in the afternoon she was coloring nicely. I got her attention and said, "You remember that Grandpa got you a Coke this morning?" Kellie said, "Yes." I continued,

"Grandpa needs his house shoes from the bedroom closet, so will you go get them for me?" I was pleased to see her interrupt her activity and go into the bedroom to fetch my slippers. Kellie brought them into the TV room and presented them to me. I hugged Kellie and kissed her cheek and said, "It really makes Grandpa happy when you do things for me, and thank you for getting my slippers." Kellie smiled. We continued to ask for services from one another, and I always reinforced her cooperation with some form of affection and a thank-you. My desire was to model how I wanted to be treated when I did something positive for her. It wasn't long before she said, without prompting, "Thank you." I was waiting for that so I kissed her cheek, gave her a hug, and said, "It really makes Grandpa happy when you say thank you when I do something for you." "Thank you" became a regular expression when I did something for her. Our bonding and attachment began to gradually improve. In a few months Kellie added smiles and hugs when I did something nice for her. I reinforced the hugs and smiles by telling her that it really made me feel good when she said thank you and hugged me. Then, of course, I gave her a hug and kiss.

Behavior shaping worked very well for Kellie. Presently, we have a great relationship with lots of mutual affection. She no longer gives me orders, and her love for me is apparent. Kellie is now nine years old. The point of the teaching story is that I specifically identified what I wanted from Kellie and then set about shaping behavior that didn't exist through rewarding small steps toward the main goal. It worked, and it was fun to do. Neither the Mariah story nor the Kellie story was nearly as complex or complicated as the Professor story. Most of the goals you choose for your child will not be very complicated either. Shaping is not complicated, complex, or difficult to execute. Shaping programs are effective and very rewarding to do. Remember that it is okay for your child to know exactly what behavior you want to shape. They do not have to be naïve like the professor.

Conclusion

It is vitally important that children learn to willingly live under parental authority. The problem that complicates this process is a lack of parental emphasis on the "willingness" part of the childrearing formula. We have previously looked at various methods of rewards necessary to teach a willingness to cooperate with parents, and it is important to remember the necessity of forming a warm, pleasant, bonded relationship with your children. A rewarding relationship is a prerequisite for encouraging a willingness to submit to parental authority.

Shaping behavior is yet another method that can immeasurably contribute to the willingness part of the guiding formula. I chose to emphasize the application of this powerful training tool to children who are experiencing merely annoying behavioral problems. Many children need to learn improved behaviors but are not rebellious, defiant children.

Behavior shaping is a wonderful method for both the rebellious and cooperative child. It is a great method to help children learn cooperative behavior that does not yet exist. A parent needs to make a list of behaviors they want from their child that either do not happen or occur only rarely. The next step is to apply the rules of behavior shaping to the desired goals. Great things should happen, and the "willingness" part of the childrearing formula will be advanced. I can guarantee you that the successful, consistent application of the behavior shaping technique will greatly enhance the relationship between you and your child.

Go forth. Do good.

Chapter 4

The 30-Second Technique

This technique is effective for children ages four to seventeen.

Tuned-out Tommy rarely does what his mother tells him to do and puts off direct requests made by his father or mother. No method of corrective punishment his parents have tried has improved Tommy's compliance to directives. Tommy doesn't intend to defy his mother or father, but he just gets busy with other things and forgets to make his bed or pick up in his room. Tommy lives by a different timetable than his parents. He will set the table, clean his room, or pick up the dog poop on his clock, not his parents. He knows he should do what they ask, and he intends to, but he has many more important things to do first, like play. It's an issue of who gets to make the rules that controls time. It's all about control. Tommy's parents think they control time and can not only tell him what to do, but when to do it. Tuned-out Tommy disagrees, tunes them out, and thus, buys time to do more important and fun things.

Unlike Tommy, Stubborn Sassy Sally is defiant when directly asked to do a chore or task that she doesn't want to do. Sally folds her arms and flatly says, "I don't want to do it. I did it last time." If her mother or father insists or threatens punishment, Sally argues, screams, or slams doors, and often embarrasses her parents in public. Sally just gets more stubborn when her parents scold or punish her. Stubborn Sassy Sally knows in her heart of hearts that she will eventually have to give in and put the dishes in the dishwasher, but only after she has demonstrated her strength, determination, and power. Her parents think it is their right to ask and expect Stubborn Sassy Sally to pick up her towel and clothes from the bathroom floor. Sally agrees that she should help her mother, but feels that she should get to make the rules about what kind of help she will provide and when she will obey. It's all about who gets to make the rules.

Parental reasoning, bribing, begging, signs of distress, anger, and threats of bodily harm have no lasting effect on Tommy or Sally. They only comply with their parents' directives when fire and smoke come out of their mothers' eyes and ears or when their fathers threaten them with banishment. Only then do Tommy and Sally comply with parental commands.

Do these stories sound familiar? Clearly, Tommy and Sally are sending a message, that is, "I will do what you say if you can make me." Children actually want to know what the boundaries are and when they absolutely must comply with parental commands. Children thrive in an atmosphere of reasonable control, but children do not naturally seek to be controlled, and they naturally move toward self-rule. They turn a simple request to perform a cooperative directive into a "who's boss" issue. Often a child's message is, "I will comply with your command if you can make me do it, but I won't voluntarily comply until you prove to me that I have to do it now." The child makes the parent assume the responsibility of making them comply. What can a parent do? The 30-Second Technique can be an incredibly useful problem-solving and teaching tool. The 30-Second Technique helps children internalize self-control and cooperation, so they will choose to cooperate rather than rebel.

The Beginning

I developed the 30-Second Technique based upon an experience that I had in my youth. I was about ten years old, and one summer day I was playing Monopoly with my two friends from across the street, Ken and Dean Carpenter. We were playing the game on the floor of their living room. The front door was open with only a screen door between me and my mother's voice. I grew up during a time when mothers screamed for their children to come home. My mother stepped out on the porch and screamed at the top of her lungs, "Jerreeeee!" Every child was, in those days, trained to recognize the sound of his mother's voice, and could hear that voice from two blocks away. I just kept on rolling the dice and moved my Monopoly piece. Mrs. Carpenter said, "Jerry, didn't you hear your mother call you?" I said, "I heard." Mrs. Carpenter said, "Jerry, don't you think you should go?" I replied, "Not yet." About fifteen minutes later, my mother stepped out on the porch and screamed my name again. I didn't move and kept on playing Monopoly. Again, Mrs. Carpenter suggested that I should go home now but I replied again, "Not yet." About ten minutes later, my mother stepped out on the porch and screamed, "Jerreeeee Richarrrrrd." I leaped to my feet and ran for the door. I had just heard my last call. I had about ten seconds to get home, or my mother would make me stay in my room for the rest of the day. I knew I could continue playing Monopoly until I heard my last call. I had trained my mother to call me several times, thus giving me extra playtime.

Children intuitively know when their parent has just given them their last call. They hold out longer and longer until they have trained their parents to transform into an unrecognizable beast and go into a rage. At that point, they reward their parents' rage with compliance. There must be a better way, and there is. I have re-thought and reorganized an old technique that most mothers typically use. Mothers have been taught by their mothers that when you count to three, children often give in and comply with a parental command. However, most parents do not know what they would do if they ever got to three. Also, children do not seem to learn a permanent lesson from the "count-to-three" method. The 30-Second Technique uses some of the count-to-three method, but incorporates the laws of learning through negative reinforcement or escape learning. The 30-Second Technique also encourages the child to internalize self-control and self-restraint in making the decision to comply with a parent's command. Now let's focus on the details of the 30-Second Technique.

How to Do the 30-Second Technique

The problem that frustrates most parents is their inability to get their children to comply with clear directives. The parent wants something done, and the child uses a variety of avoidance behaviors, such as making a promise and then delaying, partially complying, starting an argument, throwing a tantrum, or making a direct refusal. All avoidance behaviors of parental directives involve one basic theme—the child turns the interaction between parent and child into a "who's boss" conflict. Parents may confront the "who's boss" issue and win the conflict, or back away from it and refuse to engage with the child in the struggle. I recommend using both methods, thus winning the struggle and disengaging simultaneously. The 30-Second Technique accomplishes both goals and more. It requires the child to choose between two alternatives. He can either cooperate or experience a negative consequence. Each time he chooses not to cooperate, the negative consequence becomes more and more uncomfortable. For children, choice between alternatives becomes a powerful teaching tool. When a child chooses to cooperate with a parent, he also internalizes the choice. He is making a decision between alternatives from internal forces that are not entirely based upon the coercive methods used by his mother or father. Let's get started.

First, give your child a command. In order to practice the 30-Second Technique effectively, I would suggest that you stage the event. Choose a time when you are not under time pressure so that you have the time to complete the technique. For the first try, choose a task that can be completed fairly quickly. Remember, the 30-Second Technique only works for direct commands such as:

1. Clean your room.
2. Brush your teeth.
3. Get ready for bed.
4. Set the table.
5. Wash the car.
6. Do your homework.
7. Clean the pool.

Wendy's Story

A real case may help to clearly illustrate the principles of the 30-Second Technique. Wendy was seven years old when her desperate parents brought her to me for help. Wendy had a diagnosis of Attention Deficit Hyperactivity Disorder that was being treated effectively with a standard ADHD medication. Frequently, children with ADHD develop some very annoying behavioral habits. Although her ability to focus, track, and attend to details had improved, her bad emotional habits had not. When given a directive by her mother, Wendy's habit was first to ignore her mother's command. She would delay compliance until fire came out of her mother's eyes and smoke from her ears. When her mom began to scream, Wendy's next avoidance tactic was to throw a foot-stomping, screaming fit until her mother approached her. At that point, Wendy would fall to the floor and continue her fit at ten times the decibel level. She could be heard three blocks away. Wendy's mom would have no choice but to back away because she was physically unable to remove her from the situation.

I have several standard ways of establishing rapport with a child, so I used one of my methods, and soon Wendy and I had established a connection.

Wendy's parents were in the room with us for the entire session. I got Wendy busy drawing some pictures, and I asked her parents what they thought Wendy and I should work on. Both parents poured out their hearts regarding their frustration and feelings of helplessness. They gave me many examples of what Wendy had put them through. Wendy continued to draw and listen. With about fifteen minutes left in the session, I turned to Wendy and asked her to look at me. I said, "Wendy, let's work on following orders first—so I will tell your parents what I want them to do." Wendy nodded.

Wendy's mom had given me an example of a situation that frequently led to a fit. Wendy watched TV without her shoes on. When mom needed to go somewhere, she would go in and tell Wendy to turn the TV off, put her shoes on, and get her coat. Wendy would say, "Okay," but delay. She just kept on watching TV. In a few minutes her mom would come back and remind her to turn the TV off, put her shoes on, and get her coat. Wendy would ignore her. The reminder routine would repeat four or five times. By this time, Wendy's mom was frustrated and irritable, and demanded that Wendy get ready immediately. That was the signal for the tantrum to begin. Wendy knew that eventually she would have to do what her mother said, but her hidden goal was to engage her mom in a "who's boss" struggle. Remember, all fit-throwers need an audience for the fit to be worth throwing. This is an important concept to remember. The 30-Second Technique is designed to be a step-back method that will prevent a mother and father from getting involved in the struggle that the child so desperately wants.

I told both parents that I wanted them to do a careful inventory of Wendy's room. They were to make a mental list of fifteen to twenty items and then put them in a rank order from most important down to least important. I next instructed Wendy's mom to stage a situation in which she gave Wendy a command. She was to do it on Saturday afternoon when she could devote plenty of time to the 30-Second Technique. The task was to wait until Wendy was watching TV, and then to get her attention and tell Wendy, "Mommy has to go to the grocery store now, so turn the TV off, put your shoes on, and get your coat." Of course, Wendy was expected to nod as if she understood but to fail to comply with the directive. After a few minutes, Wendy's mom was to come back into the TV room and say, "I see you haven't started yet, so I'm going to count to fifteen [Wendy didn't understand time concepts very well yet], and if you don't get started, I'm going to take your coloring books [a low priority item] from your room." Here is a cardinal rule: always tell the child what item you are going to take from their room. The child needs to know what the loss will be if he doesn't comply. The choice between alternatives is very important. A choice helps a child internalize self-control. Mother would then immediately start counting.

On the day that Wendy's mother put the technique into action, Wendy began arguing with her mother, ignoring the progressing count. Her mother just kept counting. It was now just business. Wendy would either comply or lose her coloring books. Her mom had presented Wendy with a choice. Choices act as a great teaching tool. Wendy might rather continue arguing with her mother than keep her coloring books. It's a choice she could make between alternatives. Presenting choices for a child is an effective way to teach the child to internalize self-control. Wendy's mother reached the count of fifteen and immediately walked into Wendy's room and took her coloring books to Wendy's parents' bedroom. It is important to the success of the technique for the child to see something physical leave her room. It is more real if the loss is physical and personal.

Wendy's mom then went back to Wendy and said, "I will give you to the count of ten to turn the TV off and get started on your shoes and coat, or I will take your Legos [the next item up on the list] from your room."

Parents should never start with the most important thing in a child's room because they will lose their power if they take the most important item first. Usually after four or five items have left the room, the child catches on that the longer she delays, the bigger the loss will be. It is also important not to start with taking away privileges first. If you take away riding the bike, the child doesn't really know that she has lost the bike until she wants to ride the bike. It is more effective if the child sees something physical leave her room and go into her parents' room.

When Wendy saw her box of Legos leave her room, she started her typical two-stage fit. After taking the Legos, her mother went back to her and said, "I'll give you to the count of ten to get started, or I am taking your Barbie dolls from your room." Mother counted and Wendy wailed. After the sixth item left her room, Wendy made a miraculous recovery. She got up, hurried to the TV, and shut it off. She found her shoes and put them on, and ran to her room to look for her coat. When she came into the kitchen, she announced, "Ready, mommy." Her mom patted her on the shoulder and said, "Good job. I love your cooperation." Positive social reward is always important after compliance. Resist the temptation to give your child a lecture about doing what she is told to do. The 30-Second Technique represents the "last call" to a child, and at about the sixth item, Wendy correctly interpreted the counting to ten or fifteen as the "last call." She understood that mother meant business and, because she had no interactive, engaged, struggling audience (her mom) for her tantrum, decided not to bother.

The 30-Second Technique is really an elaborate version of the old tried-and-true count-to-three method, but most parents don't know what to do if they get to three. Counting to three is also too quick for older children (six and above) because they do not have time to think about the negative consequence as they weigh the relative personal value of resistance against the potential loss. Usually the old count-to-three method does not incorporate an understandable known penalty for failure to comply with the parents' directive. Negative reinforcement does work, and is a time-honored teaching method if three conditions exist. A parent must be able to catch the child doing wrong. That one isn't much of a problem until the late teens. Number two is that punishment must be applied swiftly, which is generally easy enough to do in a family. This principle is also an illustration of why the loss of privileges does not always help. A child does not know they are being punished until they want to use the lost privilege. For example, a parent may say, "Because you didn't put your clothes in the laundry basket like I told you to do, you can't play your Xbox games Saturday like you usually do." The child doesn't know the privilege is gone until Saturday, and it may be Tuesday when they got the penalty. The time between the sentence and the execution of the sentence is too long for the punishment to have its greatest impact. The third necessary condition for punishment learning to work is that the parent must have an effective punishment. For most children, scolding, threatening, and exhibiting parental anger are not really punishing to a child. They are simply annoying. Even spanking may lose its effectiveness for some children. In my practice, I have observed that for a number of children, spanking would have to come dangerously close to physical abuse in order to be effective. Furthermore, in today's world, harsh spanking can lead to a visit by Child Protective Services. Teachers, doctors, ministers, and counselors are required by law to report to CPS anything they consider to be abusive. When parents are excessively angry and evolve into an unrecognizable form of their former selves, they often choose a punishment that punishes the child and themselves. The 30-Second Technique avoids this pitfall. The 30-Second Technique fulfills all of the conditions of effective negative reinforcement without being cruel or inhumane. Children are adept at taking away the parent's ability to punish, but the complete 30-Second Technique is usually an effective punisher.

The 30-Second Technique is a front-end-loaded technique. This means that it is a lot of trouble to the parent to apply the technique the first time. Considerable time and consistency may be required. A child may also put up furious resistance the first time it is applied. A parent may be involved for an hour or longer upon the first application, but the follow-up is short and easy to apply. When a hard-playing, resistant child finally gives in and complies, the next time the 30-Second Technique is used, the child usually complies upon merely hearing the words, "I'll give you thirty seconds," or "I'll give you to the count of fifteen." He now knows it is his "last call," and he also knows that the consequences for not complying are really uncomfortable. He really understands that his parents mean business and that he must comply now. But, what if he doesn't cooperate within five or six lost items? This is a problem addressed in the last step, the "clean them out" step.

The whole 30-Second Technique is based upon the power of escape learning. The parent creates an ever-increasing state of discomfort for the child, who can escape the ordeal by complying with the directive of the parent. The penalties continue to become more and more uncomfortable until the child complies. Most children recognize by the fifth or sixth item that mother means what she says, and the penalty for resistance is becoming more costly. What should a parent do if the child doesn't comply? The parent should clean the child out and empty the room. Everything can be taken, except the bed, covers to sleep under, and some clothes to wear, although favorite shoes, blouses, or coats may be confiscated. Toys, knick-knacks, wall posters, and pictures should be removed. In forty years of practice, only two children have required the total clean-out step. Both were older boys. The chances are not great that you will have to clean out your child's room. That's good.

After the room is cleaned out of physical items, start with privileges. Continue the same routine, which is, "I'll give you thirty seconds [or the count] to get started on your chore, or I will take your TV privilege away." If your child continues to resist to the last privilege, the last act is to banish your child to her room until she complies with your directive. Later in this chapter, I will relate a case history where a teenage boy sat in his bare, empty room for three weeks before he gave in. Once you begin the 30-Second Technique, don't give in. Persist to the extreme end of the technique. It would be better to not begin the 30-Second Technique than to cave in somewhere along the way. If a parent quits when deep into the technique, it reinforces the negative behavior that is so frustrating—stubborn resistance. Quitting before or during banishment teaches that stubborn resistance or fit-throwing pays off. The child learns to increase resistance or to throw a longer, more intense fit, because it worked. It's tempting to feel sorry for the child who is experiencing extreme misery, but resist the temptation to solve the child's problem. Remember that he has made a choice to lose everything and go into isolation. Fortunately, most children will respond favorably and never reach the extreme end of the 30-Second Technique.

Brief Summary of the 30-Second Technique

Let's review the 30-Second Technique. The issue to be resolved is not compliance with a parental command. The issue is establishing who gets to make the rules that direct the ways of the family. Parents believe they have a mandate to exercise control regarding the actions and activities of children. Although children do not easily, naturally, or willingly take to efforts to control their behavior, they intuitively know that their lives will be better served if the parents assert reasonable parental control. The "who's boss" issue should ideally be resolved early in a child's life, but parents often delay in dealing with the control issues. When a child reaches his teens, it becomes very difficult to assert control. When a child reaches his teens, a parent should ideally start relinquishing control, but not abandon control. The rope needs to be lengthened, but not released. Parents often wait too long to establish a line of authority. When a child reaches age thirteen or fourteen, some parents panic because they can clearly see the danger that awaits the child. It is at that point of panic that the parent cracks down on his or her child. This often promotes and supports teenage rebellion. If you have courage, the 30-Second Techniques will work with teenagers as well as it does with preteens. The dangers for failure are greater for teens. For example, they may run away, they may get physical with you, or they may simply say, "No, you can't make me do it." Most hard-to-handle children will rely on three powerful words. They will simply say, "I don't care." When they become teens, they shorten it to one simple word, "So?" The technique works more successfully if a child argues or throws a fit. This shows that at least they care. It's those who say, "I don't care," that present the greatest challenge. They are the ones who may require you to clean them out and banish them to their room. Don't be afraid to do it, because every child will, by nature, have a propensity to respond to the laws of learning. Most children learn quickly, and the extreme end of the 30-Second Technique is rarely required. The following is a brief discussion of the needed steps of the 30-Second Technique.

1. Do an extensive inventory of your child's room. Rank in order all valuables from most important to least important.

2. Give your child a direct, understandable command. Issue this command when you are not time-pressured, because it may require an hour and a half of your time to complete the 30-Second Technique.

3. If your child obeys your command, love him and compliment him. If he does not comply with your directive, then when you are ready for him to comply, say, "I'll give you thirty seconds to get started, or I will take _____." At this point, you will name a low priority item in his room.

4. No matter what the child does next, the parent should step back and look at his or her watch, or verbally count. Do not defend your right to take something from the room. Do not teach the child a lesson with wonderful, irrefutable logic. Do not engage in a struggle with your child! Step back, relax, and let the process work. Remember, when you start counting or timing, it is just business. The child will either comply or he won't. Give your child time to decide.

5. If the child does not comply within the time limits, go get the item from the room. Most parents want to know when to give the items back. If a child complies and asks for the items back, be lenient and say, "Ask me tomorrow, and I will give them back to you." If your child asks for them the next day, say, "Sure, as soon as we sit down and have a talk." It is during the talk time that valuable moral lessons should be presented. Your child will be able to listen because he is calm and wants his stuff back. He cannot hear you when he is angry. If you have to take items again from the room, then wait a few days before returning the stuff. The penalty should become increasingly more uncomfortable the more times you must remove items from the child's room. If your child doesn't ask for his things back, then keep them.

6. If the child does not comply with your directive and you have cleaned his room out, then start removing privileges. Come back to the child

again and again, repeating the words, "I'll give you thirty seconds to get started." If everything of value has been taken away, and all privileges are gone then banish him to his room until he does cave in and comply. Room banishment is very powerful, so don't be afraid or hesitate to use it. Remember, you must leave clothes for your child to wear and bed-sheets to sleep under.

7. The last call has been set in place. Use it frequently, or your child will forget his previous discomfort and lapse back into old habits, and so will you. Every time you want compliance with a directive, say, "I'll give you thirty seconds to get started, or I will take _____."

Let's take a look at a few actual examples of how the 30-Second Technique has worked in the lives of real families.

Cleaned-Out Charlie

Cleaned-Out Charlie was sixteen years old and the son of a single mom, Charlene. Because Charlene was on long-term sick leave from her work, she was at home during most of the day, and I was working with her regarding her depressed feelings. Charlene complained that Charlie was becoming more and more stubborn and resistant to her directives. He was especially resistant to cleaning the pool. She became increasingly frustrated and depressed as he became more rebellious. I shared with her the basis of the 30-Second Technique and put a special emphasis on the clean-him-out-and-banish-him-to-his-room part. She said she would do her best.

Charlene approached Charlie and said, "I see you haven't cleaned the pool like I told you to do, so I will give you thirty seconds to get started, or I will take your radio from your room." Charlie argued that the radio was his and she had no right to take anything from his room. Charlene followed the technique and simply looked at her watch ticking off the seconds. I had previously discovered that Charlie had never physically threatened her, nor had he ever physically resisted her when being punished. Most kids simply will not physically challenge their parents. Even at age sixteen, they are like puppies and are submissive to the big dog. Charlene also nicely resisted getting drawn into arguing her right to take anything from his room. She really wanted to say, "Son, you don't own anything in your room because I bought it, and you use it at my good pleasure." When the time was up, she went to his room and took the radio.

When she walked past him with the radio in her arms, Charlie pulled out his most powerful way of resisting. He took away her punisher by saying, "Go ahead and take it. I don't care." She faithfully continued following the 30-Second Technique protocols, finally taking away his most prized possession, his computer. Charlie said, "I don't care, and that won't make me do the pool." She took away all privileges, and after an hour and a half, she finally banished him to his room. Since she was a stay-at-home mom, she was home when he came back from school at 3:40 p.m. She sent him directly to his room where he sat in a cleaned out, empty room until bedtime. His mom was determined not to budge. She even fed Charlie in his room. This went on for three long weeks, but finally Charlie said, "Okay, Mom. You win. I'll clean the pool." His spirit of cooperation for chores improved remarkably. She faithfully used the follow-up technique and said, "I'll give you thirty seconds..."

I kept up with this family for ten years. Charlie graduated from high school and joined the Navy. Since he had learned to live under authority at home, he was able to do very well in the rule-bound, controlled atmosphere of the Navy. Charlie had an older brother and sister, and when the kids would gather for Christmas, Charlie would always tell the story of the time that his mother cleaned him out. The story was told in good fun, and he always ended the story by saying, "That was the best thing mom could have done at that time in my life." Although teenagers are more difficult to teach lessons of self-control and cooperation, the 30-Second Technique produced powerful results.

Sally Sassy Mouth

Sally Sassy Mouth was a nine-year-old whose case had a twist that teaches a slightly different application of the 30-Second Technique. Sally was openly defiant. When her mom or dad told her to do something that wasn't to her liking, she would fold her arms and stomp her foot and say, "No." Sam was a working father who came home from work and hoped to get some peace and quiet before bedtime. It rarely happened. I explained the 30-Second Technique to both Sally's mom and her dad, with Sally in the room listening to the explanation. Sam wanted to try it first. He faithfully applied the rules, and they worked. However, Sassy Sally would delay for twenty-nine seconds before she would comply with the directive. While her dad looked at his watch, Sassy Sally spent twenty-nine seconds calling him every rude, disrespectful name she could think of in the time that she had available. At the last possible moment, she would get busy on the chore.

I said, "Why don't we use the same principle for her sassy mouth? Since she used the same revenge tactic with both parents, Sally's mom agreed to take this one and give her dad a rest. The instructions were to use the 30-Second Follow-up Technique and endure the demeaning, humiliating onslaught of sassy words from Sassy Sally until she finished her chore. Her mother was instructed to go back to Sassy Sally and say, "I can't let you talk to me like you did when I gave you thirty seconds to get started on your chore. I now want you to apologize to me in a way that I will believe." Children often use take back apologies like "Sorrrreeeeeeee," or the flat, "I'm sorry," while they roll their eyes. The apology must be sincere-sounding and should clarify what she did to warrant the apology. Sally's mother was to continue, "I'll give you thirty seconds to apologize to me in a way I believe, or I will take your CDs from your room." I encouraged Sally's mom to be tough and picky. If the apology didn't sound right then she should go get the item. Sally caught on quickly and put a zipper on her sassy mouth. The 30-Second Technique is versatile. Use it liberally.

Aaron the Avoider

Aaron is four years old and is fun, pleasant, and into everything. He loves to play and is very capable of entertaining himself. He is great fun until you ask him to interrupt his play and do something. He delays, delays, delays, until his mother is so frustrated that she goes over and yanks him up by the arm and marches him to the task at hand. This is a typical scene at dinner: Aaron the Avoider is playing, and his mom tells him that dinner is ready and he is to wash his hands and come to the table. Instead, Aaron decides he has to put some more Legos on his house, put his GI Joes on the shelf, or finish coloring his picture. His message is, "I will do what you say, but you will have to make me do it." He moves from one thing to another, always busy, busy, but ignoring his mother. While Aaron the Avoider is busy avoiding, his mother's frustration is growing with each passing moment. Aaron's goal is not to win, but to involve his mother in a struggle. She usually complies, and by doing so, she reinforces the very behavior she hates.

The 30-Second Technique worked well with Aaron the Avoider, and the method also made a huge difference in mother's attitude and emotional feelings. She was able to step back and become more emotionally detached from Aaron's behavior. She no longer reached out and embraced Aaron's problems, making them hers, too. She left the decision up to Aaron. He could continue to play and choose to lose more and more play things, or he could comply. It was up to him. After losing eight items from his room, he cooperated and washed his hands and came to dinner. Both mother and son were happy. Aaron's mom complimented his cooperation and she felt so calm within herself that she could actually enjoy dinner and be playful at the table. She felt a pleasant sense of confidence that Aaron the Avoider would soon just be called Aaron, her son.

Helpless Herb

The 30-Second Technique is an effective control technique to use at home, but it will work very well in public places too. You can use it at the grocery store, grandma's house, the mall, the movies, or at your best friend's house. This is Herb's story. Eight-year-old Herb was hyperactive and uncooperative with his parents and school teacher. If he thought something was too hard to do, he would go into his stubborn, "I can't do it" routine.

Herb's parents had used the 30-Second Technique on Herb with good results. He had become much more cooperative with parental directives at home. In one of our family therapy sessions, we decided to work on school performance by using the Stimulation Learning Technique (see chapter 14 on ADHD for more information regarding this learning technique). I decided to work on Reading to Remember, so I asked Herb to sit on the little stool by my chair and read a page from a simple age-appropriate book. You would have thought I had just thumped him on the head, judging by his reactions. He started moaning and crying while whining loudly, "I can't. It's too hard." I paused and observed and said, "Herb, I'll give you thirty seconds to get started on your reading." I then looked at his father and said, "Dad, what are you going to take from Herb's room when you get home?" Herb's dad was taken by surprise, but finally said, "Uh, uh...I'll take your Mickey Mouse clock [a low priority item] from your room." Herb continued to cry and complain. When thirty seconds elapsed, I informed Herb that he just lost Mickey Mouse. Again I gave him thirty seconds to get started, and his dad was ready this time. He said, "...or I will take your action figures when we get home." After twelve minutes and the loss of fifteen items from his room, Herb's tears miraculously dried up, and he picked up the book and read the page perfectly.

Herb played a hard game and lost. I doubt that your child will be as stubborn as Helpless Herb, who wasn't so helpless after all. Once a child has experienced the full 30-Second Technique at home and has lost a few items from his room, he will clearly understand the penalty that will be imposed at home for his reluctance to cooperate in public.

Children intuitively know that they can push the boundaries more in public than they can at home. The application of the 30-Second Technique should settle the control issue in public as efficiently as it does at home.

Conclusion

I have given the 30-Second Technique assignment to several thousand parents with uniformly positive results. When it fails to help, it is usually a result of leaving out a step. For example, some parents do not name the items they plan to take when they say, "I'll give you thirty seconds to get started." The parent may only imply punishment or say, "I'll take something away from you." Even though I advise against it, some parents insist on starting with taking away privileges. Some parents won't stay with the step-by-step method of the technique and will abandon it as unworkable after taking four to eight items, and some parents refuse to go as far as banishment. Raising children you want to keep exacts a huge, time-consuming investment from parents. However, the alternative of little time investment has grim results. You may save time and energy in the early years when children are more easily managed, but those late preteen and teenage years can be pure misery. It is better, I believe, to resolve the control issue early and become more lenient as they get into their teen years. The 30-Second Technique is an adaptable tool to secure compliance to directives and resolve the issue of who gets to make the rules that govern the activities of the family. Use it in good fun.

The 30-Second Technique is a great behavioral method to teach a child self-control and self-imposed responsibility. If a child decides to obey the directive, it is a result of his own personal decision. He must internally weigh the choices given him. He may decide that the resistance is worth the loss, but it is his choice. When he decides to cooperate and avoid the penalty, it's still his choice. He learns to make a decision between a good choice and a bad choice. When he makes a good choice, love him, hug him, kiss him, and compliment him on his excellent choice. Every time he makes a good choice, he further suppresses selfishness, control, and willfulness, and embraces cooperation. He gradually learns to willingly live under self-control.

Go forth. Do good.

Chapter 5

Pillow Talk

This technique is appropriate for children and adults, ages six and above.

One of the most exciting and effective change techniques I have developed is one I call Pillow Talk. It is so simple and adaptable that it can be applied to countless problems children encounter. Children do not come with a set of instructions and most parents have never taken a parenting class. Parents do the best they can based upon instinct and how they were parented. What are parents to do if their child:

1. Is afraid of the dark?
2. Can't control his temper?
3. Can't stand to be separated from his mom or dad?
4. Freaks out at test time?
5. Uses sassy, insulting, or rude words?
6. Steals, lies, or cheats?
7. Delays and makes parents late in the morning?
8. Ignores parents when they call?
9. Is chronically forgetful?
10. Picks fights with a sister or brother?
11. Has huge temper tantrums in the store?
12. Has huge temper tantrums at home?
13. Constantly interrupts when a parent is talking on the phone?
14. Has unreasonable fears?
15. Won't stay seated at mealtime?

Pillow Talk is one approach to helping a child correct these behavioral problems. It is simple, easy to apply, and effective.

How to Use Pillow Talk

The following is a short synopsis of the bare essentials of Pillow Talk. As you read the entire chapter, learning to apply Pillow Talk will become abundantly clear.

Step One: Decide what problem or misbehavior you want to change.

This sounds obvious, but it is really important. A parent needs to be very specific about what is wanted, and try not to use Pillow Talk to change a multitude of behaviors at the same time. One of the teaching stories I tell in this chapter is about a boy who steals. He stole from neighbors, stores, school children, friends, his parents, and his siblings. We decided to work on stealing from his mother's purse first. The method of Pillow Talk was applied to one specific form of stealing. When he stopped stealing from his mother's purse, we moved on to other forms of stealing. Be very specific.

Step Two: Choose one of the two applications of Pillow Talk. (Both applications will be described in greater detail later in the chapter.)

In the "Always Remember and Never Forget" form of Pillow Talk, the parent writes out a correction statement that begins with the words "I will always remember and never forget" and continues with what it is that should be always remembered. The child will read this statement three to five times before he goes to sleep for seven to ten nights. Here is an example. John is chronically late for school because he won't get himself ready. His statement is, "I will always remember and never forget that it is a really bad idea to be late for school because it drives my parents crazy and gets me punished." You may be thinking, "How is that going to help anything?" You will need to read the rest of the chapter to find out, but believe me, he will not be late. Reading the statement three to five times per night and sleeping on the statement for seven to ten nights puts the idea into his long-term memory where it belongs.

The second form of Pillow Talk is the picture-drawing method. This one is usually reserved for more severe problems like temper fits. In this form, the child will draw a crude self-picture with a speaking balloon coming out of his mouth. In the speaking balloon, words are written that describe what he does wrong. He draws his picture and writes the words in the balloon every night and the next morning he will tear up his picture and throw it away and do it again the next night.

Step Three: Require the child to put the statement or picture under his pillow and sleep on it all night long. Current psychological research suggests that what we put on our mind before sleep is thought about periodically throughout the night. Putting the statement or picture under the pillow acts as a reminder for the child to think about what needs to be changed. I call it cheap therapy because you do it while asleep.

Step Four: The child sleeps on what needs to be changed for seven to ten nights, then tests the results. If the child fails the test, meaning that the problem has not been corrected, Pillow Talk is resumed for another seven to ten nights. This cycle of Pillow Talk and testing is continued until the desired change occurs. Persistence is extremely important when using Pillow Talk. The parent must not bend or relent. Don't let your kids out-stubborn you. This step operates as an unpleasant ordeal from which a child can escape if he cooperates with changed behavior. It is called escape learning. Before Pillow Talk is over, your child will willingly want to escape this ordeal by changing his behavior to more cooperative action.

This is essentially Pillow Talk. I want to share with you two case histories that will flesh out the necessary steps of Pillow Talk.

Talkative Ted: Statement Version

Ted is eight years old. He loves attention, but he gets lots of negative attention by interrupting anyone and everyone. He is an equal opportunity interrupter. He drives his teachers crazy by speaking out in class without raising his hand. He is famous among his mother's friends for interrupting her when she is on the phone with one of them. He interrupts his mom and dad's private conversations with a constant barrage of questions and requests for service. He interrupts clerks when his mom is trying to pay for her purchases. He talks and talks, unrestrained, throughout his waking hours. Since his grades were poor and his teacher was threatening to leave the teaching profession because of her inability to stop Ted's talking, we decided to specifically apply Pillow Talk to interrupting his teacher without permission to speak.

Ted listened to me tell his parents about Pillow Talk while he played with trucks on the office floor. He interrupted me a few dozen times while I talked. I explained to Ted the general scientific part of Pillow Talk, and he semi-listened with a puzzled look on his face. Later in the chapter I will explain fully what to say about the physiological (scientific) part, and why it is important to tell the child. I wrote out three statements for Ted to read five times before he went to sleep. Here are his statements:

1. "I will always remember and never forget that talking out in class without first raising my hand and getting my teacher's permission is really a bad idea. It makes my teacher mad, and I just get into trouble."

2. "I will always remember and never forget that I can find another way to get my teacher's attention, like by raising my hand. Positive attention is good, and negative attention is bad."

3. "I will always remember and never forget that adults hate to be interrupted. My teacher is an adult. If I don't interrupt her, she will be happy and I will make better grades and won't be punished so much. So, I won't talk without permission."

I told Talkative Ted his brain doesn't sleep all the way at night. Part of it can think about important things like how to please his teacher. He was instructed to read these statements aloud to his mother five times just before bedtime every night for seven nights. Then he was told to put the statements under his pillow so he would think about them all night long. After a week, he would be tested. If he didn't interrupt his teacher and talk without permission, then Pillow Talk would be over. If, however, Ted interrupted, even once, he would do Pillow Talk for another seven nights. Ted's teacher was very cooperative and reported on Ted's interrupting behavior each school day. He failed the first two tests, but passed the third test after the third week, and has continued to raise his hand before talking in class. Pillow Talk was next applied to interrupting his mother when she talked on the phone. It worked for that problem, too.

It is important to realize that a parent shouldn't give up if the first test is failed. Persist, do not bend, and eventually your child will realize that the only way he can escape the ordeal that Pillow Talk imposes is to learn and practice what he has been reading nightly.

Disappearing Donna: Picture-Drawing Version

Donna is nine years old and is very sensitive to criticism. If her teacher criticizes her, she becomes afraid, hides under her desk, and won't come out for hours. When her mother scolds her or finds fault with her, she hides under her bed for hours. Her mom can't get her to come out no matter what she does. I decided that her problem was too severe to use the "Always Remember and Never Forget" version of Pillow Talk. Donna's fear and anxiety were out of control.

The picture drawing version seemed more appropriate for Donna's needs. Her mom and I decided that we would work on diving under the bed first. In the picture drawing version, the negative behavior is written in the speaking balloon. Here is what Donna drew every night for fifteen nights.

The assignment was longer for Donna than for Ted because her problem was more severe. However, persistent application is more important than getting the length just right. Remember, if the child fails the test, apply Pillow Talk again. Persistent application is the key. The number of nights devoted to Pillow Talk will vary in my teaching stories.

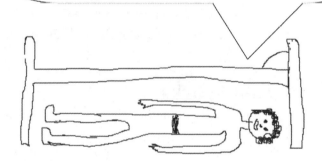

After fifteen nights of Pillow Talk, we tested. The next time her mother scolded Donna, she headed for the bedroom but never got past the bathroom door. Donna turned around, went back to the kitchen and gave her mother a hug, promising not to do again what she had done wrong that had caused her mom to scold her. Her mom gave her lots of good mother-love for controlling her behavior.

I realize it is difficult for many to see the sense of putting negative words in the speaking balloon. Later in this chapter, I will explain in detail why the negative words are so important. For now, it is sufficient to say that it is, in part, an awareness technique. Through Pillow Talk, Donna became painfully aware of the useless, purposeless behavior in which she was routinely engaging. She was forced to think about it. Donna was also instructed to find the picture every morning, read the words once, tear it up, and throw it away.

Symbolically, she was getting rid of her habit of diving under the bed and hiding for hours. Pillow Talk was very successful for the diving-under-the-bed problems, so we next worked on her diving under her desk when her teacher found some fault with her. She failed her first test, but after thirty Pillow Talk drawings, she passed. She never headed for the underside of her desk again since successful completion of the Pillow Talk assignment.

These case histories are teaching examples of the successful application of Pillow Talk. The method is so simple that its awesome power can be easily overlooked. Questions such as, "Why would Talkative Ted quit interrupting his teacher and mother just because he read a few obvious statements before going to sleep?" or "Why would Disappearing Donna quit heading for the underside of her bed or desk just because she drew a picture with a few words in her speaking balloon?" are great questions that deserve answers. This chapter speaks to these questions, but the next section talks about the scientific and physiological support for why Pillow Talk works. I think that after reading this section, the value of Pillow Talk will be clear.

Why Pillow Talk Works

There are five psychological and physiological reasons that Pillow Talk works.

1. Pillow Talk is an awareness technique. No misbehaving act can be eliminated and replaced by an appropriate behavior if the child automatically, without thinking, engages in the destructive, uncooperative, unwanted behavior. The child must first catch himself about to engage in the misbehaving act before it begins. I call it installing brakes in a child's mind. A filter must be installed that intercepts the destructive, unwanted behavior. When this happens, a child can avoid engaging in the unwanted behavior and replacement behavior can be voluntarily chosen. Think of it this way: "If you can't catch it, you can't change it." Pillow Talk helps a child catch the misbehavior so it can be changed before it happens again. (*The Emotional Brain*, Joseph LeDoux, Touchstone, 1998.)

2. Pillow Talk cooperates with what we currently know about how the brain works. The brain center called the hippocampus acts as a thought

traffic director. It sends information into either long-term memory or short-term memory. Pillow Talk tells the hippocampus to put into long-term memory what the child should always remember and never forget, which is that misbehavior leads to bad decisions and negative consequences. The hippocampus tells the brain to always remember and never forget that cooperative behavior leads to good rewards. Traditionally, parents tell and kids forget. Pillow Talk puts the responsibility to remember constructive instructions where it belongs, with the child. (*Brain Briefings*, Society for Neuroscience, April 2003.)

3.   Pillow Talk works well with the emotional part of the brain. The emotional brain does not respond well to logical command language. No matter how many times you tell Ted that interruptions will not get him what he wants, he will most likely "forget" and do it anyway. The emotional brain just doesn't get it, because that part of the brain uses a visual language, not a command language. The picture version of Pillow Talk shows a child, visually, what it is that is unwanted. The child tears the picture up and throws it away. This is a visual picture of the child getting rid of the unwanted behavior that is described in the picture balloon. If a parent wants to reduce anger, anxiety, or depression, the emotional brain must get a clear picture of what to do. One of the benefits of Pillow Talk, picture vision, is that the message is very visual.

The statement version also has a visual component to it. Putting the statements under the pillow creates a picture of the statements being transferred or absorbed into the brain. (National Institute of Neurological Disorders and Stoke, January 25, 2006.)

4.   Pillow Talk is applied just before bed for a very important reason. Recent brain research has produced some interesting support for an old concept. You have probably had to make an important decision, but you needed some time to think about it. You may have said, "I'll tell you tomorrow, but first let me sleep on it." There is a growing body of evidence that indicates that we literally do think about important things while we sleep. Albert Einstein famously would go to bed with a nearly impossible physics problem on his mind, and wake up the next morning able to solve the problem. Apparently, whatever we put on our mind before we sleep is processed while we sleep. Pillow Talk puts the problem in a child's mind at bedtime. It also imprints the corrective solution on the mind while the child is asleep. (*Neuroscience for Kids*—"Sleep and Memory," August 5, 2006.)

5. Pillow Talk is also based upon a fundamental principle of learning discussed previously. A child will tend to repeat anything that brings reward and pleasure, and will usually quit doing anything that brings discomfort. Pillow Talk, in part, is based upon ordeal therapy. Reading a set of statements three to five times and placing it under the pillow every night is an unpleasant ordeal. Drawing a crude picture and writing the details of a negative behavior in the balloon is an ordeal. The child can escape from the ordeal by giving up inappropriate behavior, but the ordeal continues until compliant behavior is attained. If the parent is persistent, the child will cooperate to escape the ordeal. When the child decides to cooperate in a desired, cooperative manner in accordance with the parent's wishes, the ordeal is over and a positive reward is given in the form of the parent's positive approval. (Note: refer to chapters 2 and 3 on creating a willingness to cooperate for more information about how to appropriately reinforce a child's compliance.)

Pillow Talk is an excellent parental correction tool that works because it is based on orderly scientific and psychological principles.

Pillow Talk is just as successful in establishing positive behavior as it is at stopping misbehavior. For example, if a parent wants a child to say, "Thank-you," for a parental service, or offer a kiss and hug at bedtime, Pillow Talk is just the right technique to establish these wonderful, positive habits.

The "Always Remember and Never Forget" Version of Pillow Talk

The "Always Remember and Never Forget" form of Pillow Talk is based upon a set of written corrective statements that are read by the child just before going to bed.

Forgetful Frank

A fifteen-year-old boy seldom remembered to turn in completed math, history, science, and English homework. He did his homework the day before it was due, but he would lose it under the bed, in the bathroom, or in his backpack. He was an exceptionally creative forgetter. Underneath his chronic forgetfulness was a pervasive fear of making a bad grade or being reprimanded for a poor homework performance. Here are the Pillow Talk statements I gave to Forgetful Frank.

1. "I will always remember and never forget that forgetting to turn in my completed homework turns my teacher off and makes my parents crazy, so I will remember where I left it, and turn in my homework."

2. "I will always remember and never forget to look for my homework papers every morning and put them in my homework folder and put my folder in my backpack."

3. "I will always remember and never forget that I am bright, smart, and capable, but forgetting to turn in my homework makes my teacher think I am dumb as a rock."

Frank read these statements three times before bedtime and put them under his pillow to sleep on. In Frank's case, I decided that he should sleep on it for fifteen nights, but in most cases, I recommend sleeping on it for seven to ten nights. Frank was told that his sleeping brain would work on remembering and never forgetting to turn in his homework. He gradually put the corrective statements into his long-term memory. Frank was told that the reason for putting the statements under his pillow was to remind his brain to think about what he wanted to correct. The paper under his pillow would rattle, fall on the floor, or he might drool on the paper, causing it to stick to his face. The point is that he would be reminded to think about what he wanted to correct periodically throughout the night.

During the fifteen days of Pillow Talk practice, Frank's mother did not make an issue of forgetting to turn in his homework. Although Frank improved, he occasionally forgot to turn in his homework. His mom said nothing. She announced that the testing period would begin after he finished fifteen nights of Pillow Talk. Here is what she was instructed to say: "Frank, it is time to test the results of Pillow Talk. I will be checking with your teachers, and if you don't turn in your work, don't worry about it because it just means that we will go back to another fifteen nights of Pillow Talk. Anyone can be forgetful, so I wouldn't be a bit surprised if you forget to turn in your homework at some time during the rest of the school year. Don't worry, Mom will be watching, and if you forget, even once, it just means we need another fifteen nights of Pillow Talk." Frank didn't forget, even once. He hated Pillow Talk! For Frank, fifteen nights turned out to be enough.

When testing, it is important to explain to the child what changes you expect to see. For example, seven-year-old Messy Matthew was told that if cups, glasses, food, plates, knives, forks, bottles, cans, or toothpicks were found in his room, he should not worry about it because he would simply go back to Pillow Talk for seven to ten nights. Matthew became tidier and remembered to pick up his stuff because he certainly didn't want to return to the Pillow Talk assignment.

One essential element of Pillow Talk is the ordeal aspect of the assignment. The parent creates an uncomfortable ordeal for the child from which he can escape if he cooperates. It is very unpleasant for a child to read the same statement three to five times before bedtime. However, it doesn't seem like a punishment to the child because the ordeal is disguised within the scientific part of the assignment.

The following are some examples of wording I have used to address a variety of problems children have, as well as positive behavior changes parents would like to see. Use these examples as your model for how to word Pillow Talk statements.

Selfish Sid. Sid is six and three-quarters years old, and he won't share his toys with the children who come over to visit with him. Here is what he read aloud to his mother for seven nights and put under his pillow.

1. "I will always remember and never forget to let other boys and girls play with my toys when they visit me."
2. "I will always remember and never forget that screaming and hitting boys and girls who want to play with my toys is a really bad idea. Boys and girls don't want to play at my house, and I always get into bad trouble with my mother."
3. "I will always remember and never forget that boys and girls have never hurt my toys, so it is okay to share them. Sharing toys is a really good idea."

At first his mom had to help Sid with some of the words, but he soon could read the script without help. Sid read these statements aloud to his mother three times before bedtime and put them under his pillow. After seven nights she tested Sid. She invited a neighbor boy over. Sid passed the test and never did Pillow Talk again, but his mother had to use a follow-up technique several times. If Sid became too possessive for his mother's taste, she would say "Sid, you're getting a little too bossy about your toys. If you keep on being bossy and selfish with your toys, don't worry about it at all, because we will start Pillow Talk tonight." Sid corrected his demanding ways because he sure didn't want to start another seven nights of Pillow Talk.

Silly Sue. Sue was a clown at heart. She was witty, entertaining, and generally a lot of fun. Sue was thirteen years old, and she would rather talk and clown around than eat. Sue's mom and dad enjoyed Sue but worried about her health. She entertained at supper and piddled with her food. Later, she would snack on chips, candy, bread, cookies, or anything within her reach. Sue was basically a cooperative child, but her clowning around at supper was driving her mother and father crazy. They had talked to her and scolded her several times with no consistent results. We used Pillow Talk in the following way:

1. "I will always remember and never forget that eating a well-balanced meal first, and clowning around second is a really good idea. It pleases mom and dad and makes me a healthier girl."
2. "I will always remember and never forget that doing what Mom and Dad want is more important than joking around and making them laugh."
3. "I will always remember and never forget to eat first and clown around second."
4. "I will always remember and never forget that when I eat food, I can listen to Mom and Dad. They have a lot of good things they want to say at the dinner table. Listening is good while I am munching on my food."
5. "I will always remember and never forget that when I eat a good dinner, I won't snack later, gain one thousand pounds, and be a sickly weakling."

Sue did Pillow Talk for ten nights, and her supper-talking habits changed significantly. About three months later, Sue became silly again and had to do Pillow Talk for another ten nights, but that was it for Sue.

Mad Matt. Matthew was an arguer. He was sixteen years old and thought he knew everything there was to know about everything. He could argue for hours. He never won the arguments, but he sure kept his parents busy and involved with him. Once he started arguing, he wouldn't stop. Generally Matt was a good kid who basically cooperated with his parents. Matthew would not admit any wrongdoing regarding his argumentative ways. We used Pillow Talk, and here is what we did. His dad took charge of this one. Mad Matt read the following Pillow Talk statements five times every night for ten nights.

1. "I will always remember and never forget that long-winded arguments are useless and purposeless. I never win the argument."

2. "I will always remember and never forget that I can find a better way to get my parents' attention than by using long, drawn-out arguments."

3. "I will always remember and never forget that the new rule is I have ten long minutes to argue my point before punishment begins."

4. "I will always remember and never forget that after I use ten free minutes, that level one punishment is a stern warning to stop arguing. If I continue, then the level two punishment is a mild take-away of a privilege, and if I still continue, level three punishment is the atomic bomb. Level three is the biggest and worst that my parents can do to me."

Matt's parents had previously discussed with Matt what level two and level three punishments were, so he knew what was coming. During the first ten nights, the parents were instructed not to use the levels of punishment. This was a learning period, and Matt needed the ten nights to get the ideas into his long-term memory so he could remember to apply them when he was told "no" about something. After he failed his first testing period, the levels of punishment were religiously applied during the period of the second ten nights. Matt's self-control improved, and he got only a few mild punishments for going past his first warning. Matt was able to control himself most of the time, and he could stop arguing with just a warning. After the second full ten nights of reading his statements and sleeping on them, he was able to pass his test. He kept his own time and stopped his pleading within ten minutes. About six months later, Matthew uncorked his self-control and persisted with his objections to a decision one of his parents made. He went back to Pillow Talk for another ten nights with a punishment imposed as an incentive to get back under control. We now call him Mellow Matthew.

This is an example of a Pillow Talk application that is a little more complicated than the common applications of Pillow Talk. This one involved a punishment element to help Matthew install some brakes on his incessant arguing. However, Matthew's case is a great example of how parents can combine the value of Pillow Talk with a reasonable creative punishment to encourage self-control. I should also mention that Matthew had weathered several counselors' attempts, using conventional methods, to help him with his arguing habit, but with little success. As you can tell from my wording, the statements do not have to be profound statements. Simple, to-the-point wording is adequate.

The Picture-Drawing Version of Pillow Talk

The "Always Remember and Never Forget" version of Pillow Talk seems to be quite sufficient for children who forget to do chores or turn in homework. The picture-drawing version of Pillow Talk is used for more severely entrenched and destructive types of problems. For example, I like to use the picture-drawing form of Pillow Talk for fit-throwing or property-destroying children, as well as children who are verbally abusive. Let's take a closer look at the details of the picture version.

The first step is to specifically identify what needs to be worked on. The mother or father then explains to the child the behavior that needs to be corrected. There should be no doubt in the child's mind about what is expected from her. Next, the mother or father should talk about the scientific part of Pillow Talk by explaining to the child, in age-appropriate language, that part of the brain does not fully sleep at night. Because the brain thinks throughout the night, Pillow Talk will be used to help her correct the unwanted behavior. This short parent-to-child talk will not only increase the value of Pillow Talk, it will also act as a disguise for the ordeal that the child will surely experience.

Next, the parent draws, as an example, a crude picture of the child with a speaking balloon coming out of the mouth of the figure. It might look something like this:

This next part is very important, so it will take some careful explaining. What I am going to tell you may not sound right, but believe me, the method is very powerful. You must put the negative in the speaking balloon. Do not put in the balloon what you want the positive change to be. Put in the speaking balloon words that describe what the child is doing that you want him to change. If your child uses rude, vulgar, sassy words, put them in the balloon. If your child hits, runs away, breaks things, or screams, then put that in the speaking balloon. When writing it in the balloon, be brief and use age-appropriate language. For example, if the child is seven years old, it would not be appropriate to say, "I frequently exaggerate my anger by using inflammatory and abusive words when I am angry with my mother." Here is another tip. It is even better when you can put the problem in words that make the child appear to really like doing the negative, uncooperative, unwanted behavior. For example, you might put in the speaking balloon something like this, "I love to lie to my mother. I would rather lie to my mother than eat jelly beans. I am a good liar too! Sometimes I even get away with it, and she never knows I have lied. Mom's punishment doesn't make me stop lying. I just like to lie too much." I know this statement will go against everything you have ever learned, and every instinct you have. It's time to trust me about this wording. If you use this format, your child will reduce lying for sure. A significant benefit of Pillow Talk is the therapeutic benefit of awareness. Little Charley cannot voluntarily install brakes on lying until he can catch himself lying. When a parent puts in the speaking balloon the problem they want to correct in negative language, it becomes a dramatic and effective way of quickly bringing a negative emotional or behavioral habit from the darkness into the light (awareness). Rest easy, little Charley will not lie more because you have written, "I love to lie to my mother," in a picture balloon.

A little humor also helps when writing the balloon words. Here is an example: Sally threw huge fits in the grocery store when her mother said "no" to something that eight-year-old Sally wanted. I put this into the balloon: "I love to throw screaming, hitting, fall-on-the-floor fits in the grocery store when mother says no to something I want. I am the best fit-thrower in the store. I feel like a movie star. I love grocery store fits, and I am good at them too. I have world-class fits. People should clap for my great fits." In only ten nights of drawing her picture and writing the words in the balloon, Sally quit throwing fits in the grocery store. Her mom greatly praised her cooperative replacement behavior to insure continuation of a better way.

Incorporated in the Pillow Talk method is a very uncomfortable ordeal from which a child can escape if she cooperates. No child I know of likes to draw the picture and write those uncomfortable words in the balloon. There is a built-in discomfort that is disguised within the scientific discussion the parent had with the child. The method truly does cooperate with how we currently believe the brain works. When a child is told that Pillow Talk helps the brain learn a better way of doing things, it is difficult for the child to identify the negative reinforcement (punitive) element of Pillow Talk. It is also more difficult, though not impossible, for a child to rebel or resist Pillow Talk. In just a few nights, little Sally decided, in her private logic, that the only way she would ever escape this unpleasant picture-drawing and word-writing ordeal was to stop throwing grocery store fits, and that is exactly what she did.

The next step is to instruct the child that the next morning, she is to find the picture, read the words once, tear up the picture, and throw it away. The parent tells the child that by tearing it up and throwing it away, she is throwing away the bad habit she wants to get rid of. She is symbolically putting the bad habit where it belongs, in the trash. This process also cooperates with what we know about the practical functions of the visual brain. Tearing up the picture demonstrates, with a visual message to the brain, that she wants to get rid of grocery store fit-throwing. The brain gets the message and corrects the problem.

There is a very powerful follow-up step to Pillow Talk that is effective and easy to do. In the initial instructions, the child was told that he would do Pillow Talk and then test the results. Here is a sample of wording for the follow-up method after ten nights of Pillow Talk. His dad says, "You have been very faithful with your Pillow Talk assignment, so it is now time to test the results. Dad will be watching and listening to you, and if you say to me 'I hate you,' 'You are mean,' or 'You're stupid,' I don't want you to worry about it. If you use those words, it just means that we need another ten nights of Pillow Talk. You didn't learn to ride a bike the first time you tried and you didn't learn to walk the first time you tried either. So, I wouldn't be surprised if you slip up and say some of these unwanted words like mean, stupid, and hate. But, don't worry about it because we will go right back to Pillow Talk for another ten nights. Okay! Let's test the next few days to see if those unwanted words are gone out of your head." So what will Sammy think the next time he is about to say, "I hate you?" He probably will think, "If I say, 'I hate you," I will have to draw that picture again for ten nights." We don't really know what a child thinks in his private logic, but we can sure observe the good outcomes of Pillow Talk.

This powerful technique can be applied in a variety of ways. It is an adaptive tool. An unexpected benefit transfers from the first success that Pillow Talk achieves. Once you use Pillow Talk successfully, the mere mention of using it again can cause dramatic and immediate change in other unwanted habits. For example, Sally stopped throwing grocery store fits, so her mother decided to use Pillow Talk to help Sally to stop throwing fits at home over the two chores she had been assigned. Sally's two chores were to help her mother set the supper table and to pick up toys off the bedroom floor every night before bedtime. When her mother told her to set the table, the fit would begin. Sally would eventually help at the table, but it was only after World War III had concluded. Here is what her mom said to Sally: "Sally, I have noticed that you throw a screaming fit when I tell you it's time to set the table. I'm going to give you a few days to fix this table setting fit-throwing habit, and if I don't see great improvement by Thursday, we will go back to Pillow Talk to correct this unwanted habit of throwing a fit when I ask you to set the table." Sally stopped table setting fits on her own and her mom never actually had to use Pillow Talk for that tantrum. She applied the same follow-up tactic with the room-cleaning chore with the same success.

The following are some balloon wordings that I have used to help children who have extreme behavioral problems.

Steve the Stealer: Steve was nine years old, and no valuables were safe when he was alone with them. He stole the neighbor boy's toys, he stole pencils and money from fellow students, and he robbed his mother blind. He took what he wanted from her purse and then denied all culpability. We decided to work on purse-thieving first. The following wording was put into his balloon:

> I love to steal money from my mother's purse. I am sneaky as a possum. I am a good stealer and most of the time I get away with it too. I am the best stealer on my block. I am so good at stealing money from my mother's purse I should have my own TV program so I could teach other boys and girls how to steal. I don't care how mad Mom gets or what punishment she gives, it's worth it. I just love to steal!

Steve stopped stealing from his mother's purse after two trials of ten nights each. We also used the same techniques for school theft, store theft, and neighborhood theft.

Frightened Fern: Fern was a nervous girl from birth. Over time, eleven-year-old Fern had acquired a variety of debilitating fears, such as fear of sleeping in her own room, fear of separation from her mother, fear that her dad would get sick and die, and fear that she would be attacked and killed while taking a shower. Fern was in family counseling, and that is where I introduced Pillow Talk to the family. This is what I put into her balloon:

I get scared really easily. I get scared of my shadow sometimes. When I take a shower, I am sure someone will attack me and kill me. That's why I have to have my mother in the bathroom at all times or I freak out. Makes sense doesn't it? I am sure all young girls all over the world freak out when they take a shower alone. When Mommy tries to get me to take a shower alone, I cry buckets of tears, shake all over, and beg and beg and beg her to stay with me. Crying and begging really work too. She always stays with me.

Frightened Fern did ten nights of Pillow Talk and then tested. Her mother sent her in to take a shower alone. Fern flunked the test. She became hysterical, so she did ten more nights of Pillow Talk. Fern failed the second test too. Her mother helped Fern do another ten nights of Pillow Talk, and to everyone's surprise and gratification, Fern showered without her mother in the bathroom. Fern wasn't perfect but she did it without the freak-out. The next shower was easier and that was the new start for confident, fragrant Fern. (People often ask if her mom sat in the bathroom when Fern was on the ten-day drawing and writing cycle. Yes, she did). We applied Pillow Talk to Fern's other fears with similar results.

An important tip for the Pillow Talk technique is that a child can request a test at any time if he believes he is ready. Give your child the option of terminating Pillow Talk. If they are ready, test for results, change, and cooperation. But if they don't get it, go back to Pillow Talk for seven to ten nights.

Pillow Talk Teaching Stories

The following stories have been extracted from my client files. All of my teaching stories are based on real children and real problems, but in these two stories, I have included the actual setting, directions, and wording. These teaching stories can serve as a guiding model that will be useful in dealing with the real life problems that your children present.

The Case of Fearful Foley

Fearful Foley was a high-energy ten-year-old who enjoyed a relatively successful life. He did well in school and had a number of close friends. He lived with his grandparents. He was cooperative with them, and they treated him well. However, Foley had a tendency to worry about things he couldn't control. One major problem in particular severely limited his activities—he had a phobic fear of eating any food not prepared in his home by his grandmother's hands. Foley planned and organized his life around being at home for food. His fear began when he overheard two respected teachers talk about a recent case of food poisoning at the local school cafeteria. He became afraid to eat cafeteria food, but it didn't stop there. Soon he could not eat restaurant food. Next, he lost the ability to eat food at his friend's house. I offered Foley some jelly beans in my office, but he politely refused. Anxiety always wants more, and it is reasonable to expect that he would gradually have become afraid of even more food-related situations. I decided to use Pillow Talk to desensitize his fear of getting food poisoning from food eaten away from his home.

Here is what happened when Foley and his grandmother came for their first session: I asked Foley what he wanted me to help him with. Foley's therapy goal was to get help with his math grade. Foley was obviously unwilling to confront his food phobia. At the fourth session, I introduced Pillow Talk. I talked to Foley's grandmother about the Pillow Talk assignment while Foley drew pictures and listened.

After his grandmother understood the general principles of Pillow Talk, I turned to Foley and asked him to look at me. I told Foley that I would help him improve his math performance, but first I would like to use the Pillow Talk assignment to help him overcome his fear of eating food not cooked by his grandmother. Foley nodded his agreement. I told Foley that I would tell him how to do Pillow Talk and I would write down the instructions for him to follow. My instructions to Foley were as follows: "Foley, you have a front mind and a back mind. Your front mind knows that you are safe from food poisoning away from home. None of your friends have gotten food poisoning from eating food away from their home. Your problem is not a front mind problem. The back part of your mind does not understand that you want to feel safe and comfortable when you eat food away from your home. We need to tell the back mind what to think, so this is what I want you to do.

"I want you to read these statements five times before you go to sleep.

1. 'I will always remember and never forget that my grandmother and grandfather know what is best for me. Grandma and Granddad are not afraid for me to eat food away from home, so I will believe them and eat food anywhere they tell me it is safe.'

2. 'I will always remember and never forget that other children do not get sick when they eat food from restaurants, school cafeterias, or from other kids' moms. Knowing this, I choose not to be afraid to eat food prepared by others.'

3. 'I will always remember and never forget that it is a really bad idea to be afraid to eat any food my grandma doesn't prepare.'

"After reading these statements five times, I want you to put the paper under your pillow and sleep on what you want to change all night long. By doing this, the back part of your mind will think about getting over your fear of food poisoning. Throughout the night, your sleeping brain will be reminded to think about what you want to change because the paper under your pillow will rattle or it will fall on the floor or you will drool on the paper and it will stick to the side of your face. The point is you will be reminded to think about your statements all night long.

"After ten nights of Pillow Talk, I want you to test yourself. I have asked your grandmother to help us by arranging to go out to a nearby restaurant. If you are so afraid you can't do it, don't worry a bit about it. You didn't learn to ride a bike the first time you tried, and you didn't learn how to read the first day you went to school, so I really doubt you will be ready for the restaurant after only ten nights of Pillow Talk. Don't worry if you don't pass the first test, we will go right back to Pillow Talk for another ten nights. Keep doing Pillow Talk, and test until you succeed. You will get the hang of it soon and you will not be afraid to eat food away from your home."

Foley failed his first test but passed his second one. After twenty nights of Pillow Talk, Foley was able to go with his grandmother to eat out. He was a little nervous but he did it. The next week, it was much easier for him to do it. In three months, he was enjoying eating restaurant food, cafeteria food, and snacks at his friends' houses.

Why Pillow Talk Works

Fearful Foley soon became Fearless Foley. I knew Foley was well when he asked me if he could get some jelly beans from my jelly bean machine. In only three weeks, his fear of eating food prepared and served by anyone other than his grandmother was over. What is it about Pillow Talk that is so powerful? There are several positive forces working simultaneously to achieve such a remarkable positive result.

1. Action is always better than inaction, especially when working with fears. Anxiety cannot be overcome by avoidance. Fear must be confronted. The child is encouraged through Pillow Talk to be proactive. Foley was doing something to work on his fear. The child is no longer ignoring the problem, but is actively addressing the concerns that his mother and dad have. It is no longer just his parents' problem to correct. By using Pillow Talk, the child is taking an active part in resolving the problem.

2. The child has an emotional and physical investment in the cure of the problem. The child is involved in the cure of the problem through reading the statements or drawing the picture, putting the paper under the pillow, and tearing it up.

3. The method of cure is time-limited. An end can be seen. Usually, Pillow Talk is applied for seven to ten nights before the first test. If the child fails the test, Pillow Talk is continued for another seven to ten nights, but there is an end in sight. The end may not come as soon as the child wants, but at least the ordeal isn't of an undetermined length. The child can escape the discomfort of the Pillow Talk assignment by stopping misbehavior and replacing it with cooperative action.

4. Parents are intimately involved in their child's therapy through Pillow Talk. They have made a commitment to help their child change uncooperative misbehavior through their supervision of the child's participation in the Pillow Talk assignment. They actively listen to their child read aloud the Pillow Talk statements, or they watch them draw their pictures and write the words in the speaking balloon. Parental

involvement is very important in the successful execution of this therapy technique. Parents are also involved with their child's therapy through their approval and praise of their child's improvement.

5. Pillow talk also involves the therapeutic use of an uncomfortable ordeal. I don't know any children who like the Pillow Talk assignment. The ordeal part of the assignment is disguised in the scientific talk that precedes the Pillow Talk assignment. Children, nevertheless, find the assignment onerous. They must continue Pillow Talk until they catch on that the only way to terminate Pillow Talk is to eliminate their misbehavior and replace it with the cooperative behavior that their parents are requesting. This is a powerful part of Pillow Talk.

6. Pillow Talk cooperates with what we currently know about how the brain works. This technique puts into long-term memory corrective steps that are necessary for the child to modify inappropriate, unwanted, uncooperative behavior. Pillow Talk has a greater impact on the emotional brain than do reason and logic.

Mean Manny Learns Self-Control: Picture Version

Eleven-year-old Mean Manny could not control his anger. It was easily triggered and reached destructive levels quickly. He was making average to slightly above-average marks in the fifth grade. Manny seemed to be able to control his temper at school and his teachers held him in high regard. Manny usually got along fairly well with his stepfather, but Manny's mother and six-year-old brother received the brunt of Manny's anger. He was rude and verbally abusive to his mother and little brother. When angry, he would throw objects and break things. Both his mother and his stepfather tried every legal means to bring Manny's anger under control, but they encountered little or no success. Because Manny's symptoms were so severe and destructive, I chose to use the more complicated picture drawing form of Pillow Talk. Regarding his mother, Manny's private, hidden agenda was, "I am the oldest son and I am entitled to have everything go my way now. When Prince Manny speaks, you will listen. I will not submit to anything without a fight first." Mom thought my assessment was "about right."

Manny's mom and stepdad attended the first session with him. As is common with children, he denied having even the slightest understanding of why he was in my office talking to me. I asked Manny to tell me what his mother told him to talk to me about, but he, again, denied any understanding of what his mother wanted him to say. His mom was obviously perplexed. I asked Manny to draw a house, tree, and person while I talked to his parents. His mom spilled the beans while Manny drew and listened. I used a few picture-drawing techniques over the next two sessions to get a better understanding of Manny's private logic. I determined that Manny was a reasonably well-adjusted boy with the exception of his excessive anger with his mother.

I told eleven-year-old Manny that he had two minds. He had a front mind and a back mind, or, as we sometimes call them, a waking mind and a sleeping mind. I continued to talk about his two minds by pointing out that he has a practical logical mind and he has an emotional mind. I told Manny that it wasn't that he did not want to control his temper with his mother and brother Joe. He really did want to put brakes on his anger, and in fact, he had probably told himself many times to stop screaming bad words at his mother and stop hitting his much smaller younger brother. I told Manny that his temper problem is under the control of his emotional brain. Manny was told that his emotional brain did not understand logical command words, and what we needed to do was to show his sleeping brain what we wanted it to quit doing. I told Manny that it was important to tell his angry emotional brain to quit being harsh and angry with his mother by drawing pictures of himself being angry at his mom. Now Manny had a general concept that explained his problem. He probably did not understand very much of the rationale about how the brain works, but it really didn't make much difference how much of the short lecture Manny understood. The purpose of the lecture was not to accurately instruct Manny on the real functions of the brain, but to present Manny with a general rationale and concept. It was also important to disguise the ordeal part of the Pillow Talk assignment.

The brain lecture raises the value of the Pillow Talk assignment in the mind of the child. A grownup, a parent, or a therapist talks about the Pillow Talk assignment with confidence, and conveys a belief that it makes perfect sense to use the Pillow Talk assignment.

My lecture planted the seed that we needed to work with the sleeping brain if we intended to be successful at controlling Manny's temper. It introduced the concept that we needed to show the emotional brain what it was that Manny needed to give up doing. Lastly, I introduced the therapeutic use of confusion as an adjunct to the Pillow Talk assignment. It is easy to resist the direct commands and direct suggestions of the therapist or parent, but it is difficult to resist corrective therapy that is disguised in the therapy talk. Manny did not fully understand the concepts I told him about. To Mean Manny, what I said sounded reasonable, even if he didn't fully understand what we were going to do about his anger. In Manny's mind, what I said must have been right because I was a know-ing adult.

We decided to work first on the angry fits directed toward his mother. When he became successful at reigning in his temper with her, we would work on his temper directed at his brother, Joe. I told Mean Manny to look at me and pay close attention because I was going to give him his homework. I said, "Each night for seven nights I want you to draw a picture of Manny getting angry at mother. We will start with mother, and work on controlling your anger at Joe later. Here is an example of what I want you to draw. You can use this example to help you draw your first picture tonight. Please copy these same words into your speaking balloon."

I love to be mean to Mom. If she tells me to do something I don't want to do, she will pay big time. I will throw a big fit, and I am a world-class fit thrower. I love to call her bad names like stupid and mean. I always say that she likes Joe better. Breaking Mom's things is fun too. But best of all I love to say I hate you, I hate you. That really upsets Mom. I love fits and I am not going to stop throwing fits no matter what Mom does to me. I am a good fit thrower.

Manny's mother was instructed on how to continue to coach him regarding what to draw and what to say in his balloon. She was to help him draw other sim-ple scenes where he commonly lost his temper. She required him to put the same abusive, rude, and angry words into his speaking balloon. This picture was about picking up his room. The rude words were the actual ones he had previously used in his temper fits. The scene may change but the speaking balloon words remain the same.

I then said, "Next, Manny, I want you to put your picture under your pillow and sleep on it all night long. Your sleeping, emotional brain will think about what you want to give up, and it will get rid of it for you. Your sleeping, emotional brain will think about what you drew because it will crinkle under your pillow, your hand will touch the picture, you will drool on it and the picture may stick to your cheek or your sleeping emotional brain will hear your picture fall on the floor. All night long, your mind will think about giving up excessive anger at your mother.

"The next morning, I want you to find your picture, look at it, tear it up, and throw it away. When you throw it in the trash, you are throwing away your excessive anger at your mother.

"The next night, repeat the Pillow Talk assignment. Your mother will help you decide what to draw. If you get angry about doing the Pillow Talk assignment and refuse to do it, then I have asked your mother to give you a reasonable punishment until you do it. You must do the Pillow Talk assignment. It is not optional."

I told his mother about the Now or Later Technique (see chapter 6) and asked her to use it to get consistent compliance. She agreed to use the Now or Later Technique, if necessary, to get compliance. Manny listened.

"Continue to do the Pillow Talk assignment for seven nights and then test your self-control. If you don't get excessively angry or go off on your mother by screaming bad words, and if you do not throw stuff or hit things, then the Pillow Talk assignment is over. Usually most kids get angry again. But if you don't do the things you drew in your picture, then you are done. But, if you get excessively angry at your mother or break her stuff, then go back to the Pillow Talk assignment for seven nights and then test your self-control. Eventually, Manny, you won't get so angry at your mother."

It is important that the child know exactly what excessive anger is. I usually ask the child's mother and father to write down what they think are signs of excessive, abusive anger. I also ask the child to tell me how he or she knows they are angry. Many times the child has some unique insights into what is too much anger. The pictures and balloon dialogue should reflect what the parents want the child to quit doing.

The Results

Manny hated the Pillow Talk assignments. He continued to throw one fit after another, but he did his drawings for four nights in a row. However, on the fifth night, Mean Manny said he was through doing his drawings. As punishment, mother used the Now or Later Technique on Manny, and after one application, Manny never missed another drawing. The Now or Later technique is invincible. Mean Manny completed his assignment of seven nights, but he failed his test. He lost his temper and gave his mother a hard time. His mom just stayed with it and made him draw picture after picture. It is important for a parent not to give up or give in. Manny was tough but the results of sticking with the program were good.

Here is an interesting part: when his seven nights were finished, his mother said it was time to test his self-control. Manny didn't last one hour. He tore into his mother because she asked him to turn the television off, wash his hands, and come to supper. His mom told him not to worry about failing his self-control test. It just meant he needed more practice talking his emotional brain into giving up being excessively angry at mom. That very night they started again on the Pillow Talk assignment. Manny accepted the inevitable, quit complaining, and completed his assignment. Again, Manny failed his test, and his mother continued with another seven nights of Pillow Talk. Remember, during the seven nights of Pillow Talk there is no punishment for fit-throwing. Fits are free during Pillow Talk practice.

After twenty-one cumulative nights, Manny and his mother again tested his self-control. He succeeded admirably. Weeks passed and Manny did not display any of the angry behavior that he put under his pillow. If he started to get excessively angry, Manny would put a lid on his anger and back off. He didn't want to do the Pillow Talk assignment again.

The strangest thing happened. Manny and his mom never did have to use the Pillow Talk assignment to control his verbal and physical abuse of little Joe. When his mom mentioned that they still needed to do the Pillow Talk assignment regarding Joe, Manny said he thought he could deal with it without doing the assignment. He was right. They never had to do it because his aggressiveness toward Joe was under acceptable control. It wasn't under perfect control, but it was under acceptable control.

More Reasons That Pillow Talk Works

The Pillow Talk assignment accomplishes the following four things:

1. It is an awareness technique. The first step in changing an emotional habit is the recognition that it exists and when it happens. Every night, Manny was required to think about his anger as he drew his picture. He became increasingly more aware of the presence of the habitual problem. Implied in the word, "habit," is the idea that the problem is beyond self-control. In fact, it can't be controlled, as long as the behavior occurs automatically. The Pillow Talk assignment makes a person aware of the

occurrence of the problem so that the behavior does not happen outside of the child's perception or awareness.

2. The Pillow Talk assignment is an excellent desensitization method. In this case, it was used to reduce the misuse and abuse of anger. The technique made it possible for Manny to use internal controls to manage anger. Internal discipline is always more effective and desirable than external control. In other words, a child who waits for his mother or father to make him face a fear or control anger is not accepting responsibility for self-control. He is not accountable for his choices or behavior because his mom and dad have accepted the responsibility for making the child get over a fear or for putting boundaries on anger. The Pillow Talk assignment transfers the control power to the child. Manny had to decide to face his unwillingness to control his anger.

3. Through the Pillow Talk assignment, children develop courage and a sense of accomplishment. Manny became encouraged because he succeeded in a difficult situation. Bad emotional habits are often characterized by years of discouragement, disappointment, and failure. The Pillow Talk assignment makes it possible for the child to quickly succeed, perhaps for the first time. Success makes the child feel empowered.

4. All of these positive learnings are possible because of the effectiveness of escape learning. Manny could only escape from the Pillow Talk assignment if he accepted the responsibility of putting self-control on his anger.

Pillow Talk Works for Adults Too

The Pillow Talk assignment is an adaptable technique that can be applied to a wide variety of problems for adults as well as children. The Pillow Talk assignment can be used with any unwanted emotional habit. Think outside of the box and use it creatively. Many parents have told me that they get frustrated with their child's behavior and lack of cooperation. For example, a parent may, while under the pressure of frustration, say or do something they later regret and that makes them feel ashamed. Ned and Nelda were such parents. Ned would lose control, spank his son or daughter, and ground him or her for the next twenty-five years. He was much too harsh with punishment when he was frustrated. Nelda was a screamer and a nagger. She could be heard three doors down because she screamed at her kids so loudly. She was sarcastic and sometimes cruel with her words. Although Nelda apologized to her seven-year-old son and her sixteen-year-old daughter, damage had been done to their egos and self-concept.

Nagging Nelda wanted to install some breaks on her tendency to speak too loudly, frequently, and harshly to her children. She wanted to think before she spoke, lessen her frustration, and reduce her impulsive traits. I told Nelda about her logical brain and her emotional brain. I pointed out that her problem was not a problem of understanding that her uncensored words cut her children deeply. She knew all of that. I told Nelda that her problem was like a bad habit, only in her case, it was an emotional bad habit. She had a predictable, patterned way of handling her children's behavioral choices and actions. She would verbally lash out when she became angry at her children and then apologize profusely. I told her about the Pillow Talk assignment and she agreed to do it faithfully. She drew a picture of herself getting frustrated over the behaviors of her children with a speaking balloon coming out of her mouth with all the abusive, sarcastic, rude words written in the balloon. Nelda faithfully did the assignment for seven nights, then tested herself. Nelda failed the test, but she did last three days without rude words before she flew into an angry, verbal snit. It happened in the car on the third day on the way to school. You guessed it. The kids began to squabble and fight, and Nelda lost it. I told Nelda that emotional habits take time to break and not to be discouraged but to keep on doing the Pillow Talk assignment.

I also coached Nelda to use a different control tactic when her kids misbehaved on the way to school. When the kids were loud and demanding or hitting and arguing, she was instructed to pull into a store parking lot and say, "The taxi to school will move again when you kids are quiet and listen to me." The first time she tried it, they were forty-five minutes late to school. Nelda went into the attendance office and told the attendance clerk that the kids did not have an excuse for being late. It had been their choice. The next time she used the technique, they were twenty-five minutes late. Both times, the school followed through and gave them extra work and detention. Now Nelda gets instant cooperation with a quiet warning that if they do not stop fighting, she will pull over into the next available parking lot. Nelda did continue the Pillow Talk assignment and she continued to fail for six weeks. This was an old habit that came out of her childhood. Nelda's mother was a screamer, and Nelda had learned well from her mother.

However, after twenty-one Pillow Talk pictures, God favored Nelda with a well-deserved miracle. Nelda has not uncorked herself for two years. She still gets mad at her children, but she expresses it in an acceptable manner.

You may be thinking, "What happened to Nelda's husband?" Ned thought I was nuts and needed more help than Nelda. He refused to have anything to do with the Pillow Talk assignment. However, Ned was perfectly willing to do the Marks assignment for anger control. (See chapter 10. When you read it, you will immediately understand why Ned took to the Marks assignment.)

What If a Child Goes Back to His Old Habits?

The Pillow Talk assignment works well with children and adults, and can also be helpful to reestablish control if the child reverts back to his old behavior. Billy the Bully was big and fearless at school. He chased, hit, cursed, and kicked about half of the boys in the seventh grade. Billy's dad made him do the Pillow Talk assignment and test seven times, and Billy the Bully finally got the picture. His temper was under good control for six months. One hot afternoon during the following summer, when Billy was in a parks and recreational program, Billy lost it. His parents called in a panic. They thought he had regressed and lost all that he gained. I told Billy's parents that it is common to revisit the old familiar place of where you used to be. Most kids don't actually permanently regress, but they may briefly revisit their old useless and purposeless behavior. I asked Billy's dad to get him back into drawing himself being angry and abusive. Billy drew three pictures and said, "Dad, I think I've got it again, so let's test." Remember, a child can call for a test any time he thinks he is ready. If he passes the test, Pillow Talk is over, but if he fails, Pillow Talk resumes with another seven to ten nights. Billy the Beautiful tested out just fine. Children with formerly strong emotions will, from time to time, revisit their old problems, but it won't last long, especially if the parent quickly reinstitutes the Pillow Talk assignment.

Conclusion

Let's again take a brief look at the essentials of Pillow Talk. It would help to review the numerous teaching stories illustrating the positive results of

Pillow Talk. Don't forget the scientific discussion about why Pillow Talk works as you review the practical applications of the method.

The first step in applying Pillow Talk is to decide what behavior you want your child to change. It's vital to be very specific at this step. For example, one mother specifically wanted her eight-year-old child to quit interrupting her phone conversations with endless questions or demands for service. Another mother specifically wanted her seven-year-old son to quit having temper tantrums in the grocery store if she told him, "No," to a request to buy something. It is not specific enough to tell a child to be nice and more cooperative every day. Be specific.

Second, decide which form of Pillow Talk to use. The "Always Remember and Never Forget" form is often used for less problematic child behaviors. The picture version is useful for more severe problems.

The third and fourth steps deal with explaining to the child the scientific/psychological reasons to use Pillow Talk.

The fifth step is to explain the need to test for results after the defined number of Pillow Talk sessions. Also included in this step are discussions that make it clear that if he fails the test, the child must go back to Pillow Talk for the defined number of nights until the next test period, and that cycle will be repeated until the child successfully passes his test.

Pillow Talk is one of my favorite psychological tools used to help parents regain control and redirect their children toward better behavior. I strongly urge you to try the Pillow Talk assignment to see if it will work as well for you as it has for me.

Go forth! Do good!

Chapter 6

The Now or Later Technique

This technique is appropriate for children ages four to seventeen, who are both rebellious and passive resisters of authority.

One of the most frustrating problems a parent can experience comes from the child who uses passive/aggressive methods to achieve his goal. The direct, in-your-face child can be far less frustrating to a parent than the passive/aggressive child. I am referring to the child who procrastinates or forgets what her mom or dad told her to do. For example, she knows she has homework to do, and she knows when she is expected to start doing her homework, but she dilly-dallies, delays, or "forgets" to get started. She uses every excuse in the book, such as "In just a minute," "I'm going to do it, but first let me finish this program." She may even tell a lie like, "I don't have any homework." She treats assigned chores in the same way. She will not say no, but the chore is put off again and again. This passive/aggressive child may be sent to her room to pick up and clean, but when her mother checks, she finds her listening to music. Of course her mother scolds her or threatens her, and Miss Passive/Aggressive promises to get on it as soon as the song is over. The room is never cleaned, so her mother nags and nags until she explodes with frustration and threatens to sell her to the lowest bidder. This type of child is a frustrating challenge!

The issue to be addressed by the parent is not the undone homework or chore. The problem that has not been settled between the parent and the child is who gets to makes the rules that affect her life. The real problem is a "who's boss" issue. It has not been fully settled in the child's mind whether the parent or the child is in charge. I use the term passive/aggressive, which means that a child is being aggressive in a passive way. Many adults use passive/aggressive methods to get their point across. For example, if a passive/aggressive adult is not served properly in a restaurant, he may leave a penny tip. He didn't directly complain to the waiter or manage-ment but he let it be known that he is an unhappy customer by leaving only a penny as a tip. That's passive/aggressive. The procrastinating child is let-ting you know that you are not totally in control. She may have to do her homework or her chore, but it will be done on her timetable, not yours.

Children cannot see very far into the future, but parents can. A parent knows that there are many, many troubles ahead for the forgetter, procras-tinator, and delay artist. Parents are desperate to teach the moral value of responsibility to their growing child. The Now or Later Technique is a par-enting tool that will creatively and thoroughly teach a child to decide to do their homework or chore now, not later. I really like this technique, and I am anxious to share it with you, but first I need to say a few more things about children.

Children intuitively know that it is best for them if their parents are in charge. Children thrive when they know where the boundaries are. They want to know the rules and they want their parents to be consistent and enforce the rules. You are probably saying about now, "This man has lost his mind! My children hate rules. In fact, my children are born-again rule vio-lators!" It may seem that your children hate rules and responsibility, but I firmly disagree. Children who live under authority and willingly comply with parental rules and directives perform much better in life as adults than children who get their way and successfully find methods to avert parental control. In fact, children become frightened of life if they are able to get away with rule defiance. Their behavioral message is, "Please control me, because I know I'm not capable to do it." I also believe uncontrollable chil-dren send the message to their parents that "I will do what you tell me to do, but you will have to make me do it, but please, please make me." The same messages apply to both the very aggressive child as well as the passive/aggressive child. Aggressive children are like army tanks. On the surface, they are blatantly obvious and blasting away. You can't miss them. They are strong and openly defy parents. Passive/aggressive children are like submarines. They are strong, with big torpedoes, but they operate out of sight and under the water. Both appear to want their way and both project the image that they hate parental rules and control. Both defy parental authority. I submit to you, however, that they intuitively know that it is not in their best interest to be in charge, and when their parents are ineffective in controlling them, it scares the liver out of them. Although I am putting an emphasis on the passive/aggressive child, the Now or Later Technique works equally well with the overtly aggressive, rebellious child.

I like the Now or Later Technique because the method presents a child with a choice. He can choose to do his homework, chore, or other parental directive now, or later. If he makes a good decision and chooses now, heaven will open up and happiness will come down. If a bad decision is made, life will take a decidedly bad direction. It is up to the child to choose between alternatives. It is a little hard to see at first, but the Now or Later Technique actually teaches the child to want to make a good choice. This is called internalization. They learn from this technique to want to cooperate with their parents. Isn't that what every parent hopes and strives for? This happens because children are given a choice to choose a good way or a bad way when given a parental directive. Good choices get rewarded and bad choices get punished.

If you sincerely want to raise a child who will willingly live under authority, the Now or Later Technique will help you do just that.

The Now or Later Technique is successful because it is based upon ordeal therapy or "escape learning." The Now or Later Technique should be used if all common control methods such as time-out, loss of privileges, take-aways, and voice control (yelling and screaming) have failed to get your child to obey your directives. If nothing seems to work, it means that your child has systematically removed all of your methods of punishment. You are bankrupt and have no effective way of controlling the behavior of an aggressive or passive/aggressive child. The Now or Later Technique is not harsh or mean-spirited, but it is strong. The first application will put you to a lot of trouble. However, after the first utilization, the follow-up technique is very quick and simple, and will get children to promptly do what they are told without a fight or struggle. Your frustration level will considerably decrease after you employ the Now or Later Technique. By using this technique, you will learn to create an ordeal for your child from which he can escape only after cooperating with you.

If you are tired of being a nagger or complainer, if you are tired of having no real authority, or if you are tired of being uncomfortably frustrated, pay close attention to the next section. I will fully explain the rules of the Now or Later Technique and will offer you several teaching stories that will encourage you and demonstrate how to effectively use the Now or Later Technique.

Before I launch into the how-to-do-it part, I want to pass along four "musts" for every parent. In psychology we are very reluctant to use words like "must," "always," "should," "ought," and "never." In this case, four firm musts are warranted. I want you to always remember and never forget that you:

1. Must put your children under reasonable parental authority.
2. Must form a caring, loving, bonded relationship with your children.
3. Must consistently reward your children for good behavior with parental approval and praise.
4. Must teach your children to make good decisions.
    With that said, let's get started.

The Now or Later Technique

The first step in applying the Now or Later Technique is to specifically decide what uncooperative behavior you want to correct in your child. This sounds obvious, but I find that parents frequently want to correct everything at once. Do you want to correct homework procrastination, washing dishes defiance, starting, but not finishing chores, or verbal disrespect? Choose one behavior, and apply the Now or Later Technique to that one specific problem. Remember, the real issue is not the chore you ask your child to do. The real issue is about rules. Your child is confused about who gets to make the rules, governing what is to be done, and when to do it. To be blunt, it is a "who's boss" issue that is being addressed.

The next step is to initiate the beginning of the ordeal. There are numerous ways to get a child to cooperate with parental directives, and I discuss a variety of other techniques in the body of this book. However, there are times when uncooperative behavior must be confronted head-on. Before replacement behavior can be rewarded by praise, uncooperative, disruptive behavior must be stopped in its tracks. The Now or Later Technique is designed to stop the continued head-butting contests that you will invariably lose. When defiance, procrastination, and delay behavior is stopped, then cooperative behavior can be substituted and rewarded. Start the process this way. Go to your child and give them a direct order. It might sound like this, "Honey, the living room furniture has not been dusted in three weeks. I would like for you to dust the furniture today. Do you understand?" Your procrastinating, passive/aggressive child will, of course, say she understands, and will promise to do it today. At that point you will leave and let time pass. You can count on your child putting off dusting. It won't be done because you are not constantly at her to get on it and dust. Remember, no reminders, and no nagging. Let time pass peacefully.

Step three goes like this. After an hour or so, go back to your child and say, "I see you haven't started dusting yet, so what I want to know is whether you would like to do it now, or later?" Any true, red-blooded American procrastinator will say, "I'll do it later." In fact, I want you to desperately pray she will say, "I'll do it later." However, if she does it right away, then compliment her on her wise choice, and tell her that it pleases you that she made a good decision by choosing to do it now. Some children are very sensitive to body language and tone of voice, and it may be that she senses that you mean business and are probably up to something. Most children will say, "Later." That's good, because it allows you to say, "That's fine, honey, and I will tell you when later is." *You always stay in charge of later.*

Step number four is the pleasant phase. You become the most pleasant mom or dad in your state. Have fun, be pleasant, but under no circumstances are you to remind your child to get on it and do the dusting chore. As you see the hours pass, bite your lip, pinch your arm, but do not remind your child to do her chore. You would be well advised to stage the Now or Later event on a Friday afternoon or Saturday morning. This technique will need plenty of time to unfold. In fact, the application of the procedure may take you into the early hours of the morning of the next day. You are going to be put to considerable trouble carrying out the Now or Later Technique. One parent sat in my office and heard the full explanation of the Now or Later Technique and said, "I don't think I want to do this. I will be punished more than my child." This may be true. You will be greatly inconvenienced, to say the least. Successful childrearing is greatly inconvenient, but that's what you signed on for. For eighteen long years, you are going to be "punished" from time to time. Remember, it's always children before self. The good news with the Now or Later Technique is that while the upfront cost for a parent is high, the follow-up technique is quick and easy. You must pay the upfront cost to earn the easy part.

Let's wind up step four. Remember, you are to be a very pleasant companion to your child until she is sound asleep that night. When you child is snoozing away, go into her room with a wet, cool washcloth and wake her up. The cool washcloth may prove to be very useful to help her fully wake up. When she is awake and semi-coherent, say to her in a kind sweet voice, "Honey, I noticed that you fell asleep before you did your dusting. I just wanted to remind you that it is later, so I want to know if you want to do your dusting now or later?" What do you think she will say? She will choose later. At this point, you will respond, "Fine, I will tell you when later is." You always stay in charge of later. Wish her a pleasant sleep, pat her on the shoulder, and kiss her good night. If your child is an aggressive procrastinator, you may get a lot of grief when you wake her up. Just ignore the insults and harsh language. We won't attempt to correct abusive language at this time. The mission is clear: you simply want to know whether your child is going to dust the furniture or not. That's all you want to know. If she says, "Later," and I am confident that, given a choice, she will say, "Later," then let her get back to sleep. You will then proceed to step five. If she gets up and dusts, then love her and compliment her on her wise choice. If your child becomes aggressive and engages you in a physical wrestling match or takes a few swings at you, then abandon the Now or Later Technique and use one of the other corrective suggestions found in the book. Most children, however, are like puppies and submit to the big dog without any physical confrontation.

Step five is the continuation method. Let your child get back into a sound sleep for ten minutes, and then go back into the room and wake her up. Use the cool rag if necessary, but be sure she is fully awake. Repeat your mantra, which is, "Do you want to dust now or later?" She will naturally choose later, because she is desperately sleepy. Keep repeating your routine every ten minutes until she angrily says, "Okay, okay. I'll do it now."

In step five, you will become the perfectionist supervisor of her dusting work. Stay right with her and make her do it right and up to your high standards. I have found the strangest, most unexpected thing happens when the child finally caves in, gets up, and starts to do her work. The unexpected outcome is that your little girl will most likely become pleasant, cheerful, compliant, and happy. Who would have thought it? Happy? Unthinkable, but that is the usual outcome. One would expect to have an unhappy, grumpy duster on one's hands. Be tough and picky about her dusting job, but be pleasant and don't give her lectures about minding you. Avoid guilt statements, like "Look how much trouble you put me to, all because you did not do your job when told." Just be pleasant and supervise her work. When finished to your satisfaction, compliment her for her good decision, kiss her, wish her happy dreams, and tuck her into bed. Do not let her sleep until noon the next day. Find a good reason to get her up early. For example, you could prepare a very special breakfast for her. The point is that this is an ordeal, so continue the ordeal by waking her up early. Use your damp, cool washcloth if necessary, but make sure she gets up!

This is the Now or Later Technique, so what do you think thus far? I can assure you that your actions will have a profound impact on your child and she will be set up for stage two which is the follow-up technique.

The Follow-Up Technique

Let's review for a moment. You made a reasonable request of your daughter to dust the living room. She procrastinated, so you gave her a choice between a good decision and a bad decision. She knew that the best decision was to dust immediately, but she made a bad decision to further delay and do her dusting later. You were in charge of later. Your beloved child went to sleep without first doing her dusting so since you were in charge of later, you woke her up repeatedly throughout the night, always giving her a choice to dust now or later. At first, Miss Procrastinator continued to make bad decisions until she caught on that you were not going to give up until she dusted "now." It may have been 2:30 a.m. before she figured out that her only sensible choice was to do her dusting "now." She finally complied and dusted. Your job was to be a pleasant but thorough supervisor. She happily finished her job and both of you retired, feeling tired but contented. She made a good choice, and you became her boss.

The follow-up technique is usually very fast and successful. It is rare that a child needs a repeat of the Now or Later Technique. Usually, once is enough, but I want you to be willing to do a grueling repeat if necessary. The next time you give your daughter a directive, simply say, "Honey, would you pick the dirty clothes up off your floor? I want to know if you want to do it now or later." Missy Put Off will have a horrible flashback to the night you kept waking her up every ten minutes, asking her if she wanted to dust now or later. I strongly believe she will get to her room now and get the clothes picked up. For discussion purposes, let's say she says, "Oh Mom, I'll get to it later." Let's say she waits one hour and does it! Your job is to love her, praise her, and tell her that she made a very wise decision and you are very well-pleased.

Let's take another scenario. Suppose you want her to do it right now. Here is what I suggest. Tell her to go to her room now to pick up her clothes and you will give her thirty minutes to get the job done. However, Miss Dilly-Dally will probably get distracted by something on TV. When thirty minutes has lapsed, go to her and say, "We need to run errands now so get ready to come along. You can pick up later." Don't say another word about her room, but make sure she has zero available time to do her room until she goes to sleep. Then repeat the after-sleep stages of the Now or Later Technique. I tell a teaching story in the latter part of this chapter to illustrate this method. Read it and laugh, because our heroine is going to learn a very painful but valuable lesson about doing a chore within the time limits you set.

Because of their first miserable experience with the Now or Later Technique, most children will simply immediately do what you tell them to because they painfully remember when later is. The follow-up technique is quick and easy. Just add "Now or Later" to all of your directives.

I'll insert here one word of caution. Be sensible and be reasonable with the application of the Now or Later Technique. For example, if your child has a medical condition, such as a respiratory infection, a heart problem, or Valley Fever, don't do a technique that could deprive them of significant sleep. There are other, less dramatic methods that can be used to get a child's compliance with parental directives. These methods are fully discussed in the body of this book. The Now or Later Technique is a great technique for a healthy child. Also keep your health in mind. Most parents just lose a little sleep and it means nothing but inconvenience, but if you have a serious medical condition, then be nice to yourself. Don't do it!

The Beginning

It's tough being a psychologist's child. A psychologist is prone to practice on his own children. The Now or Later Technique began this way. I had been toying with the concept of the Now or Later Technique for quite some time. My daughter Amanda was six, and my son Mark was four, when a set of factors came into place that allowed me to try out the new Now or Later Technique on my two young children. Amanda and Mark were still young enough to bathe together, and Roena frequently complained that when the kids bathed, they splashed water out of the tub, and she had a dickens of a time getting them to clean up the bathroom. When they finished their bath, they were tired and immediately got ready for bed. Roena was also tired and also ready for them to go to bed. When she tried to get them to pick up bath toys, towels, and clothes, they whined, cried, put off, and begged to go to bed because they were sleepy. Amanda was prone to fits, and Mark usually hid under something. It was a battle to get them to do cleanup chores. Often Roena would cave in from sheer exhaustion and do it for them after she tucked them into bed. It was faster and less stressful to do it for them.

One Saturday, I told Roena that I would like to try something, but it would be necessary for her to stay in the bedroom, and under no circumstances was she to come out to investigate what she would hear. I told the kids I would bathe them that night, and they were ecstatic. I ran a very full tub of water, all the way up to the overflow drain. The kids got their toys, and came to the bathroom when I called. When they saw the full tub, their eyes were as big as saucers. They stripped their clothes off, threw them all over the bathroom floor, and got into the deep water. They played, they squealed, and they splashed water all over the walls and floor. They were thrilled when I suggested that it would be a lot of fun to stand on the side of the tub and jump into the water. I held their hand and arm for safety, and they leaped over and over into the water. Water flooded the floor and soaked the hallway rug, as well as the bath rug and their clothes. These were happy children. When the bath was over, they dried off and dropped their towels on the floor and ran into their room to put on their PJs for bed. The bathroom was a wreck. When they were ready for bed, I went to each one and said, "The bathroom is a mess. Do you want to clean it now or later?" Both said, "Later." I told them I would tell them when later was. They said okay and climbed into bed happy children. I tucked Mark and Amanda in, said prayers, and kissed them good night. I let them get to sleep, and then I began the awakenings, but I always gave them a choice of deciding to clean the bathroom now or later. They chose later over and over until about 10:30 p.m., when Amanda said, "Okay Dad. I'll do it now." She went in and got Mark up, and they began to clean. I was amazed at how happy they seemed while they cleaned. I was a pleasant but hard task master. It took about forty-five minutes, but the job was done perfectly.

The follow-up took an unexpected turn. The next night I filled the tub full and invited them in to take their bath. They played much more quietly and splashed very little water. When I suggested that if they wanted to, I would hold their hands and they could jump into the full tub. Both declined the offer. After they had their PJs on, I went to each and asked if they would like to clean the tub and bathroom now or later. They both chose now and quickly began their cleanup job. That was about it for taking the easy way and delaying cleaning the bathroom. All I had to say from then on was, "Do you want to clean the bathroom now or later?" and for some reason, they always chose now. I complimented them on their wise choice and told Mark and Amanda that it really pleased me when they cleaned up their mess after a bath.

The Now or Later Technique was launched and I have recommended it to many, many of my clients over the last thirty years. This story illustrates another point. The earlier you start setting firm but fair rules and expectations, the better kids respond. They grow up in a home that expects kids to comply with parental directives. Both of my children are very responsible adults, and I decided a long time ago that they were kids worth keeping.

Harvey the Homework-Forgetter

Harvey was twelve years old and made mediocre to failing grades. His grades were poor because he hated to do homework. He was bright enough to make all passing grades or higher. He used every excuse known to mankind to get out of doing his homework. If required to sit down at the table to do homework, he fiddled with anything and everything for hours, until his parents said, "Okay, it's bedtime." Low or failing grades did not motivate Harvey to try harder. Harvey even, on occasion, threw up and feigned sickness to get out of doing homework. No discipline method his parents used worked.

I introduced the Now or Later Technique to Harvey's parents. They were divorced, but they agreed to cooperate together to help Harvey. His dad took the initiative and did the first Now or Later shift. He told Harvey it was time to do homework, and Harvey begged to finish his TV program. To Harvey's surprise, his dad didn't scold. He simply said, "Okay, Harvey do you want to do homework now or later?" Harvey leaped at the "later" option he was offered. His dad did the waking-up part of the technique perfectly. At about 10:00 p.m., Harvey the Homework-Forgetter decided to do his homework. His dad was an active, engaged supervisor, and Harvey did his homework, accurately, in record time.

Next it was Harvey's mom's turn. She was in touch with Harvey's teacher on a regular basis, so she knew when he had homework and what was expected of him. Harvey, of course, started his delay routine, so his mother said, "Harvey do you want to do it now or later?" To his mom's great surprise, Harvey chose to do it now because he had painfully learned from his dad when later was.

The next thing we worked on was speed. Mother set the kitchen timer for forty five minutes and announced to Harvey that he had forty-five minutes to do his homework. She continued, "If you don't beat the buzzer, you have lost your opportunity to do your homework now, so you will have to do it later, and you know when later is. If you're twelve years old, that kind of makes sense! In any case, Harvey didn't want to be awakened from a deep sleep again and again until he got up to do his homework. Harvey now finishes his homework with time to spare.

Harvey's parents put firm limits on him and backed up their right to direct him to do homework on their terms. Harvey learned that he could make a wise decision, control himself, and escape the waking up ritual. Harvey was proud of himself, and his grades improved. His mom and dad lavished praise on him for making wise decisions.

Darcy the Dragon Lady

Darcy's story is about an out-of-control foster daughter who knew no form of self-control. She absolutely hated authority figures and rebelled against any and all efforts to control her behavior. Darcy came into our house as a beautiful thirteen-year-old girl who had been in eleven foster homes before coming to live with our family. I had two teenage children about her age. On the surface, Darcy was fun and lighthearted, but underneath she was hard as nails. Darcy would comply with directives only after an intense battle. She had to be forced to do even the most minor of chores. At that point in my career, I wasn't sure if the Now or Later Technique would work with a teenager. I had used the technique with many pre-teens, but never a teenager. Since nothing else had worked, I decided to give the Now or Later Technique a try. At that precise moment in time, one of Darcy's chores was getting the evening dishes rinsed and loaded into the dishwasher. She balked, she complained, she screamed, she threatened, she cursed, and she ignored her chores. One Saturday evening, I went to Darcy and said, "I noticed you haven't done your dishes chore yet, so what I want to know is, would you rather do dishes now or later?" She, of course, chose later. We played games, teased, and had an all around good time. She said good night and went to sleep. I then began the wake-ups, always giving her a choice to do the dishes now or later. She called me every vile, filthy name imaginable, but I kept my cool and just kept waking her up. At one point, she moved her dresser in front of the door, making it very hard to get in. I pushed the dresser back a little and squeezed in. She was awake. I said, "Wow, Darcy, it was really hard to get into your room, but here I am, so what I want to know is, do you want to do dishes now or later?"

She screamed insults and threw her pillows at me. I said in a pleasant voice, "I'm going to take that as a 'not now but later.' I'll tell you when later is." At approximately 3:00 a.m., she finally said, "Okay, Uncle Jerry, I'll do it now." I was amazed at how calm she became once she made the decision to do the dishes now. We actually had a good time as I performed my picky supervisory duties. At 3:30 a.m., I hugged her good night, and she said, "I love you, Uncle Jerry." Darcy was never easy to guide, but I would say her chore duties improved about 90 percent. Every time I would say, "Darcy, do you want to do your chores now or later?" she would smile and start on her chore now. Darcy stayed with us for four years, graduated from high school, and went off to live her own life.

The Now or Later Technique will work with teenagers. However, I have found over the years that it is a toss-up whether they will internalize needed self-control and consistently make good decisions. The earlier you start getting control of a child's life, the better the long-range results are.

Dirty Harry

Harry was seven years old and he would not wipe his bottom after pottying. Harry would deny to his dying breath that he was dirty. His mom and I used the Now or Later Technique with a little creative ingenuity. She went to Dirty Harry and said, "Harry, you did not wipe after you pottied." Harry told his mother that he did too wipe. His mother was instructed to check his bottom, and if it was dirty, to ask him if he would like to get a wash rag, wet it, and clean his bottom now or later. Dirty Harry chose later. His mom woke him up fifteen times that night, always giving him the choice. At long last, Harry went to the bathroom and cleaned himself up to his mother's satisfaction. After his one Now or Later experience, all his mother had to say was, "Harry, you smell bad. Would you rather clean up now or later?" Harry would make a mad dash to the bathroom to wipe up. When he began to comply with his mother's directions, we instituted a generous rewards program for wiping first thing after pottying.

Timmy the Time-Waster

No matter what the task, ten-year-old Timmy would stonewall it to death. He was a dedicated passive/aggressive child. He was not openly defiant, but he was an unmovable, unmotivated wall. For example, if Timmy was told to pick up dog poop, he would stand around in the back yard for two hours without picking up one piece of poop. If his dad told him to get started on his homework, Timmy the Time-Waster would get his books and paper out and sit at the table for three hours without turning his hand to do one shred of homework. If his mom told Timmy to eat his green peas and he didn't want to, he would sit and stare at the peas for two hours. Usually his parents would scold him, whack him on the bottom, and send him to his room. Timmy liked that because there was plenty to do in his room!

Timmy's case is a bit different because we used the Now or Later Technique in a creative manner. Timmy was given a specific amount of time to complete a task. For example, Timmy's mom told him to clean his room and told him that he had thirty minutes to pick up his toys and put them away. She took a portable timer to his room and set it for thirty minutes. Of course, Timmy had no intention of cleaning his room. He just stonewalled. It had worked in the past, and Timmy, at that moment, saw no reason that it shouldn't work now. In the past his mom had always cleaned his room after he sat on his bed for two hours. Sure, she was mad, but never mind, he didn't have to clean his room. This time, his mom found him where she had left him, as usual, sitting on his bed, staring at nothing. She went into his room and announced that time was up and that he had to leave his room dirty and go with her to run errands. She told Timmy he would have to clean his room later, and she would tell him when later was. That was okay with Timmy the Time-Waster! His mom did not say another word to Timmy about his room. That was okay with Timmy. By now you can see where we are going with this. After thirty-two awakenings, three hours and twenty minutes after going to sleep at 9:00 p.m., Timmy cleaned his room under the strict supervision of mother.

So what's the point? His mother did not have an effective method of punishment, so she had to create one. Timmy might have been able to outlast, out-stare, and out-stonewall his mother, but he couldn't stay up as late as she could. This is what happened next. The very next day his mom gave Timmy the assignment of doing his homework now. She gave him forty-five minutes to complete his work. She very dramatically set the timer and put it down in front of him with flair. Next, she said in a sweet, pleasant voice, "Timmy, you have forty-five minutes to do your homework. If you don't complete it in forty-five minutes, you have lost your opportunity to do your homework now, so you will have to do it later, and you know when later is." I wish I could say the Now or Later Technique worked after the first application. It usually does, but in this case, Timmy played a hard game and stonewalled his mom. When the timer dinged, she went directly to Timmy, gathered his stuff up, and told him to go play. Timmy got sleepy at about 9:00 p.m. and went to bed. He was soon asleep. Two interesting things happened.

His mother only had to wake Timmy five times. The other interesting thing that happened was that Timmy beat the buzzer the next night and finished his work in about twenty-five minutes. This story has a good ending. The next day his mom gave him the chore of scooping up dog poop. She set the timer for twenty minutes and set it on the back porch. Timmy finished his chore in about twelve minutes. Later that night, his mother announced that it was now time for Timmy to do his homework. She set the timer for forty-five minutes and went through her prepared speech. "Timmy you have forty-five minutes to do your homework, and if you don't complete your homework before the timer dings, you will lose your opportunity to do your homework now, and you will have to do it later." With that, she left the room. Timmy finished his homework in record time, well before the buzzer. Mother hugged him and praised him for making two good decisions that day. To date, Timmy has beaten the buzzer every time. Both mother and child are much happier, and their relationship has vastly improved.

Timmy's mother needed to find a punishment that worked, and she found it in the Now or Later Technique. When stonewalling stopped, she could concentrate her energy on the many positive qualities Timmy possessed. Timmy is now far less passive/aggressive than he was before the two applications of the Now or Later Technique. The technique is malleable and adaptable when in the hands of a creative mind. Use it wisely.

Rudy the Rude Dude

Thirteen-year-old Rudy was very rude to his mother, but not as rude to his dad. He really tied into his mother when he was angry. The Rude Dude was also as stubborn as a mule. He was very sarcastic and argumentative with his mother, and his mom couldn't do anything right in Rudy's eyes. He always seemed to find excessive fault with her cooking, acts of service, house keeping, her looks, and how she talked. When angry, he frequently called her a bitch and a whore. Neither his mother nor his father could install brakes on Rude Rudy's mouth. I explained to his parents that Rudy was not simply rude, he was abusive in his treatment of mother. I warned them that their window of opportunity to teach Rudy how to live under their authority and live under self-control was closing fast. I explained that I would want them to use a variety of behavior change methods, but we would start with the Now or Later technique. We arranged to apply it to apologizing for rude, abusive, insulting language used on his mom. Both parents were eager to do anything that would help, but they were very skeptical about getting Rudy to apologize for anything. I asked if Rudy had ever gotten physical with his mother, or threatened physical harm to her. They both were in agreement that Rudy was mouthy, but not physical. He had never been expelled from school for violence, nor arrested for violence or threat of violence. It seemed like a green light to use the powerful Now or Later Technique. If Rudy had had a history of violence, I would not have recommend that his mom use the technique. His dad may have been able to use it safely, but I would not have recommended it for his mother.

The next time Rudy was rude, his mom was to say, "Rudy, your dad and I have discussed it, and we have decided that we will not allow you to be verbally abusive to me. I want an apology for what you just said, and you must tell me what it is you are sorry for. You must also apologize sincerely, in a way that I will believe." Sure enough, that very evening, Rudy mouthed off to his mother, and his mother gave her prepared response. I'm sure you have guessed Rudy's response. No way was he going to apologize now or ever. Of course, he said his piece in a rude and abusive manner. His mom and dad were prepared for his response. His mom continued, "Rudy, apologizing is not optional or something you decide to do or not do. What I want to know is whether you are going to apologize now or would you like to apologize later. Rudy chose neither, said nothing, and started to sulk away. Before he got out of earshot, his mother said, "I will take that to mean you want to do it later." Rudy shot back the ever popular teenage response, "Whatever." The stage was set, the lines had been drawn, and the showdown was about to begin. This was strictly a "who's boss" issue. If Rudy eventually gave in and apologized in a way his mother believed, it would be the first step to living under authority and self-control. If he could submit to one directive, he could submit to many more directives. If he apologized, there would be a glimmer of hope that Rudy could willingly live under authority. Like all children, Rudy wanted someone to rein him in and establish reasonable controls, but his message was, "I will live willingly under your authority if you are strong enough to make me. But if you are not strong enough, I will have to control myself, and I know I can't do that. I'm scared, please stop me." Both of his parents disputed my interpretation of Rudy's nonverbal messages. They were convinced Rudy lived to be in control and wanted to be the boss at any cost. Nothing more was said to Rudy about apologizing and the rest of the evening went well. Both parents were pleasant around Rudy.

Rudy was asleep by 11:30 p.m., and his mom and dad both went into Rudy's room and thoroughly woke him up. Rudy's father was there as a protective support for mom. The issue itself was to be resolved between Rudy and his mother. When Rudy was conscious, his mom said, "Rudy, it is now 'later,' and what I want to know is do you want to apologize now or later?" Rudy turned the air blue. His mom replied, "I will take that as a desire to apologize later, and I will tell you when later is." With that, she wished him a pleasant sleep. Ten minutes later, both mom and dad were back in his room waking him up. This went on and on until 4:15 a.m., when Rudy said "Okay, okay. I'm sorry. Now are you satisfied?" His mom was not satisfied, and she asked him to clarify what he was sorry for and to apologize in a sincere way.

What happened next was truly amazing. Rudy said, "I am sorry I yelled at you. I am sorry I called you a bitch, and I am sorry I disrespected you. Okay?" His mother said, "Thank you for accurately telling me what you are sorry for, but you still do not sound sincere. Take the 'Okay?' out, and say the same thing in a sincere voice." Low and behold, Rudy did it. The gunfight was over at 4:35 a.m. Rudy wasn't a new boy overnight, but he was off to a much brighter future. Occasionally Rudy would uncork himself and tell his mom "what for," but when she asked for an apology, Rudy would leave, fume around for five minutes, and come back and say he was sorry he lost control. Other control methods were also used in Rudy's case but the success of the Now or Later Technique, I believe, set the stage for other control techniques to work. Rudy is doing well at this time.

Conclusion

The Now or Later Technique is a powerful psychological tool that puts a parent back in control of her child. The child is given a choice to make. If he makes a good choice, all is well, but if a bad choice is made, there is a very unpleasant ordeal in store for him. The child can escape the ordeal, but he will have to cooperate and submit to parental authority to do so. This is a technique that helps settle the ageless question of who is the boss in the family, the parents or the child. The Now or Later Technique is especially useful for passive/aggressive children. It also works well with very aggressive children, but the aggressive ones put up quite a struggle. A parent must out-stubborn the aggressive child, so the technique may need to be applied several times. Frequently, passive/aggressive children need only one exposure to get immediate cooperation when the follow-up technique is used.

Go forth. Do good.

Chapter 7

How to Be a Good Dad in a Mom's World

In today's world, moms shoulder the majority of the childrearing responsibility. There are two major reasons that force mothers to provide most of the childcare. Reason number one is that, in the U.S., single parenting has now exceeded the 50 percent mark. The majority of children will be parented mostly by mothers after a divorce. The second reason children are mostly parented by mothers is that fathers have lost their way in the family structure. Fathers either do not know their role in the rearing of children, or they are physically present, but emotionally absent. Often, fathers who are present in an intact home are emotionally absent to their children because of their single-minded devotion to their work. They are present but absent. They represent the uninvolved father. Although more than 50 percent of first marriages end in divorce, divorced fathers can choose to continue to be involved with their children. They may be physically absent but be present in the intricate development of their children. I am choosing to focus specifically on fathers in this chapter because I feel that now, more than ever, American dads desperately need to redefine their role as parents.

As I've emphasized time and again, the best thing you can teach your children is to willingly live under parental authority. Children who learn to willingly live under parental authority will grow up to be adults who can live under self-control in a society of rules and order. Fathers play an indispensable role in teaching this concept to children. According to a survey of six thousand men and women done by *Psychology Today* magazine, Jesus Christ is the man most admired by both men and women in America. Jesus told a teaching story about authority. A captain in the Roman Army came to Jesus to ask if he would heal one of his servants from a life-threatening disease. Jesus said he would and offered to go to where the servant lay sick and dying. The captain said it would not be necessary for Jesus to go to the servant. The captain's reasoning was something like this: "I am a man who has authority. I tell a soldier to do this and he does it. I also know how to submit to authority. You, Jesus, have authority, and I submit to your authority, so all you have to do is say, 'Be healed,' and it will be done." Jesus, the most admired man in America today, said that the captain was the greatest of examples, and he truly understood authority. Because of his understanding of authority, his servant was healed. You, as a father, have great authority in the healthy development of your children. They look to you for instruction, protection, and moral value development. Use your authority to transfer the ideas presented here to equip (heal) your children. You have unusually strong authority with your children. Use it wisely.

Over the last forty years, America has seen many social revolutions. In 1965, I was in graduate school, and a sociology professor said, "There is a revolution coming in our society. Sex and death will be embraced and openly talked about in our society." The entire class gasped and said under our breaths, "No way!" Now, explicit sex is on prime time TV. Suicide and mercy death are discussed in every kind of publication across America. Another revolution is women's liberation. The feminist movement has set a fire in the hearts of women across our country. Another major social change is the dramatic change in divorce rates. Roena, my wife, remembers the absolute shock that she and other classmates experienced when the parents of one of her classmates divorced. That was fifty years ago, when the national divorce rate was about ten to fifteen percent. Today, divorce in first marriages exceeds 50 percent. There has been no greater social revolution than that of the absent father. Fathers are abandoning their families in astounding numbers.

Current research indicates that modern fathers actually want to be involved in the lives of their natural children, but there are barriers to adequate father involvement. Fathers are constantly bombarded by inaccurate popular beliefs. Fathers hear that they are not as good at nurturing children as mothers are. Fathers are accused of not wanting to be involved in the caretaking role. Fathers constantly hear that they have never learned and are uninterested in learning parenting skills. Because of these untrue but popular messages, fathers have lost their way. They don't believe they are important to children.

Fathers want to be involved with their children, but are often inhibited because of fears. Fathers often fear that they will repeat the mistakes of their own fathers. Research indicates that greater than 50 percent of all men were raised by abusive and neglectful fathers. (*Fire in the Belly, On being a Man,* Sam Keen, Bantam Book, 1992.) Fathers fear they will incorrectly discipline their children, or will indulge and spoil them. Fathers fear that they will be unable to identify and meet the needs of their children. Fathers fear they do not have adequate parenting skills. Fathers are afraid of fathering.

To put it bluntly, fatherhood is in a mess! We are forced to ask a very frightening question, "Are fathers really necessary?" There is a major force in America today who answers with a resounding, "No!" This answer is driven by four very realistic factors. First, women no longer depend on men to provide food and shelter or safety. Second, women are no longer shamed by being a single mother. Third, men are consistently described as being inherently selfish and irresponsible. Lastly, women are reluctant to trust men to stay the long haul with a family. Men have too often abandoned their families. Many women believe it is better and safer not to count on men. In my practice, it is common in a divorce situation for the mother to want to move to another state to be closer to her support system (extended family, for example) or to obtain work. When I point out that the father can't consistently visit with the children, the mother frequently replies that he is not necessary because she can do all that needs to be done for her children.

Have I painted a disturbing enough picture? Fathers want to be involved, but there are significant obstacles to their participation in parenting their children. Let's go back to the original question. Are fathers necessary? The answer is a resounding, yes!

I have read many books about fathers, but there is one book that is especially clear in the defense of father. *Life without Father,* by David Popenoe (Free Press, 1996), presents some compelling reasons that fathers are necessary. The weight of social evidence strongly supports that it is better to have both an involved mother and father. Fathers teach daughters to be independent and to take risks. Fathers teach boys to be sensitive to relationships and community values. A father teaches his sons to control their natural aggressiveness. Fathers teach boys to control selfishness and care for the welfare of the community. With involved fathers, boys are less prone to commit crimes. For boys, fathers model restraint, family loyalty, and care for others. For girls, fathers also model restraint, family loyalty, and caring for others. Boys must break away from the comfort zone provided by their mothers and become independent. They typically do this through identifying and bonding with their fathers. Sons learn from their fathers about male responsibility and achievement. Mothers cannot produce the discipline and authority that men bring to raising boys. A mother cannot control a teenage boy if he doesn't want to obey her. Fathers greatly deter delinquency, crime, and gang behavior by being involved with their sons. Fathers can teach boys and girls the concept of empathy, which is the ability to experience the thoughts, feelings, and attitudes of another person. This is an extraordinary lesson. Empathy is an important ingredient in reducing crime and promoting social harmony and societal values. In order to have law-abiding, cooperative, and compassionate adults, we must first teach children to have feelings of empathy. Dads do an outstanding job of teaching empathy.

Fathers contribute as much to the development of daughters as they do to the life success of sons. Strange as it may sound, studies have found that teen girls who have involved fathers do not get pregnant as frequently as girls who have absent fathers. Girls without fathers were far more promiscuous than girls with present fathers. Fathers protect both boys and girls, but with engaged and responsible fathers, girls develop an adequate sense of emotional and physical security. Fathers help girls to know how to relate comfortably and properly with men. Girls with supportive fathers are more successful in their careers. Fathers who are involved with their daughters' school work are exceedingly influential in developing a girl's proficiency in mathematics, verbal subjects, and science.

In general, involved fathers contribute significantly to their children's academic and intellectual skills. The male sense of rough play, reasoning, competition, and problem-solving skills are strongly associated with achievement and occupational advancement. Lastly, young adults who feel emotionally close to their fathers tend to be happier and more satisfied in life, regardless of their feelings toward their mother. Children need balance. They need both mother and father. Mothers contribute many unique values and lessons that fathers do not commonly provide. Women contribute the need to be included, connected, and related. Men offer independence, individuality, and self-fulfillment. Women provide roots. Men provide wings to children.

Are you convinced that fathers are necessary in the successful rearing of children? I hope so! Fathers are so very valuable to children. In the next section, I want to share eight keys that open eight doors to the hearts and minds of children. These eight keys to being a good dad do not represent everything a dad can do to be a good father. These eight principles should, however, get you off to a good start in learning good dad qualities that your children and their mother will appreciate.

In this chapter, I use many examples from my personal experience with being a father to my children, Amanda and Mark, rather than using only case history examples taken from clinical practice. Being a good dad is such a personal experience that I thought it best to speak directly from my heart to your heart. At the end of this chapter, you will hear from my wife Roena and from Amanda and Mark about me in the role of father, not Dr. Jerry Day, clinical psychologist. I must admit, I was a little frightened to ask my wife and children to write about me as father. I had no idea what they would say when I asked, but I am committed to publishing whatever they say, both good and bad.

There is no "good father school" that will certify you as a good dad. Learning how to father comes mostly from life experience. There are, of course, workshops on parenting and many good parenting books (like this one) to read that will help guide your real-life experience with fathering your child(ren). I greatly desire for you to use this chapter on being a good dad as one of your tools for good fathering. Fathering is a complex skill that can, with guidance and effort, be learned. To learn this complex skill you need three things. You need to want to learn how to be a better father. You apparently have this one because you have read this far. You need a good teacher with workable ideas and lots of experience. That would be me. I will teach you what I know, but you need a third element to learn to be a good dad. You need to practice what the teacher suggests. The forgetting curve is swift and radical. For the average father, three weeks after he reads this chapter he will have forgotten 75 percent of what he read. Remembering only 25 percent of the content will not make this chapter very useful. You need to practice what you learn to retain enough of the eight keys to make them practical and useful. At the conclusion of each key, a practice exercise will be offered. I would suggest that you do each suggested practice so the complex skill of fathering will be learned and put into action. Let's start our practice by getting a notebook or some paper so that you can write your personal notes. Note-taking radically alters the forgetting curve.

The Eight Keys to Being a Great Dad

Below are the eight keys I believe are critical factors in being a great father to any child. I will explain each key in detail in the next section.

Key number one: I will always remember and never forget to family-think first and project-think second.

Key number two: I will always remember and never forget to frequently and consistently bless my children every day that I live.

Key number three: I will always remember and never forget to protect my children and their mother from all harm.

Key number four: I will always remember and never forget to be firm and fair.

Key number five: I will always remember and never forget to avoid shielding my children from life's problems.

Key number six: I will always remember and never forget to get physical (playful) with my kids.

Key number seven: I will always remember and never forget to listen, listen, and listen first to understand—then to be understood.

Key number eight: I will always remember and never forget to love my children with all of my heart, mind, soul, and strength.

Empowering the Eight Keys

Always remember and never forget that these eight keys open doors into the hearts and minds of children. That's what parenting is all about—winning the hearts and minds of your children. Your kids will love the keys, and you will love practicing the keys. Let's get started.

Key number one: I will always remember and never forget to family-think first and project-think second.

A man is very prone to wake up on a Saturday morning with four projects on his mind. He puts on blinders and goes for these projects. The projects may be needed and worthy tasks, such as cleaning the garage, changing the oil in the car, pulling and poisoning weeds, and doing the laundry. For the project man, no one, with the possible exception of God, will deter these projects.

Let's get the big picture. Jake, eight years old, needs to practice his lines for the school play on Monday night. Marti, age ten, needs a ride to soccer practice at 10:00 a.m. Their mom has been wrestling with the kids all week long and needs a break from them, so she wants to shop a little on Saturday afternoon and pick up a few groceries on the way home. What should you do? Key number one suggests that you family-think. Does a clean garage contribute to the overall well-being of the family? Yes and no. It's good to have a clean garage, but it's better to have a prepared son so he won't be embarrassed and shamed for forgetting his lines at the play. Jake will think you are the greatest dad ever if you help him learn his lines. Is there a real decision here? That's family-thinking. Children want the most of what you think you have the least to give: time. Children feel valued when you give them the precious gift of time.

I remember a visit with my psychologist friend, Dr. Paul Simpson. We were talking business in his living room. His son, Woody, was causing a ruckus somewhere in the back of the house. Paul said, "Jerry, I have to take care of something with Woody, and I will be back in a minute." He left me sitting in the living room for fifteen minutes. That's family-thinking. Woody's needs were more important than my needs. Kids first.

Let's say you finally get to the garage, and Marti comes in and says, "Daddy I want to show you something." What are you going to do? Right. Go with Marti and let her read you the story she has written for Monday's class. It will take only ten minutes of your project time, and Marti will love you forever.

If you really, really want to impress your wife, significant other, or girl-friend, then family-think before you project-think. This could mean that you help out in the house with pick-up and daily chores. Your partner will be greatly impressed. The garage will get done, but not on your time schedule. Family-think!

Your assignment: For five days, family-think and observe what happens and how you feel. Then tell someone the results of your five days of family-thinking.

Key number two: I will always remember and never forget to frequently and consistently bless my children every day that I live.

Key number two is so important that I am going to take a little more time for it. Blessing a child means to be complementary, supportive, and positive with him or her. We live in a very negative world. Most of us were raised by parents who frequently told us what we did wrong but rarely praised us for what we did right. We were probably educated in a negative school setting where teachers made a big deal of our many errors without balancing them with our positive successes. A father-daughter or father-son relationship will not survive a mostly negative exchange between father and children.

Children are hardwired to want to know where they stand with their fathers. With their moms, knowing where they stand is more clear. They crave to know if their fathers approve of them, admire them, and respect them. They long to know if you accept them as they are. After safety, food, and shelter, a child's greatest need is to be accepted. What bonds married couples together is applicable to what makes for a healthy attachment and bond between a father and a child. Children thrive in a bonded, stress-free relationship between father and child. Research suggests that a one-to-one ratio does not hold or glue families together. This ratio works well in business and industry. Managers are frequently told in management courses that for every criticism, they should give a statement of praise. Turnover in business is significantly reduced when this ratio is maintained. In families, the one-to-one ratio is an utter failure. Couples who have a very loving, long-term relationship must maintain at least a five to one positive to negative ratio. Is it your habit to praise your son or daughter five times for every one criticism or negative comment? Unless you are a very unusual father, I doubt very much that you compliment five times more than you scold. It's a goal to be worked toward, and now is the time to begin the repair work. It's never too late to start this one. You can show or demonstrate your approval, but usually, we just verbally say what we like about a child's behavior and attitude. Your praise and compliments represent a blessing of your children.

There are many ways to bless your children. There are very informal blessings, such as your compliments, and there are more formal ways to bless your children. We will discuss both. The objective of a blessing is always to let your child know that he has good standing in your eyes.

Sometimes it can be a challenge to decide how to turn something that is mostly negative into something positive. My son Mark's experiences with baseball represent one of those difficult challenges. His story is a great example of a blessing I almost ruined. I was a very good baseball player in my young years. For a long time I thought I would become a professional baseball player. I played first string baseball through college, but as it turned out, I wasn't quite good enough to turn professional. I couldn't wait for my son Mark to physically develop so that I could start training him to play baseball. At about ten years old, I thought he was ready. We had been playing catch for quite some time, and I thought he was ready to learn how to catch fly balls. He could hit too! I took Mark, a bat, and a bucket of balls to the junior high baseball diamond to hit him a few fly balls. Out of thirty-five fly balls, he missed them all. He did not catch one fly ball. They went over his head, hit at his feet, and a few even hit him in the chest or on his shoulders. After thirty-five misses, I called Mark in from the outfield. Mark came trotting in from the field grinning from ear to ear. He trotted up to me with that big smile and said, "How did I do, Dad?" You probably know what I wanted to say. "Mark, you are the worst baseball player I have ever seen. You didn't catch one fly ball. In fact, I was worried that I might knock you in the head and kill you. You have no future in baseball." That's what I wanted to say, but I gulped and said, "You know, you did pretty well. Two of those balls hit your glove. Next week, you will catch one of them, and then your baseball career will be off and running." And that's exactly what happened. Mark went on to be a very good baseball player and gave me many hours of pleasure watching him catch fly balls. He could hit too!

I have wondered what would have happened if I had unloaded on him. I'm glad I will never know what the impact of a lot of criticism would have had on his baseball career and his personality. This story is an illustration of how to bless your children and the positive power of a blessing.

Blessings are powerful, no matter what the age. Susan's story is an illustration of the power of a simple blessing. My client, Susan, was forty years old and depressed. She had endless problems at work. She worked for a large missile manufacturing company on their assembly line. She confronted her managers over slights and management errors. She was a loose cannon who confronted coworkers about lazy and shoddy work habits. She had been written up over forty times and had been put on probation many times. At one visit I said, "Susan, I have noticed something important about you." She said, "What?" in a defensive, sarcastic tone of voice. I said, "Susan, I believe you are a natural leader with God-given leadership talents. Susan, you are gifted by God [she was very religious], and you need to use your gifts for God." I told her that people listened to her and naturally wanted to follow her leadership. She just needed one more thing and that was lessons on impression management. She was a new woman! She had never thought of herself as a leader. Susan was never written up again. She became a floor leader, a union representative, and effected significant changes in how missiles were assembled. One blessing and impression management changed her life. Her abusive father never once blessed Susan, and she was on a life-long quest to get a father's blessing. She got it from her substitute father (me), and the rest is history.

I love this important key so much that I could write five chapters on "The Blessing," but I will say just a few more things about the need for a father's blessing.

Always remember and never forget that after safety, food, and shelter, a child's greatest need is to be convinced that he is accepted by his father. Most children know that their mother accepts them unconditionally but fathers are a bit of a mystery. Without a father's blessing, children are often launched into a lifetime search for acceptance. As women, unblessed daughters are set up to be used and manipulated by uncaring, unscrupulous men. Unblessed men find it difficult to commit to a woman, job, or a family.

There are numerous ways to bless a child. Touch is a very good way to convey your approval. Children crave to be touched. Hugs, kisses, pats, handshakes, and incidental shoulder- and hip-touching all count as acceptance, approval, or a blessing. Painting a picture of a bright and productive future is a blessing. Children don't look very far ahead, but dads do. One day I asked six-year-old Mark what he wanted to do when he grew up. He, without hesitation, said, "I want to be a trash man when I grow up." After the shock wore off, I asked Mark what it was about trash men that he liked. He said, "They get to drive big trucks." That was my cue to paint a picture of the future for him. I asked, "Mark, do you know that firemen drive big trucks very fast?" He was fascinated as I told him about fire trucks, ambulance trucks, water trucks, and ladder trucks. Today Mark is a paramedic fireman. He drives big trucks very fast. When Amanda was young I told her she was a natural teacher and she could shape the lives of young people. She became a teacher, taught for a few years, and then became a state event planner and leader for thousands of young teenage girls. Bless your children with a picture of what isn't here yet. Paint a bright picture for them. When young, they can't see ahead, but you can. Bless your children.

Special father words can be a wonderful blessing for a child. This will be my next-to-last teaching story. Honestly! Amanda's blessing presents a great illustration of a formal blessing. I attended one of her teen events during which the fathers were asked to write out a blessing for their daughters. It was a great experience for both of us. I would recommend that you write a page-long blessing for each of your children and then give it to them. They will love it, and so will you. Years later, when Amanda bought her first house, she asked me to bless it for her at her housewarming party. It was really never about wood, brick, or nails; instead, the blessing was about who was to live in the new home. It was a great formal event and a great blessing for Amanda.

The story I want to leave you with that illustrates the power of a formal, spoken blessing is about Amanda's wedding. Amanda, the girl who loves blessings, asked me to bless her at her wedding. I have never seen or heard of a father blessing his daughter at her wedding. I wasn't sure how to do it, but I knew I wanted to do it. Here is how it went. Roena was seated in the auditorium, and I waited with Amanda to walk her down the aisle in the traditional manner. Her groom, David, waited nervously with the preachers for her dramatic arrival. I walked her down the aisle, and we both went up on the platform. Amanda and David faced one another, and I stood a little bit back but between them. We had two preachers on the platform. Henry Webb, her second dad, said some very nice things about Amanda and their relationship (a blessing). Henry then asked, "Who gives this woman to be married?" That was my cue to say, "Her mother and I." I then started the blessing. I told the audience that in days of old, fathers traditionally blessed their sons and daughters but we have lost the old tradition and I think we should reclaim this ancient ritual. I told the audience that there are many examples of blessings in the Bible but the one I like best is when God, the Father, blessed his son Jesus. I went on to describe the baptism scene that precipitated God's blessing of Jesus. The heavens opened up and God's spirit in the form of a dove came down to rest upon Jesus. Then God's voice said, "This is my Son, whom I love. With Him, I am well pleased." I then raised my hand and said, "This is my daughter, whom I love. With her, I am well pleased." I then touched Amanda's shoulder and said, "I love you, and I bless and approve of your marriage to David." With that said, I joined their hands together and left the platform. All of the women cried, and Amanda felt honored and respected.

You may never give a blessing in such a formal manner, but the point I am making is that children want and need your spoken blessing. You can speak a blessing through words written on a piece of paper, or you can speak a special blessing on any occasion, such as a birthday, Thanksgiving, after a school play or christening, in response to a report card, or on a Thursday. It doesn't matter. Bless your children by telling them how much they mean to you.

I'll close key number two with Heather's story. Heather, age thirty-five, was a client of mine whose father died suddenly and unexpectedly with a massive heart attack. Heather invited me to the family viewing of the body. I walked into the viewing room and I saw Heather leaning on her father's chest and embracing him with her arms. She was screaming words I will never forget as long as I live. "Daddy, Daddy, don't leave me! Daddy, don't leave me. You never told me you loved me. Please, please, Daddy, tell me you love me!"

Bless your children.

Your assignment: Write a blessing for your child. Hold it until the next holiday or his birthday and then give it to him. Write your blessing now while it is still fresh on your mind.

Key number three: I will always remember and never forget to protect my children and their mother from all harm.

This one may seem to be easy, given that we live in a peaceful America with very adequate police protection. Traditionally, fathers have been protectors, but what is there to protect children from now? There is plenty, and we will discuss the fact that men are still looked to and needed as protectors. Roena likes to shop, and she frequently asks me to shop with her. She knows I hate to shop, but she wants me to go with her anyway. All I do is stand around and hold packages. This has happened a half dozen times. I will be standing in an aisle, holding packages, and a clerk will come to me and say, "May I help you with something sir?" I say, "No, thanks. See that woman over there with the little boy? My job is to hold her packages and protect them from all harm. I'm just doing my job, Ma'am." She always looks at me, smiles, and goes away without another word. There are still sexual predators, robbers, rapists, and generally rude people all around us. In my job as a psychologist, I know they live and prowl because I counsel with many of their victims. However, the threat is fairly low. I think what is important is your willingness to protect to your death. That willingness does two things. First, your family feels safer because of your willingness to protect. It's really about body language. It has been estimated that 85 percent of all communication is body language and only 15 percent of communication is from words you choose to say. Children read body language exceedingly well. If, in your heart, you know beyond doubt that you are willing to lay your life down to protect your children and their mother from all harm, they will have the emotional feeling of safety and security. That is priceless. It is important to children to feel safe and secure. Secondly, your willingness to protect your family no matter the cost to you is conveyed, by body language, to predators, thieves, and manipulators. They will choose another mark because, like children, they read body language well too. I always put on my game face when I go out with my family.

Of course, there will inevitably be an occasion where you will be called upon to literally protect your children from all harm. It may not be in a face-off with a motorcycle gang, but it may be a protective act with a little less drama. Roena and I went to Mark's parent-teacher night. We met Mark's teachers and heard about his progress. Mark was in the fifth grade, and one of his male teachers was relentless in his criticism of Mark's academic and classroom performance. After hearing three thousand criticisms, I said, "I want you to stop now, and I want you to tell me five things Mark does well. I have listened to you criticize my son for fifteen minutes, and I don't recognize the boy you are talking about. Now tell me what you like about Mark." Mark's eyes were big as saucers. He had never heard anyone stand up to this teacher before. Mark felt valued and protected by me.

There is more to protection than facing off with the bad guys. Protecting your children also means safeguarding them from the bad influences of people and society. It is now thought that approximately 70 percent of all television programs display explicit sex. Excessive violence is readily available through video games, movies, and television programs. Of course, not all your child's peers or friends are good for his value development. Children are pressured to try drugs, tobacco, and alcohol. Let's not forget the pressure to shoplift. Your job is to protect children from a potentially dangerous future. Children cannot see the long-range harm involved with TV, games, drugs, alcohol, and ugly peer pressure, but dads can. You can use your male directness and straight out tell a child, "No more" and why it's harmful. You could use more indirect but equally powerful techniques such as, "Poisoning the Well" or "The Storytelling Technique" (discussed in chapters 13 and 11, respectively). Whatever method you use is of less importance than your taking protective action now. If you wait until a child is seventeen, it probably will be too late to obtain serious compliance with your wise insights.

I used "get on it now" male directness with my children regarding inappropriate TV programs. One evening, I came home from work and went into the TV room to say "hi" to Mark and Amanda, who were watching TV with some friends. There was nudity and explicit sex on the program they were watching. Mark was eight, and Amanda was ten. I said, "Hi, kids," walked over, turned the TV off, and told their guests that I didn't allow kids to watch sex shows, so they should go find something else to do. I walked out of the room. I heard one of the girls say, "He can't do that, can he?" Amanda replied, "Oh yes, he can. He does it all of the time." Mark and Amanda were accustomed to my affirmative action. Obviously this little girl's parents didn't turn off programs she watched. They found something else to do. Protect your children from bad influence.

Your assignment: Pause for a while and make a list of things you want to protect your children from. Then develop a plan of action to protect them from those things.

Key number four: I will always remember and never forget to be firm and fair.

A father has authority over children that a mother does not enjoy. I think this is so for several reasons. Men are wired differently than women. We don't come with as much aptitude for patience and tolerance as women. It's genetic. We say "no" quicker and louder than mothers. Children cannot read fathers as well as they do mothers. They lived in their mother's body for nine months, and they know their mothers like you know the back of your hand. They are pretty sure they know how far they can push their mothers. Fathers are a mystery to children, and they tend to be more careful and compliant around them. Use this to your advantage. Set firm but fair rules for your children. No means no, and there is no bargaining with Father.

I highly support the concept that children are responsible to you. When you call them to do something, their job is to comply with your directions. They are to please you by being cooperative with your reasonable requests. For example, Charles is directed by his father to carry the trash out daily. Taking out the trash is not really the child's job; his job is to please his father. Let's say he doesn't take the trash out one day. His father calls Charles by name to come to him. He is responsible to his father first. His father may send him to do a variety of chores, but Charles is responsible first to him. His father says, "Charles, come here. Look at me, Charles. I gave you the job of carrying out the trash. The trash has not been carried out. Are you going to do it or not?" It's a good lesson about who is in charge, and it is the rare child who will not immediately carry the trash out. Charles is responsible to his dad.

In this book, I have described a variety of ways to get compliance from a strong-willed child. I would recommend that you use one or more of the corrective techniques if your child consistently disregards your directives.

Remember the theme of this book. The best thing you can teach your child is to learn to willingly live under parental authority. Fathers play an indispensable role in teaching this vital life concept. Mothers discipline differently, not worse. If a child had two father-types as parents, we would have to send this child a condolence card. If a child has a mother and an engaged, involved father, we call the child lucky.

Remember to be firm but fair. Don't use strong-arm tactics. They are unfair. Grounding for a year is firm, but unfair. Balance is the key to good discipline. To help keep discipline fair, start with the least amount of punishment and then test. If your child is still uncooperative, increase the punishment a notch and test. That's fair. Be firm *and* fair with your children.

Your assignment: Go to chapter 3 and read the short section on behavior shaping. This should help with the fair part. Next, read the chapter about the Now or Later Technique, which should appeal to the firmness part of a man's nature.

Key number five: I will always remember and never forget to avoid shielding my children from life's problems.

Children do not need the details of adult problems. For example, if you are divorcing, it would be appropriate to share with the kids the fact that their mom and dad are unhappy with each other and argue way too much. They do not need to know that their dad had an affair and that their mom has a prescription drug abuse problem. That would be too much information for children thirteen or younger. The older they are, the better they can handle the details of life's problems. Overprotecting a child by shielding them from all of life's problems does not give them a chance to grow and mature as problem solvers. Children need a father who models good mental health and problem-solving abilities. If children are shielded from life problems, the implied message to the child is, "I don't think you are strong enough or mature enough to handle this."

I will never forget the lesson Mark taught me when he was nine years old. Mark started fishing with me at a very young age. He would spend a week with me on the lake beginning at the age of six. On this occasion, the truck was packed and we started across town to get on the highway to Phoenix to pick up my fishing partner, Jimmy. About a mile from our house it began to rain. This was not your ordinary rain. As we used to say in Texas, "It came a frog strangler." The back of the truck was tarped, but there was no way we could keep all of the water off of our stuff. I had pulled over to try and adjust the tarp to keep as much of our equipment and supplies dry as possible. Both Mark and I were out in the rain, soaking wet, trying to fix things. I was grumpy, muttering choice words under my breath, and slam-banging things. You can relate to this, can't you? I felt a tug on my arm. It was Mark looking up at me saying, "Don't worry about it, Dad. It's just a problem we need to solve. We have solved all of the other problems, and we will solve this one, too." I was stunned to hear such wisdom from such a little one. I loved to take my kids camping just so we could solve problems together and more closely bond. Those of you who camp understand that when camping, there is always something wrong that has to be fixed. Camping is a great way to help children mature into problem-solving adults. When camping, there is no way to shield children from experiencing a few common and uncommon problems.

Roena and I were arguing one night as we prepared to go on a two-week Christmas vacation to see relatives back in Texas and Oklahoma. Tension was high between us. We had two young children, and Roena wanted to take everything while I wanted to take almost nothing. It wasn't mean-spirited fighting, but back and forth we went. At about 10:00 p.m., I heard crying sounds coming from the formal living room. It was six-year-old Amanda sobbing her eyes out on the living room couch. I went in and asked her what was wrong. She sobbed more and said, "I can hear you and Mommy fighting, and I am afraid you and Mommy will get a divorce." My first inclination was to reassure her, put her back to bed, and tell Roena we better knock off the fighting because it was upsetting Amanda. I reconsidered and said, "Amanda, Mommy and I are mad at each about what we are going to pack for our trip to Texas. We are not going to get a divorce, but we have a lot more arguing to do before we get the station wagon packed. It may take us a long time to get our fighting done. If you want to cry some more, I would suggest you lie here on the couch and cry until you are through, then go back to bed and get some sleep because five o'clock comes very early." I told her I loved her, kissed her on the cheek, and covered her up with an afghan. She probably cried for another three and one half minutes and headed for bed. I decided not to shield her from the reality that grownups don't always get along and may at times argue and bicker. Roena and I didn't divorce, and we had a great vacation.

My son, Mark, was recently in a near-fatal motorcycle accident. When Mark was in the emergency room, hanging on by a thread, the entire family on both sides had a conference. The question was should we tell the children (ages fifteen, twelve, and eight) about Mark's accident now, or wait until we knew if he was going to live. Of course, my position was not to shield the kids from life's problems. We decided to go to fifteen-year-old Cody's high school and tell him immediately about the grave condition of his dad. The younger ones would be told immediately after school. Grandpa Ed and I headed for the high school. We talked to the counselor and told her of the condition of Cody's dad. Cody came to the counselor's office, and we told him about the accident and the danger Mark was in. Cody was tearful and quiet. We took Cody on a walk about the school grounds and let him talk and ask questions. Then Grandpa Ed and I gave him two options. He could go back to the hospital with us, or stay in school and call on his support group for comfort. We explained that Mark was unconscious and had many tubes coming out of various parts of his body. We told him that the doctors had done all they could do, and now his life was between him and God. Cody chose to remain at school and go to football practice. We assured him that if there was any change, we would immediately come back and get him. Mark did live, and is expected to make a slow but full recovery. This experience with Cody turned out so well that now I regret not going to Taylor's and Kellie's school, but we had made a firm family decision about how we would handle telling the younger children. Cody's maturity since his dad's accident has been a joy to watch. Taylor handled his dad's accident with sensitivity and confidence. Mark was on a ventilator with tubes in his nose and mouth, so we told the children that it would be a shock to see him. They were all, at first, reluctant to go into his hospital room. Then suddenly, Taylor pushed past the family crowded at the door and went on in. The first thing he did was to take the hand of his unconscious dad and tell him that he loved him. Kellie is young and shy, but she stood by his bed and touched him and told him that she loved him. Always remember and never forget to avoid shielding your children from life's problems. If you are confident that they will handle a problem well, the children will respond to your confidence in them and handle it well. Their growth will amaze you.

Don't overprotect your children.

Your assignment: Examine your own life and your family life and look for what you are holding back from your children. Have you lost your job or been laid off? Is money a big issue? Is Grandfather close to death? Are you considering a job change that will require a move? Are you seriously considering divorce? Details are not necessary, but tell your children the truth and express confidence in your kids' ability to deal with it. Remember, if you are confident and strong your children will read your tone of voice and body language and be empowered. Test the power of this Key by choosing one thing you have been holding back from your children. Tell it in the way I have described and prepare to be utterly amazed and impressed with the strong way your children handle difficult information!

Key number six: I will always remember and never forget to get physical (playful) with my kids.

Kids love to be touched. They need to be touched. Dads are famous for rough play. Keep doing it. You will be amazed at how rough play helps children. They love to be held high above your head and jiggled all over. They love to be tickled until snot comes out of their nose. They love to wrestle with their dad. They love to be chased with both of you screaming at the top of your lungs. Of course, boys forever love play fights with their dad. I hate to say this, knowing mothers will be reading this chapter. Mothers, remember, I am only the messenger, so don't kill me. Solid research clearly indicates that when given a choice, children will choose to play with their dad two out of three times. Mothers can take heart in the knowledge that if a child is hurt, he will almost always go to his mother for comfort and help.

Fathers offer a very different parenting style than mothers. Fathers put a lot more energy into play than they do with caretaking. This should not be a point of criticism. Mothers are great at caretaking, and children do not need identical mothers. Father-play is of unusual significance in the healthy development of children. Father-play involves lifting, bouncing, and competitiveness. Fathers play more physical games that require more teamwork and the testing of mental skills. Fathers don't ordinarily "let" children win. The child must take victory from the father. Mother-play is quite different. Mothers usually let the child choose the game and be in charge. They let the child proceed at their own pace and make up rules as they go along. Fathers make the child play by the rules, and the game a father chooses is usually a challenge for the child to master. Fathers roughhouse, play hard, and to the mother's chagrin, they are very loud. They highly stimulate a child, and they often do it just before bedtime.

Don't quit, Dad; it's just the right kind of play a child needs to learn some valuable developmental lessons. Psychologists have found that rough, competitive play teaches a child self-control and proper social interaction. It's a paradox. The unexpected happens. Children learn that kicking, biting, hitting, and spitting are not acceptable. Children learn quickly to put brakes on excessive aggression because dad simply will not tolerate that kind of play. They learn when they have gone too far and when enough is enough. They learn from their dad how to shut down inappropriate aggressive play. If they don't comply, the play is abruptly over until they agree to hold back inappropriate play responses. The kind of play described above is particularly helpful for boys. Fathers teach their children empathy through robust play.

Through robust father-play, children learn how to modulate highly charged emotions. Fathers help with the development of the part of the brain that regulates emotions. Rough, physical play also helps children recognize emotional reactions in others like fear and anger.

When fathers play with children, they emphasize risk-taking, competition, and independence. They hold to rules and promote fair play principles.

If you go to a children's park, you will see the stark contrast in the way men and women handle play. Women emphasize safety, and men emphasize risks. When two children are climbing the jungle gym alone, mothers will say, "That's high enough, better stop now." Fathers will say, "You know, there are only two more rungs to the top, and if you try hard, you can make it all the way to the top." Fathers hold infants at arms length and make eye contact. Mothers hold infants close to their breast and give them warmth, safety, and reassurance. Men put infants back to their chest with an arm firmly around their waist. The father walks around and the child sees the world.

Children need both parents. Both offer different learning experiences. Fathers and mothers offer balance in a child's life. One type of play is not better for a child than the other types of play. Father, play with your children as a man would because it's good for their brain development.

Kellie, my nine-year-old granddaughter, loves for me to arrest her and put her in handcuffs, which means I hold her wrists in my hands until she promises to stop pestering me. When she promises to mend the error of her ways, I release her and put her on probation. She promptly breaks probation with more pestering and must be arrested again. This game is repeated endlessly. She loves it.

Always remember to get physical with your kids and play rough, but don't hurt them or play mean. Rough does not mean abusive. Above all, don't play rough until they cry. It should always remain fun for the kids.

Your assignment: Play, play, play with your kids. Wear them out.

Key number seven: I will always remember and never forget to listen, listen, and listen first to understand—then to be understood.

Parents tend to jump to the solution of a child's problem and not listen to the child's side of the difficulty. For example, Sally is standing in her room, bawling, with a forlorn look on her face, and Fred is headed back to the TV room with the remote in his hand. Sally tells her father that Fred hit her and took the remote. Her dad brings justice swiftly and banishes Fred to his room for an hour. No TV for him. This is all done within seconds without hearing both sides of the story. Fathers do things like this without first hearing the thoughts and feelings of the offended and offender. Your first job, Dad, is to listen to understand the thoughts and feelings of your children. You will have your opportunity to be understood, but first listen. When you rush to a solution, it is a given that you haven't listened to your child. Often, dads say, "It doesn't matter what they say, the punishment still stands." Or dads will report that it's a waste of time to get the kids' version because all they'll hear are irresponsible excuses. I still submit that getting the facts and feelings straight before a corrective solution is offered makes you a fairer judge of the situation. In the example given above, would it not be helpful to know that Sally sneaked the remote from Fred while he was watching a show, changed the channel and ran to her room with the remote in hand? Fred chased her down the hallway to her room and asked her nicely to give him back the remote. Sally refused to hand it over, so Fred whacked her, snatched the remote from her hand, and headed back to the TV room. These facts could make a difference in whom and how you punish.

There is an even greater reason to listen to your children. Listening is a demonstration of respect. You will honor your child if you listen. The nonverbal message to your child is, "I respect your right to have thoughts and opinions even if I do not agree with them." Your child will love you for listening, and the long-range result is that listening creates a secure sense of willingness to live under your authority. Think about your own life experiences. Don't you hate to be around people who always talk over you and will not listen to your thoughts and opinions? Don't you avoid them as much as possible? We like to hang out with people who show an interest in what we are saying. Your children will be a lot more willing to hang out with you if you first listen. They will also be more prone to listen to you if you first listen to understand.

As I mentioned earlier, it was my habit to take long walks with Mark in the evenings. That was our ritual. It was our time together. When we first began our walks, I made it my goal to do much more listening than talking. The more Mark walked and talked, the more he talked about himself. He became comfortable sharing his personal secrets with me. I learned that he occasionally ditched school and that he lied to a teacher about something. I learned all kinds of things. I just listened and made a mental note to eventually come back to important topics. I wanted to be understood, too, but first I had to listen to understand. When Mark was in junior high school, his school brought in a counselor to conduct a series of group therapy sessions during homeroom. On one occasion the counselor asked if there was any student in the class who could tell their dad absolutely anything. He asked for hands to be raised. Mark told me he was the only one who raised his hand. That story made me proud. Eventually, the time was right for me to share my own personal thoughts. Mark listened well to me because, I think, he was first listened to.

There is more. Not only do we feel respected when we are listened to, we really like to be involved with anyone who actually tries to understand what we are saying. It is nice if someone is quiet and lets us talk without interruption, but it is twice as nice if the listener understands what is being said. Here are some starter phrases that can let your son or daughter know if you really *listened*. For example: "Son, let me see if I get your point; what you are trying to say is _____" or "I think your message is _____" and then summarize what you heard. I think you will be utterly amazed at how often you misunderstand what he is saying. But that's okay because all is not lost. When you summarize but don't "get it," your child now has a chance to correct your misunderstanding. Let's go back to the Sally and Fred incident. Without any information from Fred, you will probably assume Fred is just being a bully and having his way with Sally. In this case, that would be a dead wrong assumption. Let's say you asked Fred to tell you about what happened to make Sally cry. Fred tells you about Sally stealing the remote, changing the channel, and running away. Next, Fred tells you he asked for the remote nicely. It is now time for a summary, but for illustration, let's say you don't get it and say, "What I hear you saying, Fred, is that you're the boss of the TV and the remote, and Sally has to do what you want or she will suffer big time." Now Fred can correct you and restate his real point which is that he tried to get the remote back in a nice way. You will probably congratulate him on his heroic efforts, but point out that in this house he cannot use commando tactics to get the remote when being nice doesn't work. You also would most likely give him a better solution, such as coming to you for help in getting the remote back.

There is one more key player in our problem scenario, and that would be Sally. She needs to be listened to also. In a real situation of this nature, Sally would probably deny everything, thus muddying the water more, but for brevity and simplicity, let's say she basically tells the same story. You most likely would decide to give both of them a light punishment to teach Sally not to be rude and disrespectful to Fred and to teach Fred to respect his strength, seek help from a higher authority (you), and play nice with Sally. The point I am making is that good decisions are based on good listening. A father's power always involves listening. You will make better parenting decisions and your children will develop greater respect for you even if you end up deciding against what the child deems best and right. Listening creates a win-win relationship. Listen to your children.

Your assignment: For one whole day listen, listen, and listen to understand. If things don't go better for you on that day, call me a do-gooder quack. I don't think I will get any ill wishes from anybody. In fact, I'm sure you will like the results.

Key number eight: I will always remember and never forget to love my children with all of my heart, mind, soul, and strength.

I like this one. I have put it last because the last thoughts I want you to have as you conclude this chapter are about the power of love. Everything I have written before is relegated to the category of useless without understanding and practicing love. Love is the glue that binds all of my fathering suggestions together into a practical, useful program. Love has been trivialized by over-use. The word love has lost its former powerful meaning. Today we love everything. We love our dog, we love our country, we love coffee, we love to dance, we love the color blue, we love being in love, and we love our children. Saying I love you is like saying, "Hi, have a nice day." It means no more than a polite exchange between two people. After reading key number eight, my heartfelt desire is that you will see love with new eyes, and the word love will have a deeper more useful meaning.

When I was about fourteen years old, I fell in love for the first time. Her name was Becky, and I thought Becky loved me too. What I soon came to realize was that Becky loved ten boys, and I was the least loved of the ten. I was crushed. I lived like the walking dead for a few weeks. What I got out of this experience was that love can kill. It is too dangerous to fool around with, so I decided to only love my dog and baseball. Those loves were safe. Fortunately, I grew past these faulty early beliefs, and to my surprise and delight I discovered that love is a risk that isn't. Loving children, loving your wife, significant other, or girlfriend, puts you at risk to be hurt if they do not love you back or if they love in a way you don't want to be loved. Children can love you one day but the next day may decide that you are dirt. Here is what I want you to remember: loving children to get loved back is not the point. I truly believe that you will be delighted with how much love is returned if you love your children with all your heart, mind, soul, and strength. Your fathering job is to risk loving even if you aren't loved back. I feel confident you will be loved back, but I don't want you to require it.

Love is a risk that isn't. Before you can risk love, you must be loved. You cannot give what you don't have. At least half of the men reading this book were far from loved by their biological fathers. Research reveals that at least 50 percent of all men were raised by abusive, neglectful, or emotionally absent fathers. Are you doomed to love failure? No! You have the power to stop this cold, bloodless cycle now. You're not stuck with a love deficit. You only have to accept love from someone important to break the love failure cycle. It can be the love of a wife or girlfriend that breaks the cycle. It can be true love from a pastor or a friend that fills your love cup. Some use faith in God to know what it is like to be loved. I don't think love from your dog will break the love failure cycle, but it can't hurt either. Some break this deadly cycle by discovering the satisfying excitement of learning to love themselves. What is important is that before you can risk love, you must feel loved. It can be done, so do it. When you feel loved, you can safely love your children with all that you are, and you can teach them to love you, others, and themselves.

So, What Is Love?

Let's discuss what love is. Pop culture defines love as a feeling—some kind of warm, tingly, satisfying feeling. Truly, love is a feeling, but it is also much more. Typically the average father wants to feel warm, tingly, and satisfied before they will commit to loving anyone. It will usually be a long, boring wait. There are two steps to go through before feeling the emotion of love. Love is a decision, and love is action. Feeling love always—and I mean always—trails behind decisions and actions. Let's break this formula down and discuss the elements necessary for love. I've said love is a series of decisions, so the next logical question to ask is, "What decisions should I make?" More specifically, "What decisions are needed to make it possible to love my children with all of my heart, mind, soul, and strength?" I'm glad you asked because there are fourteen decisions to be made before you are competent to love. There are volumes and volumes of good books on love. Some of the great world faiths have a lot to say about love and how to love. The best advice I have ever read on love is the Christian Bible. The Bible is not exclusively a book about faith. It is also a guide for a good life and an instructional manual for growing healthy families. The ancient wisdom of the Bible has quite a lot to say about love. In I Corinthians 13, the Bible speaks at great length about the fourteen decisions that make love real, practical, and useful. In the absence of these fourteen personal decisions, love is simply an abstract word, an unproven theory, or worse, a polite but mundane social word. Fourteen immutable decisions make it not only possible but probable that you will love your children with all of your heart, mind, soul, and strength. These are the decisions one must make:

1. **Decide never to give up.** Children are not fatally flawed, disposable products. They may come with learning disabilities, physical flaws, and personality quirks, but they are not to be trashed like something dispensable. Love has a distinct patient quality. The father who truly loves his child never gives up on his child. I used to like to take Grandpa Bud with me when I went fishing with Amanda and Mark. He was so patient. He baited hooks, untangled endless loops of fishing line, and warmed their cold hands. He never gave up on them, and both children became good fishing partners. He was a great example to me for patience. Bless you, Bud.

2. **Decide to be kind.** This means to do good things for your children like tie their shoelaces, help with homework, and fix snacks. Here is a rule of thumb: do more good things for your children than you do for yourself.

3. **Decide not to be a boasting, know-it-all controller.** You cannot love a child if you are a pushy, bossy, blunt, controlling dad.

4. **Decide to focus on what's important.** Don't define your worth only in terms of the work you do, the important people you know, and the many nice things you have. In such a system, there is no room for a child. The loving order is child first, then your work, people, and things. You can be a love success if it is your child who gives you your value. You can't love a child if you are full of pride.

5. **Decide not to be rude.** Sarcasm, a condescending tone of voice, and a constant barrage of put-downs is the death knell for love. You can't love a child if you don't talk nice or if you use put-down language.

6. **Decide not to make everything about you.** Real life is not just about what you want, what you need, and what brings you exclusive pleasure. You can't love a child, who typically needs much, if life is all about your wants.

7. **Decide not to fly off the handle.** Anger is a healthy emotion and we should not seek to stamp it out of existence. Reasonable anger is healthy, but excessive anger is uniformly destructive. You cannot love a child if excessive anger is a way of life. I like to put anger on a scale of one to ten with one through three as numbers representing normal, acceptable anger. Four represents too much anger. Define what represents a four, and look for the early signs of excessive anger. Early warning is the key to anger control. Of course, some men go from zero to sixty in seconds and have no idea what a four is like. Whatever the case, decide to control excessive anger and find a way. It can be done, so do it. You can't love a child if you are raging.

8. **Decide not to mark wrongs.** Collecting and storing injustices in the memory bank will destroy your capacity to love a child. Injustice collection is like air pollution. It colors and taints everything. You can't love a child if you catalog and vividly remember every bad thing he does.

9. **Decide not to admire or envy bad people and bad deeds.** It amazes me that so many people admire the TV program *The Sopranos*, the movies *The Godfather, Parts I and II*, and the movies about the avenging hero who kills everyone that has done him wrong. I don't understand what is admirable about a man who publicly puts his children and wife or girlfriend in their place, which is of course under his tyrannical control. I don't know why the mafia, the put-down artist, and killers are admired, but often in our society, they are. Children cannot be taught the value of life if bad people and bad deeds are admired.

10. **Decide to value the truth.** First tell the truth, and please, please do not promote secrets. Every time you say, "Don't tell mom. This will just be our little secret," it degrades love. You cannot love a child correctly if you lie, shade the truth, or form a conspiracy of secrets.

11. **Decide to protect.** If you love, you will protect those whom you love. Protection from physical harm is the first thing we think of, but let's expand the definition. It also means shielding children from harsh or excessive criticism by teachers, friends, and neighbors. Protect children from fear. I mentioned earlier that my son Mark was near death from a motorcycle accident. He began to improve and wake up a bit from his unconsciousness. I was by his bedside as he awoke. He had tubes in his mouth. He was on a breathing machine, and he couldn't talk. He was in a hospital room and had no understanding of why he was there or what was wrong with him. He had no memory of the accident. He was afraid. His eyes darted around and his body was agitated. I leaned close to his ear and said, "This is your dad. You were in an accident. You are going to live. As long as Dad is here you will live." Almost immediately his pulse rate went down by thirty points, his blood pressure dropped back into manageable range, he closed his eyes, and his body ceased writhing. Children feel loved when they feel protected.

12. **Decide to be optimistic and positive.** Make a decision to spread hope. Reassure your child that together you will solve any problem. Paint a bright future for your child. Children like this. They really feel loved when their dad is optimistic and positive.

13. **Decide to expect the best from others.** Dad, trust people to do the right thing. Expect the best from your children. This decision does not mean you will become gullible, naïve, or see the world through rose-colored glasses. This decision means not expecting or looking for the worst first. See the potential for good. Children make a lot of mistakes. If you look for and expect the worst from your child, he will not feel loved.

14. **Decide to never give up on the power and value of love.** Stick it out, hold on, and never lose belief in the power of love.

These are the decisions that must be made to kick-start love into action. Knowing what love is, hearing about the virtues of love, reading about love, and discussing love is useless. Knowing how to love is useless. It all means nothing without action. You haven't learned a thing about love until your decisions regarding love become observable by others in your actions. Here is a way to make your decisions real. Write on two business cards two of the fourteen decisions and tape them to your bathroom mirror. Keep them there for fifteen days. For fifteen days, you will be reminded to take action on those two love decisions in action. Then, write out two more of the fourteen decisions and put them on your mirror. Practice makes perfect.

All becomes nothing without love! It doesn't matter if you are a silver-tongued lawyer who has never lost a case. It does not matter if you are a revered, successful, productive politician. It does not matter if you are generous and helpful to the down-and-out. It does not matter if you are willing to die for a just cause. All of these admirable life traits are meaningless without love.

If you are not capable of love as described above, you are a zero, a nothing, to your children. They do not need or care about the good and great of you. What your children want is your love. No child values the good you do and the great you are if you cannot convincingly *show* them they are loved. If you love your children in the way the book of wisdom teaches, then all the good and great you are has weight, value, and significance to your children. Without love, you do not exist as an important and valuable person in their life. In their eyes, you are nothing, unless you love them with all of your heart, mind, soul, and strength.

Here is the heart of love. What follows in this next paragraph is the good of love. Fathers, you are protector, provider, authority, and the sender to do good work. Mothers are the nurturers, caretakers, and relationship builders. Together, you are stronger than you could ever be individually. Even if divorced, you can come together in providing your child with these necessities. Children can be strong, secure, happy, and confident if they know that both their dad and mom love them without reservation, without qualification. You may wonder how your children will know they are loved. Saying, "I love you," is not unimportant, but it is the least of the ways to convey love to a child. Look at the list of fourteen decisions again. Children will know they are loved when they experience your love decision in action. They will know love if you act loving.

For a child that is loved by dad, rejection is painful but tolerable. If a teacher scolds and rejects, it is okay. If a friend rejects, all will be right. If a neighbor rejects, it is no matter. If a boyfriend or girlfriend rejects, it can be overcome. This all becomes possible when a dad loves his child with all of his heart, mind, soul, and strength.

One hot summer morning, I was in the backyard doing some yard work when the trash collector stopped at my trash can. I poured an ice cold glass of tea and offered it to the man lifting my trash into the truck. To my surprise he said, "I wouldn't drink anything your white, elitist hands have touched. You are just trying to put me down because I am black. You are a snobby racist man, and I hate you for it." With that he headed for his truck. I went into the house and told Roena how much I was upset by what the man had said. Roena said, "Jerry, you are the kindest, most generous man I know. Now who are you going to believe, me or the trash man?" If you really love your children and someone says to your boy that he is a stupid sissy, but you say to him, "No, you are smart and manly," who do you think you son will believe? If someone says to your daughter that she is fat and ugly and you say, "No, you are beautiful and kind," who do you think she will believe? If your child has seen your love in action, she will feel your love emotionally and your opinions will be the ones that shape her life.

Your daddy-love is not an elective that may be taken occasionally as needed, but your love is a life-giving vaccine that inoculates your children from the destruction the world presents.

Conclusion

In the first section of this chapter, I painted a dark, morose, discouraged picture of fatherhood. I asked the question, "Are fathers necessary?" I hope by now you'll agree that the answer is an emphatic, "Yes!" Involved fathers make unique contributions to their children's lives that cannot be duplicated by anyone else. When it comes to father figures, there are no effective look-alike substitutes. Dad, you are it, and even if you want a stand-in, one just can't do what you do. My message is this: Biological fathers, step up to the plate and take your swings, because you are fated to get a lot of hits." To help children get the best their father has to give, you must engage and be an involved dad. No more absentee dads.

Do you remember the movie, *Top Gun*? The fighter pilot Maverick, played by Tom Cruise, flew close to a fierce battle, but he is afraid to join in the dogfight. The voice of his copilot keeps pleading, "Maverick, engage. Maverick, please engage. Engage, Maverick." If you have read this far, you know where the battle is and how to contribute to the developmental needs of children. Right now, you should be hearing the voice of your child in your mind pleading, "Father, engage. Father, please engage. Engage, Father." You can do it, so do it.

You may already be a committed, faithful, engaged father, so I say, "God bless you, Dad," and I hope what I have written in this chapter will be helpful as an enrichment to your fathering skills.

Most fathers are doing well to consistently live up to the possible. To live up to the possible is good, but there is a kind of dad who doesn't have the slightest idea of what is reasonable and possible. He doesn't know where his limits are, so he lives beyond the possible. This dad does not live by the rules everyone knows and agrees with. This dad flies with eagles, high and beyond the reach and grasp of rule-bound humans. This dad does not ask permission from authorities because they are much too slow with their approval or blessing to proceed. This father is a hero whom I very much admire. I am referring to the adoptive father. The father who adopts children not his own is a man who marches to the beat of a drummer few can hear. Sometimes this dad adopts infants whose mothers and fathers either can't, or don't want to, raise a child. Sometimes this unusual man adopts older children whose biological fathers have abused or abandoned them. This is a man I instinctively like and love. The eight keys that open the eight doors to the hearts and minds of children should be exceedingly helpful to this courageous father. Go for it, man!

If you are divorced or separated, do not be discouraged, because it does not disqualify you from being an adequate father. It means you will have to try harder and live smarter. Remember you can be a good dad, even though you're divorced. Hang in there, and live the eight keys. You can do it, so do it.

The eight keys that open the eight doors to the hearts and minds of children present a fascinating concept. There are actually many more than eight doors that need to be opened into a child's heart and mind. I originally identified twenty-seven doors and keys, but this is a chapter on fathering, not an entire book on the subject. The eight keys I included in this chapter represent some of the best and most practical ways to influence children for good. Fathering is all about winning the heart and mind of a child, and these keys will help you do that. Winning the heart means creating a comfortable, stress-free bond between you and your child. When the heart is won, there is a willingness to cooperate with you and live under your authority. When the mind is won, the child is equipped with behavioral tools that will help them to live under self-control in a society of rules and order. Fathers equip the mind of a child through their modeling of the actions of a healthy male. Remember, action is always better than inaction. Living the eight keys will give your child an example to live up to. Modeling a healthy adult helps your child to learn to live like a healthy adult.

Go forth. Do good!

What My Family Has to Say about Me

Since I've given you all this advice about what it takes to make a great father, I thought I should share with you what my family has to say about me. Of course, I'm not perfect, but I know from experience that the insights that I have shared with you will have a tremendously positive impact on you and your family.

Here's what my wife of forty-five years, Roena, had to say:

Being married to a psychologist has been an adventure, especially when that psychologist is Jerry Day. In our partnership of parenting, I have seen my husband use some unusual approaches with our children. You have read many of them in this book. One day I was home with two preschoolers with colds and four feet of snow outside. I greeted my husband at the door with the plea, "Please, speak to your children." I just knew he would see the floor littered with toys, hear their high-pitched squealing voices, observe my exhausted appearance, and realize they needed some discipline. Jerry held his arms out and with a smiling, happy voice said, "Hi, kids," scooped them up in his arms, and spent the next half hour playing, talking, and listening to our children and, after a while, invited them to help him pick up toys, and they did!

What I believe makes Jerry a great father is that he has always listened to the children. He gave importance to their opinions, and his love has been expressed by the gift of time he spends with each one. The verbal, "Good job," "Go for it," and "I love you," let them know he was in their corner no matter what.

During the school year Jerry would take a day each semester to spend special time with the kids. They could choose whatever they wanted to do. I was at the middle school to pick up Mark for his Day with Dad. I told the assistant principal that I was going to take Mark to meet his father, go to lunch, and to a baseball game. He paused and said, "If more dads would take their kids out of school to spend time together, my job would be easier, and our kids would be better."

Looking at our children today and watching them incorporate some of the life rituals that we practiced as a family and their philosophy of "family" reassures me that the children we raised are the kind of children we want to keep. Jerry has had an active role in the daily lives of our children, and add the camping trips, Days with Dad, Family Nights, spiritual guidance, and just having fun being together…priceless!

From my daughter, Amanda:

People often ask, "What it is like to have a father who is a psychologist?" and I always respond, "I don't know. He's just my dad."

Jerry: What was it like being a child in our home?

Amanda: I know I was not the easiest child, so let me thank you for not leaving me on the side of the road or moving and not leaving a forwarding address. Our home [was] full of love, and you accepted always. Home [was] a safe place. Many of our friends wanted to live with us because our home was safe, fun, and loving. I don't remember if we had lots of money, but we always had what we needed. There was a tremendous sense of family. Individuality was encouraged, and all ideas were accepted, but not always used.

Jerry: What are some of your favorite memories from your childhood?

Amanda: Date night. You worked a lot but you always found time for me. I remember going skating and attending school plays. *Talking*— walking and talking, ice cream and talking, coffee and talking, long distance calls and talking. I enjoy our talks about everything. Perhaps that is one reason we are so close and have an unbreakable bond. *Writing and leading conferences together*. During one of the conferences, we did an activity, with those attending taking two sticks and looping them together creating a type of figure eight. Those sticks hang on my wall, and I am often asked about them. I tell people how they represent our dad/daughter bond and the only way our relationship can be destroyed is if we destroy our bond.

J: Parents often wonder if they teach their children anything. Did I?

A: Besides the obvious—look both ways before crossing the street or tying your shoes or how to throw like a girl—yes. Perhaps the greatest gift you gave to us was how to love one another always. Your children love each other and talk daily not because we live close but because we want to. Your children love their mother and would fight to the death for her. Your children love you too. The second gift you gave me is how to love others. I have a good marriage because you taught me how to love a man and how a man should love a woman by loving mom. The third gift you gave me was to love myself. The fourth gift is to have strong faith. The fifth is to give all you have to help others. There are many more but those are some of the highlights.

J: Did you feel loved as a child? What was said or done to make you feel loved?

A: Yes, I felt loved because you told me and showed me. When I was little, you always tucked me in bed. Come to think of it, you have even tucked me in as an adult. Rocking for hours and perhaps miles, told me you loved me, and made me feel safe. Mom said you would come home for dinner or at bedtime to spend time with Mark and I, then go back to the office—thanks. I require lots of attention and time and you always have time for me. No matter how tired you are or how many problems you have heard during the day, you make time for me.

J: Did you receive enough affection as a child?

A: Yes, and as an adult.

J: What do you mean "as an adult"?

A: Affection as a child is important, but it is just as important for an adult. You still give hugs and kisses, but you often just put your arm around me in a group of people and that makes me feel loved and cared for as well. I know you are proud of me because you tell me and are specific.

J: If you could change me what would it be?

A: That is a tough question. You work a lot, which did not leave much time for family vacations. What you did do was find time to develop our relationship around your work schedule.

J: Any final thoughts?

A: I used to think everyone grew up like I did, but the older I get the more I realize it is not so. I am thankful I grew up in a home where I [was] loved and accepted and encouraged.

From my son, Mark:

1. What was it like being a child in your father's home?

It was very comfortable growing up in my father's home. There were expectations of us, chores and rules, but they were achievable. I never did worry about money or eating or taking a vacation. Everything was always taken care of.

2. What are the three best lessons your father taught you?

Trust must be earned, not given. Always treat women with respect. Trust in God, and He will provide.

3. Name three positive memories from your childhood.

Staying up late with my dad, fishing trips with my dad, and church.

4. Did you feel loved as a child?

Yes.

5. If you felt loved, what was said or done to make you feel loved?

By the way my family treated me, parents and grandparents alike, and the way we were spoken to, not down to.

6. What could have been done by your father to make you feel more loved?

My only wish is that my father actually said it more. I know he did [love us], and he showed it, but rarely said it.

7. Did you get enough physical affection as a child and teenager?

Yes.

8. How did your father express physical affection to you?

He would usually place his hand on my shoulder or rub my head but rarely hugged [me].

9. What could your father have done better regarding physical affection?

I think he did a fine job. I always knew that he loved me.

10. If you could go back to your childhood and change your father, what would you change most about him?

Although we did many things together, it seemed as though he was always at work.

Final Thoughts

My children are now forty-one and thirty-nine years old, but asking them to look back at their childhoods was a scary, humbling experience for me. I learned a few things about myself. My work as a psychologist is very demanding and time-consuming. Both of my children mentioned that I worked too much and was away from them too much. Dads, if your children are young, take heed and learn from what my children said, "You worked too much." Children want more of what you have the least to give, TIME! It is not too late to reorder your priorities, so do it.

I was raised by an "old school" father. Back then, you hugged and kissed a girl and shook a boy's hand. My son Mark needed more action-focused love. He needed more hugs than he actually got, and he wanted to hear me say directly, "Mark, I love you." Fathers, pay attention. Hug your boys and tell them you love them. Mark felt loved and valued, but he longed for more demonstration of my love for him.

Roena is so very supportive. She is the perfect "doctor's wife," supportive, loving, caring. She is funny, too. I loved her story about being overwhelmed with childcare and expecting me to come in and set those demanding kids straight. Roena has done a great job of raising the kids. Where I am weak, she is strong. I like that about her. I also agree with her that we have raised two kids that we are eager to keep.

Fathers, I would suggest that you ask your children to give you feedback from time to time about how you are doing as a father. Also, ask your kids' mother (even if she's your ex-wife) about your fathering skills. You, like me, may learn a few things that will help you become a better father or grandfather. It's never too late to learn to become a better father, so do it.

Go forth. Do good.

Chapter 8

The More Not Less Technique

This technique is appropriate for children ages three through seventeen.

Do any of your children have bad habits? Of course they do! Have you ever wondered how you can help your child break those bad habits? Of course you have! Have you ever felt frustrated, stuck, and helpless to do anything about your child's bad habits? Probably you have felt these nagging feelings. The More Not Less Technique may be exactly what you need to break your child's bad habits once and for all. It's that good.

Let's look at the life of a six-year-old boy who threw fits if he was even slightly inconvenienced, denied what he wanted, or was told no by his mom or dad. Fitful Ferguson was relentless, and he knew no limits. He threw a bawling, wailing, kicking, hitting, throwing, spitting fit anywhere. Ferguson's mom and dad were exhausted. They were not good at discipline, and they had no control. Ferguson ruled.

His parents were desperate, so they were ready to hear about new control tactics. They promised that they would do anything I told them to do, if I thought it would help. They almost fell off the couch when I told them that we were going to make Ferguson throw more fits, so he would throw fewer fits later. I said, "We are going to make Ferguson do it more so he will do it less." They were speechless. However, after hearing the plan in detail, they became enthusiastic supporters and were more than willing to go the distance.

The Birth of the More Not Less Technique

I developed this habit-change technique many years ago, based upon an experience with Mark, my youngest child. He rarely turned a light off once he turned it on. You know how parents are when it comes to the utility bills.

You may say to your child what I frequently said to Mark, "Turn the lights off! Do you think I own the electric company?" I also used standard, common punishments, such as scolding, take-aways, and time-outs in hopes that he would learn to turn the lights off. Nothing worked with Mark, so one evening I decided to try out a budding idea I had been working on. I went to Mark, who was about six years old and said, "Mark, I have noticed that if you turn a light on, you usually go away and leave the light on." Mark replied quickly, "I know, Dad. I just forget. Don't punish me." I continued, "So I have decided that we need to practice some 'remembers' and get rid of those 'forgets.'" Mark stared at me blankly. I went on to explain practice. "So, Son, I want you to stand here at this light switch and turn the light on and off one hundred times." He didn't like it, but he did what I said to do.

The results were not as good as I had hoped for. His memory improved some, but he still left the lights on more often than I could tolerate. After more thinking and evaluation, I asked myself a question. "What if I required him to do more of what he does wrong, so he will eventually do it less?" What he did the most was turn the light on, do something, leave, and forget to turn the light off when he left.

Here is what I did next. I went to Mark and told him that he had improved some but not enough, so we were going to practice, but this time we would do it a little differently. Mark said, "Oh, Dad!" in a disgusted tone of voice. I took that as a good sign. I said, "Mark, there are lights in the kitchen, so I want you to turn both on and pretend to get yourself a drink of water." He complied by turning on both lights and pretending to get a glass of water. Next I said, "There are lights in the bathroom so leave the kitchen lights on and let's go turn the two bathroom lights on." We headed for the bathroom. I told him to turn on the lights and pretend to take a whiz. He dutifully complied, and in fact, he seemed to be having some fun pretending. We left the bathroom lights on and went to his bedroom. He turned the lights on, including the closet light, and pretended to play with something in his room. By this time, I was sure he was making a fun game of the whole procedure. He left his bedroom lights on, and to my surprise, he very helpfully reminded me that there were lights in the laundry room, where we headed next. We soon had every light on in the house. I said to Mark, "Now, Mark, I am going to do what I always do. Go to your room and pretend play, and I will go to the family room and pretend to read my newspaper." He headed for his room. Next, I yelled from the family room, "Mark

Day, every light in this house is on. You get in here and start turning lights off!" Mark eagerly complied. He was having fun.

The next part wasn't half as much fun. We went through the whole routine again, with Mark turning off all the lights he had just turned on. When we finished, I said, "Well that was better, but I think we need some more practice." So we turned on every light in the house again. After the tenth practice routine, Mark was pleading with me to stop. Now I had the little forgetter where I wanted him—frustrated. We continued turning the lights on, and pretending to do the distraction things he usually did when he forgot to turn them off. At practice number twenty, and just before Mark went up into a huge puff of holy smoke, I said, "Mark, that will be enough practice for tonight." Mark was relieved. I then put the final touches on the technique by saying, "You know, Mark, you didn't learn to ride a bike the first time you tried; you didn't learn to read on the first day of school; and I know you didn't learn to walk the first time you tried. So Son, I wouldn't be a bit surprised if you don't forget and leave a light or two on before you go to bed tonight. But, don't worry about it at all if you forget and leave a light on. Dad will be watching, and if you forget, I don't want you to worry at all about it, because it just means we didn't get all of the 'forgets' out. If you forget even once and leave a light on, we will just practice some more until you get all the forgets out of you, so we can put some remembers in."

What do you think Mark thought about every time he touched a light switch? Right, "I'd better turn the light off, or my crazy dad will make me practice." That was it for Mark. There was no more forgetting to turn lights off, and the More Not Less Technique was born. I next practiced my newfound technique on Amanda to check it for accuracy. I even used the technique on myself, and it worked very well for me, too. It is a user friendly tool that can be applied creatively for hundreds of child, teen, and adult bad habits. It has become a great method to help children break bad habits that parents just hate.

Before I get to Amanda's More Not Less story, consider this: I have found that the More Not Less Technique can markedly help children with Attention Deficit Hyperactive Disorder. ADHD kids are famous for their many behavioral problems. They are starters, but not finishers. They are impulsive interrupters and consummate procrastinators. The More Not Less Technique can help them break bad habits in these areas. It helps re-train the part of the brain affected by ADHD, namely, the prefrontal cortex. I will say a bit more about this area of the brain later.

One could call the More Not Less Technique a saturation method. Suppose I asked you to open your mouth to receive six large tablespoons full of pure sugar on your tongue. Further assume that I instructed you to let the sugar melt and then to swallow it. Next, assume you feel a little nauseated. After you've dissolved and swallowed the six tablespoons of sugar, I take a sweet Snickers bar out of my pocket and ask you to share half of it with me. I predict that you would politely decline my invitation to eat something sweet. You have had it with sweet taste. The More Not Less Technique operates in a similar fashion. Mark did not want to ever again experience saturation light-turning-on practice. The best way for Mark to avoid saturation practice was to remember to turn lights off!

Amanda's More Not Less Story

I perfected this technique by using it first on my own children. Fortunately these experiences happened early in my career as a psychologist. Over the ensuing years, I have taught several thousand parents the More Not Less Technique with uniformly good results.

Amanda was eight years old, and her bad habit was that when she opened a door or drawer, it stayed open. No punishment curtailed her bad habit of forgetting to close doors and drawers. I told Amanda that we needed to practice forgetting to close drawers and doors so she could remember to close doors and drawers. I set aside plenty of time, and we began. She was instructed to open all the doors she could reach in the kitchen, including the refrigerator. Next, she opened all the drawers in the kitchen. I sent her out to play on the swing set then I went into my part of the drama. I went to the door and pretended to be angry, as I called her in and said, "Amanda Day, I have told you a thousand times to close the doors and drawers. Get yourself in here right now and close those kitchen doors and drawers." Like Mark, she at first enjoyed playing the pretend game with me. Next we went to her bedroom and opened all the doors and drawers. I sent her to the kitchen to pretend to eat a snack. Remember, you are the director of the drama, so it is important to have a clear understanding of every action and mistake your child makes. Your job is to make her practice what she does wrong, so she will do it less in the future. I angrily called Amanda to get to her room to close doors and drawers. We went to every room in the house and repeated her mistakes. I made her do it over and over again until she was ready to get a new dad.

When she had had it with practicing her mistakes, I went to the final step. I told her that I would not be surprised at all if she forgot, even that night, and left a door or drawer open. I told her not to worry about leaving a door or drawer open because I would be watching, and if I saw a door or drawer open, it just meant we would have to practice some more. I was astounded at the results. No more drawer or doors were left open. I am sure that Amanda must have privately said in her mind, "I better close the door, or my rude dad will make me practice some more!"

There was an interesting twist in Amanda's story. Remember, little kids tend to think concretely and literally. She did close drawers and doors in all of the rooms we worked on, but she still left the front door and back door open. I presume that she thought that since we didn't practice on the front and back door, it was okay to leave them open. To deal with this oversight, I went to Amanda and said, "I really appreciate that you are remembering to close doors and drawers all over the house." She beamed. "But I have noticed that there are two doors you still forget to close, the front door and the back door." She looked worried. "So, here is the deal, I am going to give you two days to get this problem fixed. If, after Thursday, you are still leaving the front or back door open, we will practice forgetting until you remember." To my pleasure, she self-corrected the problem without further practice.

The experience led me to develop the easy-to-use follow-up technique. If your child begins again to do what you practiced, say, "I have noticed that you are beginning to forget to pick up your towel and clothes from the bathroom floor after your shower. So here is what I am going to do. I will watch you for two days, and if you forget again, don't worry about it, we will practice again." Usually the child will have a flashback to the practice session and start to comply again.

If you have had at least one long, grueling practice session, you can use the follow-up technique in a new and creative way. Let's say you want to work on the bad habit of getting up after bedtime and asking for parental services, such as a glass of water, a back rub, another kiss, or a check on the monster that lives in the closet. Say to your insomniac child, "I have noticed that every night you get up after bedtime two, three, or four times and ask Mom or Dad for something. So here is the deal, I will give you two nights to fix this problem, but if after Thursday, you get up after bedtime, even once, we will have a practice session like we did with forgetting to brush your teeth at bedtime." You will be surprised at how many problems children can self-correct if you threaten them with another practice session to correct a new problem. Next, let's look at the seven steps necessary to carry out the More Not Less Technique.

More Not Less Technique Summary

1. Work on one bad habit at a time.
2. Allow plenty of time for practice. Don't start it if you have a dental appointment in an hour. It may take a while to wear your son or daughter out. Be patient.
3. Explain to your child what you are going to do and why practice is needed. For example, you might word your explanation like this to eleven-year-old Joe. "Joe, I have noticed that you turn your radio up too loud in your bedroom, then leave to go somewhere else to play, and leave your radio blaring in your bedroom. Here is what we are going to do. We are going to practice everything you are doing wrong more, so you will do it less. So, let's get started."

   If a child is eight or younger, I like to draw a picture of a child with a rather large chest. In the chest portion, I draw a bucket and fill it with the word "forget" written again and again. I use the same wording as above but I turn to the picture and say, "Son, we have to empty your bucket of forgets out before I can put any remembers in, so we are going to practice your forgets out of your bucket." That picture lives in their head as they practice. Some kids will even say during practice, "Dad, is my bucket empty yet?" That's a good sign.
4. Practice, practice, practice. You need to think about all of the things your child does wrong in regard to that specific problem. Think of every word and every action that is associated with your child's bad habit. Think of your role as parent. Think about what you do and say in response to your child's bad habit, which will include your good and your bad actions and words. Do not require your child to practice the positive replacement behavior that you so desperately want to see happen. First, he must become painfully aware of every little nuance of his problem. What you practice are the words and actions you want him to get rid of. It's the negative actions and words you want to practice out of him. When he can control his negative behavior, then he can replace it with positive, cooperative behavior.

The practice, for best results, must become very burdensome to your child. Practice must be an ordeal for the More Not Less Technique to work. By including the little picky details, and practicing over and over, you help the practice session to move beyond being a fun exercise and instead become an ordeal that the child won't want to repeat. Only then will your child think before he repeats the bad habit you worked on. Remember, I am not encouraging you to be mean or cruel, just meticulous. During the practice, keep a pleasant demeanor. Your child may cry or whine, but don't scold or lecture him on the virtues of doing what you tell him to do. Resist saying things like, "This will teach you a lesson, you little forgetter," or, "Now you know how I feel." That kind of talk is demeaning and unnecessary. Just practice, practice, practice, and stay pleasant and in a good mood. Follow the examples given to illustrate the proper use of the More Not Less Technique. The teaching stories presented are your models for success.

5. Always conclude the session with the finishing statement. When your child is very uncomfortable, and when you are ready to conclude the practice, always finish with this vital statement. "Jill, I think that will be enough practice for today, but I wouldn't be a bit surprised if you didn't forget and leave a light on, but don't worry about it. You didn't learn to ride your bike the first time you tried, you didn't learn to read the first day you went to school, and I know you didn't learn to walk the first time you tried. Don't worry. Mom and Dad will be watching, and if you leave a light on, it just means we need to practice some more." Memorize this finishing statement and use it at the conclusion of every practice event. The finishing words are necessary to use for the More Not Less Technique to work effectively, so use them.

6. Look for opportunities to use the follow-up technique. The More Not Less Technique should serve you well in helping your child break a bad habit. After the technique has been successfully employed, you can approach other bad habits you would like to see eliminated in this way. Suppose you successfully eliminated your child's bad habit of standing up to eat supper. Now he sits quietly in his chair to eat. Next, you would like for him to work on his habit of starting to clean his room, only to get distracted and not finish the project. Go to Joe and say, "Joe, I have noticed that whenever you start to clean your room, you never finish the job. I'm going to give you one hour to start cleaning your room and finish

cleaning your room. If you don't finish the job in one hour, don't worry about it, we will just practice all of those 'don't finish a jobs' out of you." Most likely he will finish the job of cleaning his room. Use the same follow-up wording for other tasks he is assigned but doesn't finish.

7. The last step is to out-stubborn your kids. Most children toe the line after one very long practice session, but not all kids. You may have one or more of these stubborn children that, for unknown reasons, don't improve after one application of the More Not Less Technique. Repeat and repeat again if you have to. Stay with it until your child changes her bad habit enough to please you. The worst thing you can do to your child is to back off and let her win. If you step down once you have started, the only thing your child has learned is that they can keep things the same by being more stubborn than you are. If you do not have the will to carry on to a successful conclusion, it would be better for your child if you had not started the use of the More Not Less Technique. Be tough. Be persistent.

A List of Applications

The following twelve areas represent some of the common problems to which I have successfully applied the More Not Less Technique. However, this list is not definitive or exhaustive. Be creative, and add some of your own child's bad habits to the list.

1. Forgetting to complete a regular, assigned chore.
2. Not using proper table manners, like using utensils and saying, "Please," and "Thank you."
3. Dilly-dallying or failing to get ready to leave the house for school, appointments, or to run errands.
4. Performing purposeless rituals. Some children have annoying rituals they feel they must do or something bad will happen. Your child may have an Obsessive Compulsive Disorder that requires professional treatment. However, many children only have some traits and features of OCD but not to the extent that their rituals reach the diagnostic level. The More Not Less Technique certainly cannot hurt and is likely to help, so use the technique. Note the teaching story of the boy who had to have smooth bed covers before he could sleep as an example of how

to use the technique on rituals. Professional help may be required to help an OCD ritual, but do not be reluctant to try the More Not Less Technique first. I have never found the technique to cause harm, and frequently it successfully corrects even extreme rituals.

5. Starting tasks and failing to finish them.

6. Not sitting still or concentrating when required. Some children cannot sit in a chair long enough to finish a task like eating supper. ADHD must be suspected and ruled in or out (see chapter 14 on ADHD). Even if your child has ADHD, use the technique. It should help.

7. Hitting, kicking, biting, pulling hair, etc. Use the technique here, but remember that they are to practice by hitting a pillow, not an actual brother or sister!

8. Using hurtful, abusive, or inappropriate language with a parent.

9. Not coming to a parent when called, or coming late.

10. Chronically interrupting or blurting.

11. Procrastinating about doing homework.

12. Being extremely disorganized.

Note: Here is an important caution when applying the More Not Less Technique. Never, I mean never, require your child or teen to do repetitive behavior that may cause physical harm. Do not require your child to engage in any form of practice behavior that could cause shame, humiliation, or guilt. For example, do not ask your ten-year-old boy to jump off the roof of your house into the swimming pool, so he will do it less. Do not require your five-year-old daughter to repetitively slap your face so that she will hit less. I am sure both will jump less and hit less, but the danger of physical harm and shame offsets the gain.

Using More Not Less with Teenagers

Teenagers can present a serious problem to the parent who has decided that the More Not Less Technique should be used to break a bad habit. Often teens believe the technique is stupid and refuse to do it. Here is how to handle a reluctant teen. Let's say you want to correct your teen's bad habit, but scolding, voice control (yelling and screaming), take-aways, and loss of privileges have not made a dent. If your child is a standard teen, he won't willingly engage in the technique. Parent, it is not optional; it is not his choice to make. He must do it, because you have directed him to do it. As a back up to your authority, I would suggest you use the Now or Later Technique. He will do it with you after one application of the Now or Later Technique, guaranteed. (See chapter 6.) Let me hasten to say that most teens will eventually go along with the technique, although they won't like it. That's fine, because they aren't supposed to like it! Just putting your foot down and being firm is often quite enough to get compliance under protest. Teens start the technique mad and disgusted, so it usually takes fewer repetitions of the negative than what would be required for a ten-year-old boy who has the same bad habit. Don't let teens' negativity put you off. Go for it!

Parental Concerns

Before a successful application of the technique, parents often question the wisdom of repeating the negative over and over in practice. We have been taught to de-emphasize the negative and accentuate the positive. Parents wonder if this technique won't simply add fuel to a burning fire and reinforce the negative bad habit. It does seem that way at first look. It doesn't make logical sense to practice the negative. It does seem to be more reasonable to practice, practice, practice the positive thing you want your child to do. This technique presents a paradox. The very thing you would expect to happen doesn't. In fact, the opposite occurs, and the child gets better, not worse.

First of all, this is an awareness technique. One cannot change any habit that happens automatically without preplanning and thought. You can't change what you can't catch yourself doing before you do it. Confused? I hope not.

Here is an example of what I am talking about. As a young psychologist, I was part of an evaluation team whose job was to evaluate the performance of a high school. My job was to evaluate the counseling department. When we finished our evaluation, the ten team members went to a room to write our report. The supervisor of the team came over to me and said, "Jerry, what's wrong?" I said, "Nothing." A few minutes later he walked by and said, "Jerry, is there something wrong?" I said, "Nothing is wrong." He came by a third time and asked the same question. I said, "The only thing wrong is you keep asking me what's wrong, so why have you asked me three times?" He told me I had the worst scowl on my face he had ever seen. He said my forehead was furrowed into a deep line between my eyes. I was driving home, and I adjusted the mirror so I could see my face. Sure enough, there it was. He was right. For the next month, I looked for the frown and found it often. Eventually I could feel my face beginning the scowl. I gradually corrected it and today, many years later, I cannot even make my face scowl. I couldn't correct the scowl until I could learn to catch myself beginning to frown. Here is the point. Until your child is fully aware of his bad habit, he can't correct it. The More Not Less Technique is a surefire way of bringing his negative habit into his conscious awareness. To correct a bad habit, your child must think before he acts, and that takes awareness.

Part of the power of the More Not Less Technique is that it is crafted around escape learning. The parent creates a big ordeal for the child by means of excessive practice. The child can escape the ordeal, but he will have to cooperate with his mom or dad to do so. The practice is so dramatic and uncomfortable that the child seeks ways to escape or get out of future practices. To be able to escape, he must find a way to break the old bad habit. The child does this by installing a filter in his brain that causes him to think for a split second about the consequences (practice) that will occur if he engages in the old habit. Remember the story of Mark? When he touched a light switch, his filter slowed his actions and reactions down enough that he could think, "If I don't turn the light off when I leave the room, Dad will make me practice." Mark is now thirty-nine years old and still remembers and talks about the time I made him turn lights on.

The More Not Less Technique is a negative reinforcement technique, but punishment must not and cannot be your only corrective tool to teach a child the error of his ways. We need to use positive reinforcement, too. Balance is the key. Children need five times as much praise, love, and caring as they do punishment. Refer back to chapters 1, 2, and 3 for instruction and examples of love, praise, and positive reinforcement. These positive experiences are absolutely necessary as a foundation for the success of the use of negative reinforcement. When your child stops his old bad habit, praise him frequently and lavishly. Children want to know when they are doing right and pleasing their parents. Parents are quick to point out the wrong a child does, but not so swift to invest at least as much time and energy in recognizing the right a child does. The ratio of positive to negative is always five to one. A child must experience five positive exchanges or more between child and parent for every one negative exchange in order to experience the best mental health and a strong relationship between parent and child. Always remember and never forget that the premise of this book is based on a balance between willingness and compliance to authority.

A child will be willing to obey if the five to one ratio is valued, practiced, and honored in the home.

Using the More Not Less Technique creatively, wisely, and frequently will make a huge contribution to raising a child you want to keep. The following teaching stories are designed to provide tactics, methodology, and encouragement to press on.

Forgetful Frank

Frank, eleven years old, had three standard weekly chores to do. His jobs were to carry the trash out every day, pick up dog poop in the yard on Mondays, Thursdays, and Saturdays, and load the dishwasher on Sundays after supper. Forgetful Frank forgot one or all three on a regular basis, and his mom was turning into a nagging shrew. She had tried all common and reasonable punishments, but nothing consistently worked. I introduced the seven steps necessary to carry out the More Not Less Technique, and after hearing the whole story, she was determined to do all the steps perfectly. Frank was more forgetful about picking up dog poop than he was about the trash and dishes. Although he needed to work on all three chores, we decided we could not adequately attend to all three using this technique, so we applied it to Frank's yard duty. Frank's mom went through the steps with Frank, and they practiced and practiced all of his excuses and avoidance actions. His mom, the drama coach, went through her part, too. She made him sit in the living room, pretending to watch TV, and she would storm in, chew him out, and send him out to do his chore. Frank pretended to pick up the poop, and then his mom sent him to his room to lie on his bed and read comic books. She then flew in, reamed him out, and sent him out to pretend to scoop poop. She sent him to all of his usual loafing and recreational places over and over and over, until he was ready to have a meltdown. Finally, she used the finishing words and told him she would be watching. If he forgot to do his chore, he wasn't to worry, because they would practice some more.

Frank became Mr. Reliable regarding poop. We next tackled trash, and his mom used the follow-up technique. She gave him two days to get it straight in his mind that if he didn't carry out the trash everyday, they would go back to the practice method. He mended his ways and remarkably remembered to carry it out daily without being told.

Getting Frank to do the dishes was the easy task. His mom just said that he needed to remember that Sunday was his day to do dishes, and if he forgot again, they would practice to improve his memory. Frank didn't forget. Frank's mom likes herself again, and she and Frank are closer then ever before.

Bad Manners Mona

Mona is eight years old and has terrible table manners, both at home and out in public. Mona was prone to pick up food with her fingers and resisted using a fork. She rarely said, "Please," or, "Thank you," at the table. She would say, "Give me the beans," and when the food was passed, would not say, "Thank you." Her parents had tried everything. No punishment had any long-term effect. I explained the steps of the More Not Less Technique, and her dad said he would like to give it a try. Her mom was too angry with Mona to approach the technique in a calm and pleasant manner. Her dad followed the steps and soon had Mona pretending to eat with her fingers. He made her ask for imaginary dishes on the table and forbade her to say, "Please," or "Thank you." He dutifully went through his part. He lectured her about table manners, using her fingers, and saying, "Please," and "Thank you." Then he would start the drama again. Forty-five minutes later, Mona began to sniffle, so her dad said that would be enough for tonight. He applied the finishing words and told her he would be watching at the next meal, and if she forgot and used her fingers, or failed to say, "Please and Thank you," she shouldn't worry. It just meant they would need to practice some more.

To her dad's surprise, Mona failed the test! In a day or two Mona had lapsed back into her old habits. Her dad reminded her that they had agreed that if she forgot, even once, they would practice again. He set a time to practice, but this time, he drew a picture of Mona with a big pot of "forgets" inside her tummy. Dad said they would practice until her pot was empty so he could put some "remembers," and "please" and "thank yous" in her bucket. They practiced for fifty minutes that time. Mona was cured, and she didn't forget again.

Dilly-Dally Sally

Sally, age ten, dilly-dallied every school day morning. She just couldn't or wouldn't get herself ready soon enough to make it to school on time. Her mother was a nervous wreck, rushing around in a manic state, trying to get Sally to hurry up and get her stuff done. She had also become an angry, yelling, scolding, critical parent. Because of her mom's frayed nerves and Sally's "What did I do wrong?" attitude, we decided to use the direct and powerful More Not Less Technique. Sally's mom needed immediate improvement.

She carefully thought through all of Sally's morning antics, including her words and attitude. She also carefully went over her unbecoming words and actions that she used in response to Sally's dillies and dallies. She was ready. Sally's mom explained what they were going to do and why. Sally was required to practice every getting-ready delay tactic, starting with her resistance to getting out of bed. Let's use this one as an example of the many behaviors her mother made her practice. Sally's mom's responsibility was to act as Sally's drama coach. At 3:00 p.m. on a Saturday afternoon, she made Sally put on her night-gown, get in bed, cover up, and pretend to sleep. She went into Sally's room, turned the light on, went to the bed, and shook Sally awake. Sally pretended to be asleep, kept her eyes closed, and turned her back to her mother. Her mother kept shaking Sally. At her mom's command, Sally opened her eyes, sat up on the edge of the bed, and said in an angry voice, "Okay, okay, I'm getting up." Her mom laughingly retorted, "You'd better get up young lady! You will be grounded today if you don't." She then left Sally's room and pretended to fix breakfast. Sally was instructed not to come when called, so her mom went back into the bedroom and directed Sally to crawl under the bed and pretend to sleep. Remember, this was a play, so it was important to reenact Sally's common mis-takes and acts of defiance. Sometimes her mom would find Sally in the closet asleep, or on the bathroom rug asleep. (Note: Sally went to bed at a decent hour and appeared to sleep well through the night.) She made her practice that, too. She made Sally practice every antic she had ever observed. Her mother was the coach so she said, "I always pull you out from under the bed, and I am furious with you. I always say, 'You little, ungrateful imp! I do everything for you, and you do nothing to help me!'" She made Sally say her usual reply in her whiny, insin-cere tone of voice, "Sorry, Mom. I'm just so sleepy I fall asleep again. What's the big deal?" You get the idea. Everything was practiced, including bathroom delay tactics, dressing resistance, breakfast delays, and packing-her-stuff-for-school-in-her-backpack slowness. They went over every detail again and again for one and a half hours.

Finally, to Sally's great relief, her mom said, "Okay, that will be enough prac-tice for today. She used the finishing words, "Sally, I wouldn't be a bit surprised if you are late for school on Monday morning. But don't worry. You didn't learn to ride your bike the first time you tried either. Mom will be watching, and if you are late, don't worry about it, because all it means is that we will need to prac-tice again."

I instructed Sally's mom that after she awakened Sally with one call and one good firm shake, she was not to remind Sally to do anything. It was up to Sally to get herself organized and out the door. Often, the More Not Less Technique produces a miracle cure for bad habits, but it did not in Dilly-Dally Sally's case. Her mom had to practice with Sally two more times before Sally got it. Sally discovered that the only way she could escape the practice ordeal was to cooperate with her mother and get herself ready to leave on time. After the third More Not Less practice, Sally made a remarkable change. She got ready on time with no prompting from her mother. Sally pleased her mother very much because she internalized the responsibility of independently preparing herself to be ready on time. Her mom lavishly praised Sally, and both enjoyed a much calmer, stress-free mother-daughter relationship.

There is more! Because her mom also practiced her unbecoming, negative, ineffective, useless, nagging, scolding, put-down words and actions, she became aware of her useless words and behavior. She installed some brakes, too, and corrected many of her negative responses to Sally's misbehavior. The More Not Less Technique helped both mom and child.

Hateful Harry

His dad was a bit of a mystery to Harry, age nine, so he was pretty careful about what he said and how he said it to his father. His mom was another story. When she corrected Hateful Harry or said, "No" to him, he would fly into a rage and call her every vile name an eight-year-old boy could think of. He would rail at her and call her "stupid," "bitch," "idiot," "shithead," and even worse. His mom had tried every punishment known to mankind, but to no avail. Hateful Harry continued his tirades. I explained the steps of the More Not Less Technique, and his mom agreed to give it a go. She first made a list of all the naughty words she had ever heard Harry say. She waited until Harry was in a good mood before she explained the basics of the technique. It was hard on her, but his mom made Harry say aloud each word in the usual manner in which he delivered the ugly words. At first, Harry refused to cooperate, but his mother was ready for this act of stubbornness. I directed her to read the chapter on the 30-Second Technique and apply it to Harry if he didn't want to cooperate. She told Harry that it wasn't his choice and he had to say the words. She gave him thirty seconds to get started, and then she named an item from his room that she would take if he didn't get started in thirty seconds. Harry got mad about the loss of toys from his room, and he spontaneously went into his ugly word routine. After the loss of eight items, he caught on that his mother was not going to cave in, and his losses were growing. He agreed to practice. The 30-Second Technique was good for both

Harry and his mom. She was gaining power and leverage, and Harry was learning to submit to her authority. For thirty long minutes she made Harry practice saying bad words, in the places he usually said them, in the voice he usually said them, and under the same circumstances that usually triggered his tirades. Mom went through her angry and hurt responses also.

She used the finishing words and sent Harry on his way. Harry's word choice improved some but he still would, too often, slip up and call her a few choice words. I asked his mother to repeat the technique, but this time repeat it for an hour. She also taught Harry to take three to four deep breaths when he started to get mad. By doing so, Harry was much more able to keep his temper in check. After the second application of the More Not Less Technique, Harry stopped cursing his mother out, and found other, more acceptable ways to let his mother know he was not happy with her.

Ritual Ralph

Sixteen-year-old Ralph had three rituals that he performed to protect himself and his parents from harm. One ritual was exceptionally annoying to his parents. He had to have every wrinkle smoothed out of his bed covers before he could sleep. If there was a wrinkle, he was sure something bad would happen to him that night. Reason and logic had no lasting impact on Ralph. He smoothed his covers over and over for fifteen to thirty minutes before he could lie down to sleep. He also felt he had to plug every appliance in three times, or something bad would happen. He couldn't tell me what bad thing would happen, but he insisted that it would be bad. He also had to count to three every time he touched a door knob. The bed cover wrinkles ritual was the most intrusive, so we tackled that one first. I went over the More Not Less Technique steps with his parents. His dad agreed to employ them. Ralph, who was surprisingly cooperative, was asked to smooth his covers perfectly, then mess them up and smooth them again. Father and son practiced for two hours on a Saturday afternoon. (It was important that his dad did not practice with him at bedtime.) Ralph thought it was a great exercise for about the first hour, but he found the second hour to be miserably boring. He lost much of his Saturday fun time, which added to the quality of the ordeal. Ralph understood that he was doing his ritual to get rid of his ritual. At the end of the two hours, Ralph's father used the finishing words. He told Ralph he would be surprised if he had practiced enough to fix the problem, but not to worry if he smoothed his covers again. All it meant was they would need to practice more next Saturday afternoon. That was it for cover-smoothing. Ralph went to bed, covered up, and drifted into sleep. We used the same technique for the plugs and door knobs, with similarly good results.

The severity of Ralph's problem may initially be a source of discomfort for some parents reading this, who could easily think that this was a clear case for a counselor, not a parent. However, insight-oriented therapy that digs down to the root of the problem rarely helps children with OCD-type problems. Behavioral therapy, such as the use of the More Not Less Technique, on the other hand, offers great hope for a safe and reliable resolution to the problem. With coaching, Ralph's parents were able to successfully execute the technique and deal with Ralph's useless nightly ritual.

The chances the More Not Less Technique will help in a situation like this one are very good, even with severe problems. If the technique doesn't work, no harm will have been done, and you can always refer to a qualified psychologist.

Conclusion

The More Not Less Technique has proven to be a valuable tool to break up any bad habit that a child has acquired. There are seven necessary steps to learn in order to make the technique effective. The key to success is the "practice, practice, practice" step. The child must practice the negative thing he does over and over again, until it becomes an ordeal. The finishing words put the *coup d'etat* on the practice session. Without the finishing words, the technique loses much of its power. The finishing words consist of some version of the following statement. "You probably haven't practiced enough yet to get this bad habit out of you, but don't worry. Mom and Dad will be watching, and if you do it again, we will just practice some more until the habit is broken, and you don't do it again." These words make the child think before habitually or impulsively engaging in the bad habit again. The child installs an inhibitory filter in the brain that helps him impose self-restraint before acting out improperly.

The prefrontal cortex is the part of the brain involved in most bad habits. The More Not Less Technique is a helpful tool to help a child wire this part of the brain more efficiently. When rewiring is successful, a child can better impose self-control over his bad habits. Try it. It works.

I have presented a number of teaching stories to help a parent with how to creatively use the More Not Less Technique. This technique should be used when common behavioral methods such as time-out, scolding, or take-aways have failed to break a child's bad habit. The technique is front-end-loaded, which means that it puts a parent to considerable trouble at first, but the follow-up technique is quick and easy. I do not hesitate to recommend this technique to parents. It is my opinion that parents made a tacit agreement at the child's birth to adequately parent her, no matter the cost in personal time. My teaching stories not only expand a parent's awareness of the many, many ways to apply the More Not Less Technique, but the stories also supply creative wording that can be used when applying the technique in your home.

Give the More Not Less Technique a sincere try. It works!

Go forth. Do good.

Chapter 9

How to Get Your Parents to Give You Anything You Want (Within Reason)

This technique is appropriate for children ages ten to eighteen.

Message to Parents

Don't let the title deter you from reading this chapter. You will like this method. This chapter is about manipulation. We are manipulated almost every day by spouses, friends, salespeople, neighbors, and children. We hate bad, improper manipulation, but we warm to good, proper manipulation. This chapter is about good manipulation.

This chapter is also about helping children grow up to be responsible, mature, independent adults. Our job, as parents, is to provide a way to help our children mature, and to show them how to gain independence in a healthy manner. When children reach their teen years, they want to push against parental rules and limits. Our job is to lengthen the rope and give them ever-increasing freedom to make more and more of the decisions that affect their life. Of course, we don't want to drop the rope at age sixteen and say, "Good luck, and I hope you do well." This chapter is about extending the rope.

Parents often become nervous critters when kids hit the teen years, because they are not sure their teens are ready to make major life decisions. If your teen will follow the guidelines suggested in this chapter, you won't feel as tense about giving him more freedom. The worst thing you can do for a responsible teen is to pull him back and shorten the rope. It is unfortunate, but some irresponsible teens often deserve a shortened rope because of their rebelliousness and rudeness. This chapter can be very helpful to any parent who wants to avoid the rude and aggressive manner some teens use to obtain freedom from parental control.

Children are born with the princess and prince mentalities. They want what they want when they want it, and they erroneously believe they are born with the right to get what they want. Children need to learn how to get what they want in a socially acceptable way. It is my suggestion that you first read the entire chapter before you discuss with your child how he can get you to say, "yes" to his request for services and privileges.

If your child is twelve years old or younger, I would suggest you read this entire chapter aloud to your son or daughter. It is short, so they should be able to listen to it in one sitting. After reading it to them, explain what it means, and suggest that they use the methods to train you to say yes to their requests. Younger kids will simply look at you with a blank stare. They have no idea how to organize well enough to get started, so tell your youngster that you will help him. I have found that ten years old is a good age to start with this technique.

If your child is thirteen years old, or older, give him this chapter as a reading assignment. Set a date for completing the reading assignment. Remember, once you give it as a reading assignment, it no longer is optional. It is a parental directive, and they must complete it. If they rebel, use one of the methods discussed in this book. I would recommend the Now or Later Technique, but the 30-Second Technique would work well, too. Suggest to your teen that it would be a good idea to use it on you. Also inform your teen that you will help them get started.

The getting started assignment is critical to the success of this new experience. The following steps will make more sense to you after you have read the entire chapter. Always remember and never forget that you are always and forever your child's mentor. I think both you and your children will enjoy putting this method into practical application. The following are the seven steps to use in getting them started.

1. Help your child choose a reasonable goal. The goal must be specific like adding three dollars to the child's allowance, extending curfew by an hour, or buying a new computer game that costs $55. Children have trouble setting specific goals, and kids tend to think in the present, not the future. Help your child set a realistic goal.

2. Break the big goal down into smaller pieces. For example, if your child wants a $3 increase of allowance, start with $1. If your child wants to stay up one hour later on weekends, start with fifteen minutes.

3. Discuss how your child can reward you for saying yes to his or her request. The reward is for your child to say thank you, show appreciation, and do what he/she agrees to do. Emphasize how good you will feel and how rewarded you will be.

4. Do the program for a few weeks, and if your child is consistent with the rewards, then up the ante. Suggest that it is time to ask for more. If your child has not frequently said thank you or has not kept his end of the bargain, then discuss how he could do it better. Remember, you are always the coach, always the mentor.

5. Continue to up the ante until the total goal is reached. This means that from time to time, you suggest that he ask for a bit more.

6. Reward for success. If your child thanks you, as the method suggests, and commitments have been met, then give your child your praise and your approval. He needs to know that the technique is working, your trust is growing, and you like the way he is handling things.

7. When the child has successfully completed the project, suggest that he choose a new goal, but this time not tell you what it is. Encourage him to go for it alone and see if he can get what he wants by applying all of the rules. If he falters, then help him again by going over steps one through five. Keep repeating until he gets it. Practice makes perfect.

Let's get started. Either read the chapter to your child or give an assignment to read the chapter and discuss it later.

Introduction

It is a parent's responsibility to train children in the way they should behave. It is also a child's responsibility to train parents to say yes to reasonable requests. This lesson is about the care and feeding of your parents.

Parents can be trained to give you anything you want, but you've got to be smart about it. After you read this, you will be smart enough to train your parents to want to give you anything you want. Remember, if you ask your parents for something illegal, unethical, or immoral they are supposed to say no, but anything else can be yours for the asking.

Before I give you the power to train your parents to say yes to you, there is something very important you must understand. There is a four-year gap between how you see yourself, and how your mom and dad see you. They generally treat you like you are two years younger than you really are. You think you are two years older than you really are. This gap must be narrowed, or you are in as much trouble as a tightrope walker on a windy day. Read on, and you will learn about the power you need to narrow this four-year "generation gap."

The Power

All human beings learn in an orderly pattern. We tend to repeat any behavior that brings us reward and pleasure. We tend to stop doing anything that brings us pain and displeasure. What you want is for your parents to say yes to anything you want. If you try to get what you want by screaming, pouting, demanding, or threatening, it causes your parents to feel pain and displeasure, so they naturally say no to you, because there is no reward for giving in to your requests. If a parent says yes to you after you have screamed, pouted, kicked and spit, they only feel pain and displeasure, and they are more and more likely to simply ignore requests you make in the future. Ah, but if you know how to reward them when they do say yes to you, they will feel pleasure and want to say yes again. The problem for you is to find a great reward that you can control and afford. You can't afford a boat, home, or car, so those rewards are out. However, there are two rewards that any child controls that are more precious to your mom and dad than silver or gold. Read on, and I will tell how you can reward your parents.

Before I get there, there is one more thing I want to tell you that you must understand. When you want something from your parents, you must be very careful about asking for the whole thing all at once. Ask for part of what you want. For example, if your weekend curfew is 10:00 p.m., but you want to stay out until 1:00 a.m., do you think your parents will say yes to a three-hour extension of your curfew? The answer is, "No." Ask for part of what you want. Let's say you ask for an additional thirty minutes. They will be much more comfortable with that small request and will be much more likely to say yes. What's the point? The point is, you want your parent to say yes, so that you can reward them for saying yes to your request. Ask for a little bit of what you want, and a few weeks later, you can ask for more. Your parents are going to be more inclined to say yes to your next request when you have rewarded them for saying yes to your first request. (We will get to the rewards part in a minute.) It is slow, but sure. Most young people make the mistake of wanting all of what they want right now. Smart kids learn a better way, because it gets them anything they want. Let's put it all together.

The Goal

The first thing you must do is select your goal. What do you want from your parents? It is very important to be specific at this point and decide just what you want from your parents. Do you want more money? How much more money do you want? Do you want a later curfew? Specifically, how much longer do you want to stay out? What would you like your new curfew to be? Do you want to start dating or get three new outfits? It is an absolute must that you decide *very specifically* what you want to get from your parents.

The Rewards

Remember, everyone tends to repeat behavior that brings them pleasure. Your parents will actually want to say yes to your requests if by doing so, they will receive pleasure and reward. You have two very powerful rewards. Pay attention now!

Reward number one: Show or tell how much you appreciate what your parents do for you. "Thank you" is a tremendous reward for a parent.

Reward number two: Do what you promise you will do. If you agree to do something, then do it. Your cooperation proves to your parents that they can trust you to keep your word.

Let me explain why these rewards are so powerful. Many parents have sat in my office and complained that all they expect from their children is just a bit of appreciation for all they do for them. It may seem small to you, but it is true that a parent is an A-1, king-size sucker for "thank you." Incredible, isn't it? Parents often feel that they give and give, but their children do not appreciate their efforts. Say, "thank you," often, and the world is yours.

Now let me explain the second reward, which is to do what you say you will do. Do not ever promise to do something that you know you will not do. Most parents feel a great responsibility to raise you to the point that you can leave home and take care of yourself in the outside world. Their life is dedicated to the satisfying reward of getting rid of you. So, they look and look for signs of cooperation, maturity, and trustworthiness. They desperately want to know if they can trust you, so they continuously test you. For example, if your parents tell you to be home at a certain time, and you come in at that time, they feel really good, because it is a sign to them that they can trust you. So, your demonstration that you can keep your word is very rewarding to a parent because it tells them they can trust you, and that you are turning into a responsible adult.

Reviewing the Concept

Choose your goal and be specific. Describe what you want. The greatest rewards you have to give to your parents are thanking them and keeping your word, which means cooperating with them and doing what you say you will do. These two rewards are better to your parents than cars, clothes, money, or boats.

Ask for a small part of what you want to get. I know it is hard, but you must be patient at this point. Your patience will pay off later. For example, if your curfew is 9:00 p.m., and you want to stay out until 11:00 p.m., then start by asking to stay out to 9:30 p.m. It is a beginning. The point is, you want your parent to say yes to your request, so start small. If they say yes, you can then reward their yes. You can ask for more later, after you have reinforced or rewarded your parents for giving you an extra half an hour.

It Works Like Magic

Now, let's wrap it up. We must now put all of this information into a program. Read this example:

Sixteen-year-old Jim had recently gotten his driver's license. Jim's goal was to be able to take the family car and drive over to his friend's house. His parents thought he was too young and too inexperienced to go that far away in the car without an adult present. Here's how Jim handled the situation.

The first step in getting anything you want is to know exactly what you want. Be specific. Jim wanted to drive over to Fred's house, twenty-five blocks away.

Step Two is to ask for only a small part of the goal. Jim brought the issue up at the supper table while both parents were present. He said, "Mom and Dad, I have been a pretty good driver so far, haven't I?" They both agreed that was the case so far. Jim went further. "Then would you let me drive to the store for you when you want something? It is only five blocks away." They agreed that it would be okay, but he would have to be careful and agree to come straight home. Jim agreed. In a day or two, Jim's mother needed a loaf of bread and some milk, and she let Jim drive to the store to get it. Jim drove straight to the store and straight back. He didn't fool around one bit. When he came in, his mother seemed pleased that it didn't take very long, and Jim said, "Thanks, Mom, that was fun!" When Jim went to the store, he always went straight there and back and said, "Thank you," when he came home. Jim ran errands for his mom and dad for three weeks before he asked for more.

Clinching the Deal

Now let's take a look at Step Three. Jim approached his parents at the supper table by saying, "Mom and Dad, I have been driving to the store for you, and everything has turned out okay, hasn't it?" They both agreed, and thanked him for his help. Next, Jim said, "I would like to get some practice time in by driving around our neighborhood, so would you let me drive around our area for twenty-five minutes two times a week?" What could they say? It was just a little more. Jim had already demonstrated his cooperativeness by going to the store, and after all, he only asked to drive around, close by, for just twenty-five minutes. Every time he finished his drive around the neighborhood, he said, "Thank you. That was great." On top of that, Jim showed his cooperation by coming in three to five minutes early! To his parents, that meant they could trust him.

Parents are strange about time limits. If a parent sets a return time for you, they are very upset if you are even five minutes late. To a teen, that five minutes is nothing, but to a parent who is testing their child, it means everything, so watch it. You should always come back a few minutes early and express your appreciation to your parents for letting you go. Your demonstration that you can do what you promise to do and say, "Thank you," are mighty rewards for them, and they will have a hard time refusing your next request because you have shown cooperation and appreciation. You see, you are training your parents to enjoy giving in to you. They will love it.

Jim did the neighborhood thing for three weeks, and then came the big request. "Mom and Dad," said Jim, "I have been driving around the area safely, so would you mind if I drove over to Fred's house? I will be gone only an hour and a half, and I won't drive anywhere else but straight over and back." They could hardly say no, because Jim had proven that he was trustworthy. Jim applied the rules, namely, he did what he said he would do, which was to drive straight over to Fred's and come back home five minutes early. He always expressed appreciation to his mom and dad for letting him go. Later he asked for more time at Fred's house.

Long before Jim was seventeen years old, he was allowed to take the car virtually anywhere. None of Jim's other driving friends had anywhere near Jim's car privileges. Jim earned his privileges, and his parents were happy to give them to him because they felt he was mature enough to be trusted.

See how easy it is to apply the rules of learning? You literally must train your parents to give in to your goals and like it. Train them to say, "Yes, yes, yes!"

How to Extend Curfew Hours

Let's look at another example of how it works. I will be brief!

Mary was fourteen, and she felt that her curfew deadline should be extended. Mary had to be in the house by 8:30 p.m. on weeknights and by 11:00 p.m. on weekends. Mary's new curfew goal was 9:30 p.m. week nights and 12:00 p.m. weekends. Mary asked for only part of her goal, namely to add thirty minutes to her curfew. Her parents agreed to it. However, if they had refused, all would not be lost. Mary would just have had to drop back some more and ask for only fifteen minutes. It doesn't matter where you start, because you will get more if you follow the learning rules. Mary made it a strict rule to come home five minutes earlier than they really expected her to be home. She made it a point to come in by 8:55 p.m. and 11:25 p.m., and when she came in, she never forgot to thank her parents. She rewarded her parents with cooperation and appreciation for five weeks before she asked for fifteen minutes more. Gradually, she got more and more until she reached her goal. It works if you apply the rules.

How to Get New Clothes

Let's suppose you want a whole new outfit. You ask your mom and dad if one or both of them will go with you to shop for some new clothes—just looking, of course. First, try on the most expensive clothes you can find, but don't buy them, no matter how much your parents want to buy them. If they are really in a buying mood, just pick out one inexpensive item and have them buy that. Don't forget the magic. Say, "Thank you. I appreciate your generosity." There you have it. You cooperated by voluntarily limiting your desires, thereby protecting their pocket book, and you demonstrated appreciation by saying thank you. Soon, they will trust you to shop by yourself, and to buy more and more. Parents love to give in to their children when it brings them reward. I can hear your mom now talking to her best friend. "My daughter is so practical. Why, the other day we were shopping and I wanted to buy her an expensive outfit, but she insisted that we should buy something more within our budget. She is a joy to shop with."

If you think about it, you can apply these three principles—goal, reward, cooperation—to anything you want. It is so much more effective than demanding your rights. Parents really resent power plays. When you demand the car because you think it is your right, parents see that as rebellion, and they are very prone to show you who is boss by saying an unthinking, "No!"

Pete's Story

Pete was ten years old, and his chore was to dust the living room furniture every Saturday. Pete hated dusting, and he frequently asked if he could have another chore. His parents always said no. After I talked to Pete about "How to Get Anything You Want from Your Parents," Pete went to his mom and said he hated dusting. His mom said, "I know." Pete told his mom he was willing to do a trade off of two for one. He would do two other chores if he could get rid of one chore. His mom wanted to know what two chores he had in mind. Pete said he would clean the upstairs toilet and sink, and pull at least twenty weeds in the backyard every Saturday. His mom quickly agreed. Pete said,

"Thank you, Mom. It means a lot to me to get rid of dusting." Pete kept his word and did what he agreed to do. From then on, when chores were reassigned among the children, Pete was always given a choice of what chores he wanted to do. His parents were impressed with the mature way Pete handled the dusting problem.

Jill's Story

Jill was eleven years old and wanted to get a weekly allowance. Her goal was to get $5 per week to spend on herself. She approached her dad at the supper table. Jill said, "Dad, I have been thinking about an allowance." Her dad was prepared for Jill to ask for $15 per week, and was poised to say a quick, "No!" Jill said, "I've been thinking of starting at $1 per week." Jill quickly added, "And I will save twenty-five cents of the dollar for a rainy day." Jill's dad liked the idea of her saving some money each week, so he said yes. Jill thanked him then and every week thereafter when she got her dollar. She also got a jar to put her quarters in. She wanted her dad to see the quarters grow. She kept her promise and saved a quarter every week. Two months later, Jill asked for more. She asked for $1.50 and promised to save the fifty cents for a rainy day. Her dad was impressed and proud of his daughter. Before the year was over Jill was getting a $5-per-week allowance. She reached her goal. She was happy, and so was her dad.

Mark's Story

Mark is my son, and when he was thirteen years old, I told him about "How to Get Your Parents to Give You Anything You Want." I told him to use it on me, and I would help him with his first goal. He wanted a new baseball glove, so we worked out a deal where he did an extra chore to earn enough money to buy the particular glove he wanted. Everything worked great, as it was supposed to. He kept his word about the chore, and he thanked me every time he got his pay. He enjoyed his glove for many years.

That's not the end of my story. Mark was very good with his thank-yous and doing what he promised to do. When he was fourteen years old, I said, "Mark, I would like to set a new long-range goal." He was curious. I told him that by the time he was in the second half of his senior year in high school, I would like for him to make all of his decisions on his own without supervision from me. I told him to continue with his appreciation and keeping his promises, and it would come true. At Christmas time during his senior year, Mark came to me and said, "Dad, do you remember saying that when I reached the second semester of my senior year, I could make all of my own decisions?" I told him that I remembered. Mark reminded me that the second semester was about to begin and he was ready to make all of his own decisions. I asked him what he had in mind. He said he thought he would start with no curfew. I said, "No curfew!" Mark said, "Right, and if I want to stay out all night, I will do it." I said, "I don't know, Mark. That's pretty scary for me." Mark replied, "Let's think about it. Haven't I always kept my word and done what I promised?" I agreed that he had. He went on to remind me that he always thanked me for what I did for him. I agreed that he was very good with that one. Then Mark put the clincher on and said in a manly voice, "So, I promise I will not do anything that will get me into trouble, so that should settle that." I agreed and said, "Okay, it's done." I think he stayed out until 5:00 a.m. two times that semester. The other times, he was home and in bed by 12:00 a.m. Mark never did get into trouble, and he enjoyed making his own decisions. Mark was ready to leave home and go on his own after he graduated from high school. Mark turned out to be a great man and very responsible. I am proud of him.

Good forth. Do good.

Chapter 10

The Marks Method

This technique is appropriate for children ages five through seventeen.

The Marks Method is easy to apply and deadly effective. It is helpful in correcting any repetitive, uncooperative behavior in your child.

Let's briefly examine a few examples of therapy cases where the Marks Method was successfully applied. These cases fall into four broad categories: fear, anger, control, and depression. My purpose for sharing these cases is to illustrate the broad application of the Marks Method. My hope is that you will see applications for your family.

Fear

Children are very susceptible to a wide variety of fears like:

1. Fear of the dark.
2. Fear of bugs.
3. Fear of strangers.
4. Fear of the unknown.
5. Fear of failure, like bad grades.
6. Fear of fire.
7. Fear of fights.

As a parent, what would you do if your child was afraid to go into any room in the house without a parent at his side? That is just one of Phobic Pete's problems. He also won't go to the bathroom by himself, nor will he sleep alone. Is there anything a parent can do to help eight-year-old Pete? There is, and it is gentle, deceptively easy to apply, and very effective. It only requires a mark on the arm, and the reading of a nursery rhyme. It is called the Marks Method.

Nine-year-old Nel is as nervous as a pregnant fox in a forest fire. If a stranger comes to visit her mom, Nervous Nel is nervous for the entire visit. She is anxious about the unknown. She is nervous when her dad takes her to a new restaurant. She is nervous when her mom takes her to a new shopping mall. She is a nervous wreck when her parents take her to see one of her older brother's school plays. She is even nervous about new foods served at dinner. Can her parents help Nel? Yes, if the Marks Method is used.

Shy Sue is ten years old and very socially backward. Sue avoids social contact unless it is with close family members. She does not attend classmates' parties or Sunday School social events. If mom has guests over for dinner, Sue won't say a word. Sue won't answer the phone or the doorbell. Sue is terribly shy, but the Marks Method will help her.

Anger

A significant number of children have anger control problems. Parents are often frustrated about how to get their child to rein in his temper. If children are near to or in the teen years and have anger problems, it can be very frightening for a parent. Children can become angry over:

1. Being told no about anything.
2. Lost items.
3. Failed tests.
4. Term papers.
5. Parental rules.
6. Being criticized.
7. Broken promises.

Many children have not learned to control their anger. They uncork this anger at the least provocation. Their adrenaline is quick to be released and once they release it, they have great difficulty reigning in their anger. The Marks Method has been proven to be a wonderful helping tool for children who:

1. Throw fits.
2. Use rude, sassy, insulting language.
3. Scream.
4. Hit and kick.

5. Throw and breaks things
6. Run away.
7. Hide out.
8. Slam doors.
9. Punch walls and doors.
10. Pout.

Angry Angela is thirteen years old, and her anger is triggered if either of her parents denies her anything she wants. She thinks like a spoiled princess and will not tolerate a parental "no." If she wants to shop for a new pair of gym shoes and her mother can't take her right away, Angry Angela throws a screaming, stomping fit. If she is at a friend's house and calls to request an hour extension, but her dad says no, he gets an earful. If she is asked to do a chore, like help her mother prepare supper, she becomes incensed and ties into her mother. The Marks Method will really help Angela.

Cruel Carl, who is nine years old, is cruel to pets and hits his brothers and friends. He kicks the dog and pulls its ears if the dog doesn't do what he wants. He whacks his brother for almost no reason, and he is very aggressive with children who come over to play. If a playmate doesn't play just the way Carl directs him to, you can hear Carl scream out his anger from three blocks away. Carl is also known to be a school bully. Carl doesn't seem to catch on that he makes a horrible impression on others. He really needs the Marks Method.

Explosive Edward is a walking, talking time bomb. He explodes in vindictive anger if anyone crosses him. His specialty is explosive anger. He is especially explosive with his mother. In Edward's eyes, she can do nothing right. After an explosion, he feels remorseful and apologizes, but by then, the damage has been done. He wants to control his anger, but he does not have the slightest idea how to do so. The Marks Method can really help Explosive Edward.

Control

Some children just live to control. They want to be the boss of everything, or they feel things getting out of control and feel the need to micro-manage. Both types of children want to control:

1. Parents, friends, and teachers.
2. Their parents' time and energy.
3. Making perfect grades, test scores, term papers.
4. Parental directives involving chores and rules.

Arguing Arthur is exceedingly competitive and wants to win and dominate. He incessantly argues with his parents. Whatever his parents ask of him, Arthur will argue about. His mother often says that ten-year-old Arthur should become a lawyer when he grows up! Arthur is not much fun and is often a real pain. He just won't give in and stop arguing his point. He has little respect for anyone in authority, and he strives to take charge of all family situations. His constant arguing will end once the Marks Method is applied.

Ida the Interrupter is seven years old and loves attention. If her parents give their attention to someone else, Ida interrupts in some manner to wrest the attention back to her. If her mother talks on the phone, Ida suddenly needs her mother for seventy reasons. If her dad wrestles and plays with her four-year-old brother, Sam, Ida is all over her dad until he turns from Sam and gives her his undivided attention. Ida constantly interrupts parents' conversations. Ida will do almost anything to control her parents' attention. Later, I'll show you how the Marks Method can work in this situation.

Eleven-year-old Forgetful Francis represents an unusual form of control. Francis forgets to do anything her mom asks her to do or at least puts off compliance with mother's directives for as long as possible. If mother asks Francis to set the table, Francis says, "In a minute." Her minute can last forty-five minutes. Francis has two chores. She must feed the dog and clean the bathroom. However, Francis rarely does her chores unless mother makes her. When asked to explain, Francis simply says, "I forgot."

Depression

Children do not usually experience depression in the same way adults do. Sometimes, depression in children takes the form of anger, withdrawal, and negative fault-finding. These three children were depressed, but not in the usual, expected form.

Negative Ned, eight years old, can't be made happy. He complains about almost everything. When his mom bakes chocolate chip cookies, Ned says they are too hot, too small, or they don't have enough chocolate chips in them. When his mom surprises Ned with a new video, Ned finds some reason not to enjoy the movie. Ned is negative about everything. The Marks Method will be very helpful in curbing Ned's form of depression.

Mopey Millie seems sad a good deal of the time. She spends a lot of her time alone, and her parents rarely hear spontaneous laughter from her. She mopes a lot. The Marks Method will derail Millie from her depression track.

Four-year-old Weepy William will cry at the drop of a hat. The slightest criticism brings tears. If William colors outside the lines, he cries. If William spills his juice, or drops graham crackers on the floor, he cries. William seems to be happiest when he is unhappy. William cries a lot, but the Marks Method will help William dry his tears.

How to Apply the Marks Method

It is important to remember that a child cannot change a repetitive habit if he is unaware of it happening. The nature of a habit is that it occurs automatically. Children usually do not think before they act. Most parents have said to their child, "Think. Just think a second before you do that." Unfortunately, children often repeat the same behaviors that have gotten them into trouble before. The child's way of thinking or behaving has become an emotional or physical bad habit.

The following represent some of the behavioral problems of children who have responded well to the Marks Method.

1. Rude, sassy, cruel, abusive verbal responses to an adult in authority
2. Explosive angry outbursts or temper tantrums
3. Arguing with adults in authority
4. Obsessive-compulsive rituals
5. Unreasonable fears
6. Forgetting to do homework, chores, and promises
7. Interrupting
8. Phobic fears
9. Anxiety, tension, and nervousness
10. Depression
11. Symptoms of Post-Traumatic Stress Disorder
12. Harsh, mean self-criticism
13. Tears over hurt feelings

The method I am going to recommend will seem, at first look, to be too simple to be effective. Don't sell it short. I have recommended this method to several thousand parents with uniformly good results. There are only four easy-to-remember steps necessary to successfully apply the Marks Method.

Step One: Identify

All problems cannot be addressed at once, so carefully select a well-defined problem that you want to address with the Marks Method. You will need to build skill and confidence in the use of the Marks Method, so choosing a specific problem to address will provide an opportunity to get experience with the method with the greatest chance of success. Discuss with your child what you want to work on, and give your child many practical examples of the habit or behavior you're talking about. Describe exactly what you will be looking to correct.

Step Two: Marks

Every time the behavior you are working on occurs, tell your child to immediately put an ink mark on his arm. The mark should be about one half inch long. Your child will wear his mark or marks all day and all evening long. There is something very personal about marking one's arm. He will be extremely aware of the one or more marks on his arm. Before the evening is over, your child will be frequently reminded, for example, of how many times he lost his temper. Self-awareness regarding the frequency that this unwanted behavior occurs is very important to the success of the technique.

Children of all ages tend to resist marking their arm. Do not let your child talk you out of putting a mark on his arm. No matter how he presents his objections, don't give in. If a child begs and whines, don't give in. If a child flat out says, "No," don't give in. Pre-plan a set punishment to use if a child says no. Usually the 30-Second Technique will get compliance from the young child, and the Now or Later Technique will work for defiant older children. Review the chapters that fully discuss these techniques. Marking the arm is not optional. The child must mark his arm every time you tell him to. The success of the Marks Method depends, in part, on marking the arm.

Step Three: Poem

In the evening before bedtime sets in, ask your child to read a nursery rhyme five times for every mark he has on his arm. The nursery rhyme is "Hickory Dickory Doc." This poem has three imbedded meanings. Only emphasize the main meaning of the poem. Let's look at this poem and then discuss the main meaning of the poem.

Hickory dickory doc
The mouse ran up the clock
The clock struck one, the mouse ran down
Hickory dickory doc
Now isn't that a silly thing for a mouse to do?! (This line is my addition.)

Ask your child what is silly about the mouse's behavior. Some children get it pretty close right away, and some kids never get it. Don't belabor the point. To give a hint, ask a child what is on top of a grandfather clock. The following is a typical parent/child dialogue. Use it as an example of how to word your discussion of the poem.

Most children say, "I don't know." That's your cue to say, "I don't know either. That's the point. There is nothing on top of a grandfather clock. The mouse's behavior is useless, pointless, and doesn't help the mouse in any way. If the mouse was running up the kitchen cabinet, we would say, 'Go for it!' because there may be something to eat. But, since there is nothing on top of a grandfather clock, his behavior is pointless. You are a lot like that mouse. Throwing a fit is purposeless and useless to you. Mom or Dad get upset, and you usually just get punished."

No matter the age or intellectual capacity of the child, I always launch into a brief discussion of how the brain works. If they don't catch on to very much of what you say, at the very least, they'll understand that what you are asking them to do must be very important. Tell your child that their brain has two sides. I tell the child that his left brain (I touch the left side of his head) is his thinking brain. It's the brain that talks and solves problems. "Your left brain already knows that fit-throwing is purposeless and useless and shouldn't be done anymore. In fact, you have told yourself many times to stop it. The problem is not in your left brain. We need to talk to the part of your brain that controls your habits, attitudes, and emotions. Those are in your right brain." I always touch the right side of the head at this point. I go on and tell the child that the right brain doesn't understand commands like,

"Don't do that anymore." So we have to use a language the right brain understands, like poetry. I continue on by saying, "So, I want you to tell the right brain that fit-throwing is useless, purposeless, and doesn't get you what you want. I am going to ask you to read the 'Hickory Dickory Doc' poem aloud five times for every mark you have on your arm." Your child will probably look at you with a blank stare but at least they know it must be important because you are talking about the brain. "We have to tell your right brain that what you are doing is purposeless and useless and you want to stop doing it."

There is another reason for the short discussion about how the brain works. It also acts as a disguise for the ordeal part of the technique. We are going to create an ordeal for your child from which she can escape but will have to give up the useless and purposeless behavior to escape. Reading the poem aloud five times per mark, up to twenty times per sitting is a serious ordeal. For example, when Ida the Interrupter decided that the only way she could get rid of reading the poem was by refraining from interrupting her parents, she just internalized a healthy system of self-control. It was her decision.

Reading the poem accomplishes two objectives.

1. It influences the correct part of the brain. The problem is not solved by reason and logic because those techniques work on the wrong part of the brain. It's not a left side problem. The part of the brain that needs to be influenced is the part that deals with emotions, attitudes, and habits. The right brain loves poetry, and the poem is telling the child to give up useless and purposeless behavior.
2. The poem is also an ordeal because it must be read over and over. Our greater objective is to encourage the child to voluntarily give up the useless, purposeless behavior. The ordeal increases the child's motivation to think before she acts or speaks.

Step Four: Count

It is a parent's responsibility to keep an accounting record of the number of marks your child has put on his arm each day. You can either count them yourself, or require your child to count his own marks. It is important to the technique to establish a weekly baseline to compare against. For example, if a fit-throwing child has a total of eight fits the first week of the program, the baseline is eight. From there, we can measure the success of the Marks Method. For example, in the second week, there may be six fits, and that notes improvement. We should see the marks reduced each week until he has zero marks.

Ida the Interrupter

As I mentioned earlier, seven-year-old Ida shares a problem with many children. She hates to be ignored and will do pretty much anything to be noticed. Sometimes these children are referred to as attention-getters. They do require, and get, a lot of attention from their parents, but it is my opinion that the real issue is a strong desire to always be in control. They love to be in control and remain in charge of their parents.

Ida was this type of child. She was nice, fun, and cooperative until the focus of her parents was directed somewhere else. Ida's most serious problem was constantly interrupting her parents. If her dad was talking business with a coworker, Ida constantly interrupted him with a million questions. If her mom chatted with a friend, Ida interrupted over and over. If either of her parents gave any special attention to her four-year-old brother, Ida did anything to wrest attention back to her. Ida's parents were often angry and frustrated with her. They were at their wit's end when they came to see me about Ida. I taught Ida's parents how to use the Marks Method to address Ida's interruption problem. Her mom handled this one, and the following is her report.

Step One: Identify

Ida's mom told her that she had noticed that Ida interrupted her a lot with questions and requests to do things for her. She gave Ida many examples of how she interrupted mother. The list included:

1. Whining when her mother washed clothes.
2. Saying, "Mom, Mom, Mom," when her mother talked on the phone.
3. Tugging on her mom's sleeve when they shopped.
4. Getting close to her mom's face and asking questions when her friends visited. Ida would ask useless questions, such as "Can I play with the dog?" "Can I get a drink of water?" and, "Should I wash my hands?" Ida really knew the answers before she asked.
5. Asking her mother for acts of service when her parents were talking to one another. "Mom, help me put my socks on," or "Mom, help me find my doll, Ginny."

6.   Openly playing with forbidden items when her mom talked on the phone, entertained guests, or took a leisurely bath.

The list was much longer as I recall, but you get the idea of what Ida's mom had to contend with. Ida was relentless. Her mom identified the problem and what she would be watching for.

Step Two: Marks

Next, Ida's mom told her daughter that every time she interrupted her when she was busy with someone else, she would ask Ida to put a mark on her arm with a ball point pen. To demonstrate, she reminded Ida that she had interrupted her when her mom was paying for groceries at the store, so Ida had to put one mark on her arm of about one half inch in length. Ida's mom reminded her that only ten minutes ago, she interrupted her phone conversation with her grandma, so she handed her the pen to put another mark on her arm. Next, she reminded Ida that she had, just moments ago, interrupted her mom while she was telling her what they were going to do about Ida's interruptions, so she had to put a third mark on her arm. Ida had had it with this mark thing, so she protested and refused to put a third mark on her arm. Her mom used the 30-Second Technique and said, "Ida, I will give you to the count of ten to put the mark on your arm, or I will take your radio from your room. Ida didn't comply, so her mom got her radio. She repeated the 30-Second Technique sequence three times before Ida submitted. Ida marked her arm for the third time.

Step Three: Poem

Ida's mom instructed her that every hour, they would count the marks on Ida's arm and Ida would read a poem five times per mark. Ida didn't really catch on, but her mom continued the instructions. She called it to Ida's attention that she had three marks on her arm, so she would have to read "Hickory Dickory Doc" fifteen times. She told Ida that the poem had a very special meaning that was just right for her interruption problem. She said, "Ida, let's read the poem and see if you can figure out the meaning of a special message that is just for you." She had copied the poem on the back of a business card and she read it aloud to Ida.

Hickory dickory doc
The mouse ran up the clock
The clock struck one, the mouse ran down
Hickory dickory doc
Now isn't that a silly thing for a mouse to do?

She asked Ida to tell her what the mouse did that was silly. Ida didn't know. She asked, "What is on top of a tall grandfather clock?" Ida didn't know, and her mom said, "I don't know either. That's what's silly about this mouse. It just keeps running up the clock and down the clock, up the clock and down the clock, for no good reason. Now, if the mouse were running up the kitchen cabinet, we would say, 'Go for it, mouse!' because there might be something to eat on top of the kitchen cabinet. Ida, your interruptions are just as silly, because they don't get you anything good. Mom and Dad just get mad and often scold you when you interrupt. It's kind of silly to keep doing something that is purposeless and doesn't get you anything good. When you interrupt, you are being silly like the mouse, so you are going to read the poem to remind yourself not to do silly things like interrupt Mom and Dad."

Every hour her mother asked Ida to count the marks on her arm. She made Ida read her poem five times per mark, up to twenty times.

More than twenty readings is unnecessary. Ida was young, and a very frequent interrupter, so I advised her mother to monitor her interruptions every hour. Usually, I recommend counting marks in the evening and reading the poem five times per mark at the end of the day. For example, a child that has an anger problem will, unlike Ida, have five or six marks, at most, by poem-reading time. Ida, on the other hand would often have five or six interruptions per hour. Her mother would make her read the poem twenty times, and then wash the marks off of her arm and start the process over the next hour.

For Ida, the results were pretty amazing. The number of marks on her arm dropped radically. The first day, Ida accumulated sixty marks. This sounds like an awful thing to impose on a child until you break it down into smaller, more understandable units. This broke down to an average of five marks per hour for a period of twelve hours. A seven-year-old child can read the "Hickory Dickory Doc" poem in fifteen seconds or less. This means that every hour, Ida would read her poem for a maximum of five minutes. What really happened was that Ida did not get five marks on her arm every hour. One hour she would get eight to ten marks, but in another hour, she would get only three marks. Some hours, she would receive zero marks. For example, when she played with her friend Sally, she got zero marks for an hour and a half. Since the Marks Method was started on Saturday, Ida took an afternoon nap and received no marks during that time. Remember, the maximum number of times she will be reading the card is twenty times per hour, regardless of the number of marks on her arm. One hour, Ida would read the poem twenty times but in another hour, she would read the card only ten times.

The Marks Method was not too harsh when applied to Ida, but it definitely created an unpleasant ordeal for her. Most of the self-control methods I recommend to mothers and fathers incorporate an unpleasant ordeal from which a child can escape, but they must cooperate to do so. No ordeal that I recommend is excessive, abusive, or too harsh, but they are unpleasant, or they wouldn't be ordeals. Remember that Ida's mom and dad had already tried voice control (yelling and screaming), time-out, and many take-aways. Nothing slowed Ida's interruptions.

Ida improved very rapidly. The first day (Saturday), she accumulated sixty marks, but on the second day (Sunday), the marks were cut in half. Monday, Tuesday, and Wednesday (school days), she averaged six marks. For Thursday and Friday, she averaged two interruptions per day for the five hours after school until bed time. Saturday, she had zero marks, and Sunday she had one mark. During the second week, Ida had to read the poem ten times (i.e., two marks for the week). In week three, Ida made none of the targeted interruptions that she typically made. The bottom line is that in only two weeks, Ida self-corrected a very annoying, longstanding problem. The Marks Method served this family very well. In the third week, Ida's parents put her on a positive rewards program. Because Ida was able to control her interruptions, her mom could start rewarding her for cooperation. Often parents must first stop uncooperative, destructive behavior before a child is willing to work for reward. Ida's parents made a deal with her that if she did not interrupt, they would play a short game with her before bedtime. Ida was ecstatic to get her parents' positive attention. Ida didn't interrupt anymore.

Angry Angela

Angela was a brand new, hormonal teenager. She had always been explosive, but when she reached the teen years, Angela's aggressiveness radically accelerated. If her mom told Angela to help her set the dinner table, a battle ensued. Angela couldn't control her mouth if either parent told her no to a personal request for parental services. Angela didn't hesitate a bit to demonstrate her anger. She would, when angry, slam doors, stomp her foot, fold her arms, and break things. Angela was angry and too out of control to get control. Angela wanted to be boss over her parents so that she could have anything she wanted. There was a definite struggle about who got to make the rules that governed the actions of the family.

Step One: Identify

Angela's mom took her through the steps one at a time. First, she identified what she would be looking for. While Angela was calm and there were no current issues to be dealt with, her mom discussed what Angela did that offended her parents. Her mom was kind, but very specific about what she wanted Angela to work on.

Children intuitively know that life is really better when their parents are in control of family affairs. Angela listened to her mom define the problem because she knew in her heart of hearts that her mother was right. I told Angela's parents that her message to her parents was, "I will do what you ask me to do, but you will have to make me. Please, please, make me control my temper, because I can't." Angela's dad was somewhat dubious about this message being true. Her parents wanted to put limits on Angry Angela, but they just didn't know what to do.

Step Two: Mark

Angela's mother carried out step two by telling her that every time she got excessively angry, she would require her to put a mark on her arm. To help Angela understand when she would get a mark and what excessive anger was, her mom explained the ten-point anger system. She explained that she was allowed to get angry, because everyone has a right to be angry and to express their displeasure. It was excessive anger that would get a mark. On the ten-point scale, ten represents the screaming, slamming, and breaking kind of anger. Everyone knows what a ten is, but what is a four? Four is the beginning of too much anger, so Angela and her mom discussed the early signs of too much anger. They came up with these early warning signs that would let Angela know that she had crossed the line and her anger had become excessive.

1. Angela's voice begins to elevate.
2. Angela feels her face flush and get hot.
3. Her mind begins to think really fast, and she speaks more rapidly.
4. Angela uses the word "so" in a defensive manner, as in, "So, you don't want me to talk to my friends ever. So, you think I'm a baby and you have to tell me what to do all of the time. So, you think I'm lazy and stupid." Of course, Angela's mom would always get derailed and begin to defend herself, which Angela liked.
5. Angela's heart beats faster.
6. Angela either folds her arms or puts her hands on her hips.
7. Angela leans forward and scowls.
8. Angela's voice sounds different.
9. Angela uses sarcasm, saying things such as, "Yeah, you think you are Queen Mom and can have anything your royal heart desires."

Angela's mom explained that the earlier Angela could catch herself becoming excessively angry, the better she could control her anger. With that in mind, she informed Angela that she would try to help by asking her to put a mark on her arm at the first signs of excessive anger. In anticipation that Angela would angrily protest her mom's instructions to put a mark on her arm, she explained the rule. Remember, girls usually do not like to mark their arm, and Angela certainly did not like to be told what to do, ever.

This is a formula for an angry outburst. I want to remind each parent that my personal experience shows that the Marks Method does not work at all unless the very personal mark is put on the arm.

Angela's mom explained that Angela did not get to choose to mark or not to mark. If she refused to mark her arm, her mom would employ the Now or Later Technique, which involves waking her up every ten minutes until she marks her arm (See chapter 6). By now, Angela was getting pretty nervous.

Angela's mom actually did have to employ the Now or Later Technique the first night of the first day of the Marks Method. Angela, in a fit of rage, refused to mark her arm. Her mom simply said, "Angela, do you want to mark your arm now or later?" As Angela stormed off to her room, her mom quickly said, "I will take that as a 'later' answer, and I will tell you when later is." Her dad enforced the Now or Later Technique, and woke Angela up every ten minutes until she agreed to put the appropriate number of marks on her arm and read her poem the prescribed number of times. Both of her parents felt encouraged, and more importantly, they felt empowered. Who would have expected it? Angela gave in!

Step Three: Poem

Angela's mom explained step three, which was the use of a poem to train her emotional brain to quit doing something purposeless. She gave her the written poem, and the two had fun guessing what was so silly about the mouse's behavior. That part went well.

Step Four: Count

Angela's mom explained that in the evening, they would count the marks on her arm, and Angela would be required to read "Hickory Dickory Doc" five times for every mark she had on her arm. By reading the poem, Angela would be training her emotional brain to live under self-control. Again, in anticipation of resistance, her mom told Angela that reading the poem was not optional. She had to do it. If she refused, either her dad or mom would use the Now or Later Technique until she did it. The Now or Later Technique had already been explained to Angela, so she knew what to expect.

The interesting thing about explaining the details of the Now or Later Technique before it is needed is that it often is not needed. A child often reasons, "Why bother with stubborn resistance if that's what I will have to go through?" (See chapter 6 on the Now or Later Technique.)

Her mom also kept a weekly total of the number of times Angela marked her arm. This became a baseline to measure progress. Without getting a baseline, the improvement from ten marks the first week to eight marks the second week would be difficult to catch.

Results

My experience with the Marks Method has been very positive, and I have recommended it to several thousand parents with uniformly good outcomes. In Angry Angela's case, it was very helpful in reining in her anger. Angela internalized a large measure of self-control in a few weeks and rarely became excessively angry. Over a six month follow-up, Angela would occasionally hit a four or above, and her mother would require her to mark her arm and revisit the Hickory Dickory Doc poem.

In the first seven days Angela had a total of twelve marks. The next week she slipped up four times, and the third week she exceeded level four only three times. In the fourth week, she only uncorked her excessive anger once. In fact, her mom was convinced that the mere fact that they discussed the steps reduced her anger expression before she even began the program. She will swear that Angela had far more than twelve angry attacks per week before they began the Marks Method. Angela's parents were taught how to reinforce her progress through generous praise and approval. She learned to willingly live under self-control, and that did wonders for their parent-child relationship. All three simply liked each other better than they had before the Marks Method began.

The Marks Method consists of three parts. Part one is an awareness exercise. Children cannot correct a bad habit if their behavior occurs automatically without the benefit of pre-thought. Part two involves a voluntary influence upon the emotional part of the brain. Part three is based upon a parent creating a subtle but powerful ordeal. The child can escape the ordeal, but to do so, she will have to correct the unwanted behavior. There are four steps that explain the Marks Method.

1. **Identify**

   It is the parent's responsibility to specifically identify the problem that will be addressed. You may identify ten problems that need to be corrected, but choose only one at a time to work on. Fully discuss with your child specifically what it is you will be asking him to correct. The child must know what you will be looking for. Remember, this is an awareness technique; therefore, a child must be fully aware about what he must correct.

2. **Marks**

   After clearly defining what you want your child to stop doing, move to explaining the marks part of the method. Let's say you want your child to stop singing and dancing at the dinner table. You would tell your child that every time you catch him performing his routine while eating, you will require him to put a one half-inch mark on his arm with an ink pen. You'll tell him that he will wear the marks until just before bedtime, at which point he will read a poem.

3. **Poem**

   Before your child is too tired in the evening, tell him it is time to read his poem. The poem is "Hickory Dickory Doc." Next read the poem to him, and tell him that there is an imbedded meaning in the poem. Coach your child to understand the silly thing the mouse is doing. The basic imbedded meaning is that the mouse is engaging in useless behavior by running up and down the grandfather clock. It just doesn't make sense, because the mouse is doing something useless and purposeless. Continue by telling your child that his behavior (his bad habit) is useless and purposeless. Performing his dinnertime revue doesn't serve him well. It is purposeless and usually just gets him into trouble with his parents.

   Tell your child that he will be required to read the poem five times per mark on his arm, up to twenty times. He must read the poem aloud to either parent. The reading of the poem is not optional. Your child does not get to choose if he will read the poem. The method does not work if the poem is not read five times per mark, up to twenty times. Kids hate this part of the Marks Method, which is good. We want to create a sizable ordeal to encourage the child to escape the ordeal by controlling his bad habit. If you are too busy to listen to your child read the poem aloud, it is permissible for the child to write the poem five times and show it to you later.

4. Count

In order to be able to measure improvement, either a parent or the child must tally the daily marks. Once you get the final tally of marks for the week, you will have a baseline against which you can measure improvement over the next week's use of the Marks Method. For example, if a child has a total of fifteen marks the first week, but he has a total of eleven marks the next week, we know he has made good improvement. Without the baseline, it would be difficult to identify improvement, because there isn't an obvious enough difference between fifteen and eleven. In reality, a difference of four is really quite significant.

The Marks Method is an incredible correction technique to help children change bad habits and become children you want to keep. Use the Marks Method frequently and have some fun. It works, so use it. (Note: I have checked with a number of dermatologists and they assure me that marking the arm with an ink pen does no permanent harm to a child.)

Go forth. Do good.

Chapter 11

The Tell a Story Technique

This technique is appropriate for children ages three to seventeen.

Parents teach children 24/7. We teach through body language, tone of voice, and the words we choose to say. Parents can't help it. We are going to teach kids something of value, or something useless. How we teach children is something parents can control. Stories can be a great method of teaching. We can teach morals, values, principles, and self-control by the use of stories. Stories have no expiration date. They can guide a child and continue to influence her throughout her adult years. Your children will very likely tell the same stories they hear from you to their own children.

The objective of this chapter is to equip parents with an adaptable psychological tool that can greatly enhance their influence on their children for good. It is not the easiest psychological tool to use, but the stories are incredibly powerful. There are times when only a story will teach a child a valuable lesson. When boys and girls reach their teen years, they often become parent-deaf. Parental advice sounds to a teen like "blah blah blah and blah blah." A story is another matter. A story can bypass stubborn resistance and stonewalling. If a teen is not ready to hear the message, there is no harm done, because it was just a story. If the teen is ready to receive the message, it is irresistible. A teen has no defense against it.

Some children come to us with very sensitive nervous systems. Scolding, confrontation, and pointed lectures can have a negative effect, quite the opposite of the positive intentions of the parental message. These children get their feelings hurt easily and they quit listening to well-intended parental advice. Storytelling is a Godsend for these sensitive, easily hurt children. Sensitive children or rebellious children will remember your stories long after they have forgotten confrontational parental advice.

Telling stories is a resourceful and creative way to teach morals, values, and self-control, such as:

1. Treat women with respect.
2. Tell the truth.
3. Do not steal from others.
4. Don't use street drugs.
5. Don't abuse alcohol.
6. Don't be a bully.
7. Have good self-confidence and high self-esteem.
8. Don't have premarital sex.
9. Don't have unprotected sex.
10. Cooperate with others.
11. Be willing to live under authority.
12. Exercise good social skills.

Stories may be from your life, what you have observed or experienced. They may also be blends of fact and fantasy. The meaning of the story can be directly offered. I usually discuss the meaning of the story with children between the ages of three and twelve. For teenagers, I believe stories have greater impact if the moral or meaning is not discussed. With teenagers, I prefer to tell the story to someone else, with the teen as the audience.

Allan in the Alley: A Story for Parents

This story from my childhood is about boys, but the meaning applies equally to both sexes. I was in the fourth grade, and because I lived only a mile away from school, I walked to and from class every day. It was about two years after World War II. Sugar was still rationed, so it was rare that we could buy candy or gum at the little store across the street from the elementary school. Back in those days, we bought long stalks of sugar cane as a cheap substitute for candy. The little store had received a new supply of sugar cane, and I had purchased a long stick and was headed for home. On the way, I passed by an alley and saw another fourth grader, Allan, with his back against the fence, surrounded by a group of fifth-grade boys. They were taunting Allan and insulting him. Allan was shy, skinny, short, and scared. Allan was not a friend of mine, but I did know him, and I knew that he would not hurt a fly. I observed what was going on for a few minutes and then walked over to the group of boys and asked them what they intended to do with Allan. They told me that they were going to beat him up. I walked between two boys, sugar cane in hand, put my back against the fence beside Allan and said, "Now there are two of us. Do you want to beat both of us up?" They did and the fight was on. I whacked with my sugar cane stalk, kicked, hit, spit, bit, and yelled, but those five boys beat the holy crap out of both of us. Allan did his share of hitting, kicking, and spitting, but there was no way to win the battle. The older boys finally backed off and left. I was bloody and my shirt was torn off, but worst of all, my new stalk of sugar cane was rendered a limp, split, and broken mass of fibers. I checked on Allan and found him to be alive, so we caught our breath, talked for a couple minutes, and parted, beaten and defeated kids.

The strangest thing happened after that day. Allan and I became bonded friends, and Allan stood almost in awe of me. Other fourth graders admired us, and the rumor spread that we had single-handedly taken on the entire fifth grade. As it turned out, winning was not what was important. The fact that we stood against the bullies and oppressors seemed to be what counted for Allan and me. The bond between us was unbreakable.

There are four points I want you to get out of this story.

1. This is a story about courage. Over the years that I've been in practice, I have counseled with thousands of parents and found that some parents cannot confront their children. They indulge or give into a strong-willed child far too often. It takes courage to put your back against the fence and say, "Enough!" to the child who bullies through fits and abusive language. Some children are not openly defiant, but they disrespect their parents through delay and put off tactics. The methods that I recommend in this book are strong techniques that will quickly establish parental control. However, no matter how much I emphasize the destructiveness of indulgence, some parents will water down or dismiss the suggested method I would like for them to use. It takes courage to establish fair rules and to firmly enforce them with the techniques I teach. Have courage, and put your children under your authority. The payoff is rich.

2. The second point is to help the weak. There is always someone in your circle of influence who is weaker than you, such as your child. From time to time, he will need your protection. For example, your child may face abuse from neighborhood kids or classmates, and you may need to make

a visit to their parents and have a parent-to-parent talk about these children being sexually, physically, or verbally abusive to your child. Children find it almost impossible to confront an adult. Most school problems between teacher and student should be left to the school to work out, but there are times when a parent must make a school visit to protect a child. Have courage and protect your child.

3. The third point is that those who are helped love the helper. A strong bond develops between a child and parent when a parent has the courage to stand up for them against abusers. My forty-year-old daughter still tells the story about the time her mother went to school and removed Amanda from the room of an abusive, mentally ill teacher, against the objections of the teacher and the school principal. The next year, this abusive, mentally ill teacher left the teaching profession, much to the relief of many parents. Amanda had a very positive experience in her new school. The friendship bond between Amanda and her mother is very strong to this day. A substantial part of that friendship bond can be attributed to the times Roena put her back against the fence and stood firm in the protection of Amanda.

4. Those who are helped by the stronger do not feel weaker. In fact they feel empowered. Allan did not walk the halls of Horace Mann Elementary School with a hung head and a defeated look. Allan physically looked like a truck ran over him, but he held his head up, and told everyone who would listen about the fight he lost. Allan was never again the shy, shamed, wimpy kid that he had been before his beating. Those who are helped get stronger.

Have courage, and when necessary, put your back against the fence and help your children. They will feel safe, the friendship bond between you will grow, and your children will feel empowered.

I made four points:

1. Have courage to be firm with your children, and teach them to willingly live under your parental authority.
2. Help those who need help, particularly children.
3. Those who are helped love the helper, and relationship bonds grow stronger.
4. Those who are helped by the stronger do not feel weaker; in fact, they feel empowered.

Wasn't it easier to get and relate to the four points because you read the story, "Allan in the Alley?" Keep this in mind as you use stories to teach your children.

Teen Stories

Let's deal with the hardest group first: teenagers. It is in the teen years that the importance of independence from parents grows in value. A common problem among teens is their sudden onset of deafness. They become parent-deaf. They often do not seek parental advice, nor do they receive and understand parental advice. A story is another matter, and teens have difficulty protecting against the message in a story. My preference is to tell a teaching story to a spouse or friend and let the teen become a part of the listening audience. Supper is an excellent time to tell a teaching story. While a teen is munching on his green beans, he has nothing better to do than listen to a "boring story." I have advised parents to tell teaching stories in the following critical areas.

1. The dangers of drugs
2. The difficulty of teen pregnancy (emphasis on abstinence and protection)
3. School achievement and advancement
4. The value of higher education and vocational school
5. The dangers of out of control behavior
6. Guidelines for dating
7. Respect for authority (mothers, fathers, teachers, police)

The list could be a thousand topics long, but I am sure you get the idea. Let's take a tough problem for a tough population and formulate a good story.

Teenage Pregnancy

Jewel is the mother of Kimmie, age fourteen, and William (Bill), age sixteen. Jewel knew that Bill was sexually active, and she strongly suspected that Kimmie had recently become sexually active. She was worried that Bill might get a girl pregnant, and she prayed that Kimmie would not become pregnant. Neither child welcomed Jewel's wisdom and advice like they used to. She was a single mom, but she had a serious boyfriend, Elo. With guidance, Jewel formulated a teaching story about teen pregnancy that she told to Elo while they were all were seated for a family dinner. Elo was quite willing to be the straight man and go along with the story. The following story that Jewel told is totally fictional.

While all four were seated at the supper table, Jewel told this story. "Elo, do you remember my friend Eva?"

Elo's script called for him to say, "No."

Jewel continued, "I knew Eva in high school; she married a guy, and they moved to Phoenix. Eva called me a few days ago all in tears, and she told me what happened to her fourteen-year-old daughter Jill. Apparently, Jill got a boyfriend who was much too old for her."

"How old was he?" Elo asked.

"Well, he was a senior in high school so I guess he was seventeen or eighteen years old. Anyway, they started dating over the objections of Eva, who thought he was much too old for Jill. The boyfriend, Tom, was in that stage when all he could think about was one hundred ways to get into Jill's panties. You know about that stage of life, don't you Elo?"

"I sure do," Elo said, right on time.

"Well, they did the deed two or three times, and Jill, bless her heart, got pregnant. Can you believe it? She's pregnant at fourteen years old! Eva asked Jill why she didn't use protection if she knew she was going to have sex. Jill said the strangest thing. She said, 'What kind of protection?' Apparently Jill had never bothered to ask anyone about condoms, or the Pill."

Elo said, on cue, "Whoa. You mean she had never heard of rubbers?"

Jewel said, "Elo, not in front of the children."

Mission one was accomplished. Jewel had just emphasized two points. First, don't date older boys when you are fourteen, and secondly, if you are going to have sex, use protection. Now for mission two.

Jewel continued, "My mom always told me that the best way to prevent pregnancy was not to do it until I got married. I know that sounds old fashioned, but look at what happened to Jill."

Elo said, "Well, what did happen to Jill?" (Elo was good!)

Jewel painted this horrible picture of the pregnancy aftermath, "Well, first of all, Jill was depressed for two months, knowing she had to tell her mother, and time was running out. Next, Jill had to decide if she wanted to keep the baby, get an abortion, or put the child up for adoption. Of course her 'boyfriend' was long gone, and he denied any responsibility for the child. Jill decided to keep the child and raise it herself, which really means that she and Eva will raise the child. I don't know if Jill will ever be able to move out on her own and support the child, too. She dropped out of school and went to one of those alternative schools. As for Tom, they plan to get a lawyer, get DNA samples from Tom, and prove that he is the baby's father. Then they'll sue him for child support. Can you believe his stupidity, just thinking he could walk away and pretend it never happened? He will be paying child support for eighteen years. Let's see, he will be thirty-five years old when he makes his last child support payment."

Elo concluded the story right on cue by saying, "Teenagers! Will they ever learn to plan ahead?"

Jewel said, "Yeah, I know, but Jill's counselor says that in a year or two, she should be able to get over her depression, and with any luck, she shouldn't get pregnant again until she marries."

"I hope so," said Elo.

Jewel powerfully made her points. Kimmie learned that teenage pregnancy has some painful consequences, and Bill learned that if he gets a girl pregnant, he can't just say, "Oops!" and walk away. He too will experience some very painful and negative consequences.

The results of this teaching story were interesting. About a month later, Kimmie came to her mother and said her cramps were really getting bad, so she wanted to talk to their family doctor about the Pill. As for Bill, he never did say anything to his mom about sex. However, one day while Bill was in the shower, she decided to do laundry, and when she took Bill's wallet out of his dirty jeans, she saw a large round circle on the leather of his billfold. Jewel couldn't help herself, so she looked. As suspected, it was a condom, safely tucked away in a zipped pocket of his wallet. As of this writing, Kimmie has not gotten pregnant, and Bill has not fathered a child. So far, so good.

Other teen sex stories might focus on "hooking up," which often involves oral sex, or the grim prospects of STDs.

Children Stories: Ages Three to Eleven Years

Children are easier to tell stories to than teens. They actually like parental teaching stories and will usually ask for more stories. I like to use theme stories, which means that certain elements of the story remain the same. I must have told my children one hundred stories about three bears that live at the bottom of the Grand Canyon. We lived near the Grand Canyon and often took trips there. However, as the children got a little older, I switched to stories about the groose, a strange-looking forest animal that does everything backwards. I like the groose stories because they always have a wise old owl in them who gives the weird groose wise counsel and advice. The wise old owl, of course, is me, but the owl could just as easily be you. I believe there are some very fertile areas regarding morals, values, and cooperation that stories can highly influence. Teaching stories could be told in the following areas:

1. Stories about love and trust
2. Stories about self-confidence and self-esteem
3. Stories about cooperation with teachers, parents, and others in authority
4. Stories about seeing the needs of others and helping them
5. Stories about politeness and saying please and thank you
6. Stories about making good decisions
7. Stories about truth-telling and honesty.

After describing a groose and telling the child that a groose does everything backward, I say, "Let's pretend you are a groose, and you do everything backwards." Children love this groose game. Here is a sample of the wording I use.

"A groose has gorilla ears, eyes like a bird, teeth like a lion, a nose like a donkey, two humps like a camel, a tail like a monkey, hind legs like a deer, and big front legs with flat feet like an elephant, so the groose could run very fast slowly. A groose hears everything backward and does everything backward. For example, if Ms. Flips, his teacher, says, 'Everyone, stand up and count aloud to ten,' the groose sits down and says the alphabet. If mother says, 'Come here and give me a goodnight kiss,' the groose runs out the front door backward and kisses a tree. The groose does everything backward.

"Let's pretend you are a groose named Sally that does everything backwards. Here we go. 'Sally, don't stand up.'

"What's Sally going to do?

"'Sally, don't turn around fast three times. Sally, the groose, I forbid you to hop across the living room.'"

After the child is consistently doing every command backward, I begin telling the groose story. The practice game is a good way to get the child's attention and prepare the child for the real story.

Let's look at a typical story about a groose who wouldn't say please and thank you.

The Groose Who Wouldn't Say Please or Thank You

Once upon a time, in a land far away, lived a groose named Ruth. In those olden days, a groose looked very different from anything you have ever seen before. This is what a groose looked like. A groose has gorilla ears, eyes like a bird, teeth like a lion, a nose like a donkey, two humps like a camel, a tail like a monkey, zebra stripes on one side and leopard spots on the other side, hind legs like a deer, and big, round front legs with flat feet like an elephant, so the groose could run fast very slowly. You have probably never met a groose, so let me tell you something very important about a groose. It is true that a groose looks very strange, but the most unusual thing about a groose is that it does everything backwards. If mother groose says, "Honey, put your dirty school clothes in the laundry basket," the groose will put her clothes in the trash can. If her teacher says stand up, the groose will sit down. If the teacher tells the children to put the toys gently and quietly in the toy box, the groose will throw them on the floor loudly. If a mom tells her groose son to turn the TV down because it is too loud, what do you think the groose will do? Right, turn the TV up really, really loud. A groose can't help it. No matter how much he wants to change, he just does everything he's told to do backwards. (Do the practice exercise here.)

This story is about Ruth, who is a groose, and Ruth's teacher who is not a groose. Ms. Flips is Ruth's fifth grade teacher in Forrest School District Four. This is what happened. Ms. Flips walked over to Ruth's desk and said, "Ruth, I have noticed that you never say 'please' when you ask for something from me, or 'thank you' when you get something from me. Ruth, it would make me very happy if you said 'please' when you want something from me, and 'thank you' when I give it to you." Most children would feel very sad if their teacher was mad at them, but not the groose. Ruth smiled, laughed, and was very happy because, as you know, the groose does everything backward. Ms. Flips continued, "Do you understand what I want you to do Ruth?" You guessed it, Ruth said, "No, Ms. Flips, I didn't understand a word you said." Ms. Flips got madder and madder.

Ruth didn't know what do to. She wanted to please Ms. Flips but every time she asked Ruth the groose to do something, Ruth did the opposite. That's just the way grooses are. Ruth the groose wanted to say, "Ms. Flips, could I please get a drink of water?" But it came out, "Ms. Flips, get me a drink of water now!" Ruth the groose knew she should say thank you when Ms. Flips gave her clean paper to write on, but she didn't. Ruth was very happy, I mean, sad.

The wise old forest owl heard all of this through the open window. As usual, Ruth was playing alone because the other children didn't like to play with a child who does everything backwards. The wise old owl flew down and sat beside Ruth and said, "Ruth, do you know who I am?"

Ruth said, "Yes, you are the wise old owl."

The owl said, "What did you mother tell you about me?"

Ruth the groose said, "Mom said I should do everything you tell me to do because you are very wise."

"That's right," said the owl, "and this is what I want you to do. You are a groose, and you do everything backwards, but you are not stuck there. You can change and be like all the other forest animals and say please and thank you, but you have to do something in your groose mind first."

"What's that?" asked Ruth the groose.

"You have a reverse button in your mind, and you can push it anytime you want. So this is what I want you to do. When Ms. Flips brings you clean paper to write on, you must say in your mind, 'I will never say thank you,' but I want you to immediately push the reverse button which will make you say, 'Thank you, Ms. Flips.' Always remember and never forget that you must say in your mind, 'I will never say please or thank you.' Keep hitting that reverse button and you will reverse your no-thank-you thought and no-please thought to thank you and please. That's it, Ruth the groose. All you have to do is hit the reverse button, and you will become the most polite student in the fifth grade. Can it get any easier than that? Practice for a week, and I will talk to you later."

The wise old owl flew away.

In a week, the wise old owl flew back to the school ground and was amazed at what he saw. There was Ruth the groose, happily playing with the other children, and pinned on Ruth's blouse was a big badge that said, "Good Student of the Week." The wise old owl decided not to interrupt Ruth the groose, and flew off with a tear in his eye and a smile on his beak thinking, "Boy, that reverse button sure does work!"

How to Tell a Groose Story

The fundamentals of the story always remain the same. The groose is described as a very strange-looking forest animal. The groose gets into trouble because when he is told to do something, the groose hears it backward and does it backward. There is always a wise old owl who helps the groose reverse his backward ways and do it right. The wise old owl is always pleased with the good results. Other characters may be added to the story, such as a princess, a prince, a teacher, and other boys and girls.

Choose what you want to teach and have the groose do it backwards. The wise old owl understands how a groose works, and all grooses have been told by their mothers to do what the wise old owl says. The owl tells the groose to do the wrong thing, knowing that the groose will reverse the owl's instructions and do it the right way.

The Six Elements in "The Groose Who Wouldn't Say Please or Thank You"

Let's review the six important elements that will guide your development of a groose story.

1. **The groose is described**

    The groose is described as a very strange looking forest animal.

2. **The problem is described**

    In this story, Ms. Flips, Ruth's fifth grade teacher, takes on the role of describing the problem. She brings to Ruth's attention that she doesn't ever say please or thank you.

3. **The wise old owl intervenes**

    The wise old owl needs to have an opportunity to intervene. In this story, Ruth the groose was playing alone because the other children didn't want to play with Ruth because she does everything backwards.

4. **The owl always establishes his credentials**

    The wise old owl needs to establish his credentials as a wise owl. The owl asks Ruth what her mother has told Ruth about him. Ruth answers that her mother says he is wise, and she should always do what the wise old owl tells her.

5. **The owl always offers a solution involving a reversal**

    The solution needs to be offered. In this story, the wise old owl tells Ruth the groose to reverse her thoughts when Ms. Flips does something for Ruth. She wants to say please and thank you, but Ruth the groose reverses the positive and thinks the opposite. "From now on and forever more," the owl advises, "I want you to say, 'I will not say thank you or please' when Ms. Flips does something nice for you, or you ask her for something." Of course the groose who does everything backward will say, "Thank you, Ms. Flips," and, "Please, Ms. Flips."

6. **The owl is always very happy the solution worked**

Reversing works, and the old owl is happy. That's a groose story.

Let's look at another groose story about Joey, who makes a lot of common student mistakes.

The Groose Who Needed to Fix Some School Stuff

If you ever see a groose deep in the forest, you will be pleased with what you see. A groose is very different from all other forest animals, but very beautiful in its own way. Many of the groose's unusual body parts serve very useful purposes, as you will see in this story.

One look at Joey, and you would know he is a groose. He has the round face of a strong mountain gorilla, teeth like a lion, a long nose like an anteater, zebra stripes on one side and leopard spots on the other side, the muscular arms of a gorilla, two humps like a camel, the long neck of giraffe, a short wiggly tail like a pig, big round elephant legs in front, hind legs like a deer in back. Like all grooses, he could run very fast, slowly. All of the girl grooses thought Joey was really good-looking. Best of all, Joey had very long, big, pink, soft, fuzzy rabbit ears. This really helped Joey in Ms. Flips' classroom. Joey could hear the teacher's direction and instructions better than any student in the room. Joey never missed anything Ms. Flips said.

Joey's eyes were big, black, and kind, like a panda bear's, and he had the clear, keen eyesight of an eagle. An eagle can see a little mouse scurrying across the desert floor from way, way high up in the sky. Joey could see better than other kids, so he never missed anything Ms. Flips wrote on the board. When Ms. Flips wrote homework directions on the board, Joey could see them all and write them down in his notebook. Joey never missed a word Ms. Flips wrote on the board. Joey could hear and see better than anyone.

The wise old barnyard owl flew down to the forest animal elementary school to check on all of the students. He sat on the window sill and listened and watched. Soon he saw that Joey had a problem that the wise old owl could help him with.

An unusual thing about a groose is that if you tell him to do something, he will always do it backwards. A groose will hear his teacher or mother tell him what to do, then reverse it in his mind and do the opposite of what he was told. Grooses are in trouble a lot. These were Joey's problems.

1. Ms. Flips always told her class to listen to all of her directions before they started to work on the assignment. Joey thought Ms. Flips said to get started on the work as fast as a rabbit and forget about listening to instructions and directions. Joey thought Ms. Flips said listening was a big waste of time, so don't do it and just get going on that assignment. Grooses can get into lots of trouble listening backwards!

2. Ms. Flips told all the students to go on to the next assignment when they fin-ished the one they were working on and never bother the other students who were still working. "Above all else," said Ms. Flips, "tell the truth when I ask you if you are finished." Of course, Joey, being a groose, does everything backward. He really wants to go on to the next assignment, and he doesn't want to play with and tease other kids. But something gets flipped, and he does it anyway.

3. Ms. Flips told her students to hand in their work immediately after they finished it. Joey thought she meant to always hold on to the work and never turn it in, and to pretend you were still working on the assignment when the teacher asked you if you were finished. Poor Joey, he was so con-fused! He really thought he was doing everything the right way, but it was all backwards.

4. Ms. Flips always told her students to write down homework assignments in their notebooks. Joey thought she said never write your assignment in your book.

Wow! Hearing backward can really be frustrating for a groose! Someone needed to talk to Joey in a way that he would understand.

At recess, the wise old owl flew down to Joey the groose and sat beside him. The wise old owl said, "Joey, I am the wise old owl, and your mother has always told you to listen to me and do whatever I say, right?"

Joey agreed that he was supposed to listen and do what the old owl said because he is very wise. The wise old owl said, "Joey, I notice that you are, at times, in trouble with your teacher and your mother about school things."

Joey sniffed some snot back up his anteater nose, and a huge tear came to his panda eye and splashed down on one of his leopard spots and washed it com-pletely off his tummy. Joey was sad. Knowing that a groose listens backward the old owl said, "I can help you Joey, but what I will say to you will make you very sad, and you won't like doing what I tell you."

Joey immediately broke out into happy laughter and was very eager to hear and do what the old owl said. Grooses can be very funny sometimes. The old owl smiled for he loved grooses better than almost any other forest animal.

There are four things the wise old owl wanted Joey to remember to do. The wise owl knew how a groose thinks, so he knew Joey wouldn't remember to do any of the four things if he told Joey to remember. But if the wise old owl told Joey to forget the four things, he would remember them all. The wise old owl also knew Joey would hear backward and do the opposite of what the wise old owl told him.

The wise old owl said, "Do these four things everyday and your teacher and your mother will be very happy with you and proud of you. Ready? Here we go:

1. "Joey, never, never listen to all of the directions from Ms. Flips, your teacher. Start working real fast way before she's finished giving her instructions.

2. Joey, when you finish one assignment, never, never, go on to the next one. Make Ms. Flips come over and check your work and make you start on your next work.

3. Never, never turn in the work you have completed. When the teacher looks at you, pretend you are still working on it. Always play with and tease other kids until your teacher makes you stop.

4. Joey, never, never, ever write your homework assignment in your notebook. Never let your mother know what your homework is about. This will greatly please your mother.

"Good luck, little groose, I know you will hate doing everything I told you to do!"

That wise old owl sure knew how a groose thinks, didn't he! Since grooses think and act backward, Joey did the very opposite of what the wise old owl said. Here is what happened. Pay attention now.

1. Joey looked right at Ms. Flip's eyes and heard every word she said before he started to work on his assignment.

2. As soon as Joey finished one assignment, he went on to the next one right away. Ms. Flips was proud.

3. Joey always turned in his completed work right now. It just totally slipped Joey's mind to play and tease other kids while they were working. (Wasn't that owl wise?)

4. Joey couldn't figure out what happened to him, but as soon as Ms. Flips wrote out the homework assignment, Joey whipped out his notebook and wrote down every word. He took it home to his mother, too.

Good things began to happen to Joey. The principal came to Joey's room and gave him a balloon and free passes to eat pizza and play games at Klukky

Cheese. Joey was one of the five best students in his class. Joey was so proud. All of the boys and girls in his class wanted to be just like Joey. Well, maybe the girls didn't want to be just like Joey, but they did like the way he studied and made great grades. Joey's teacher was so proud of Joey's top-five award that she danced a jig in front of the class, stepped into the waste basket, clanked around for a few seconds, fell into the principal, and they both fell down. All the kids laughed until they cried. Ms. Flips was not hurt. The principal was embarrassed.

When Joey went home and showed his mother his award, she became very sad and bawled like a baby, ran backward out of the house, and hugged and kissed a tree in the backyard. Remember, Joey's mother is a groose, too, so she does everything backward. For non-grooses this means that mother was so happy for Joey that she laughed and squealed for joy. Then she ran over to Joey and gave him many hugs and kisses.

This story has a really good ending, and the old owl had a smile on his beak and a tear in his big old owl eyes as he flew back to the forest.

The end.

Let's analyze this groose story, using the how-to-tell-a-groose-story formula.

1. The groose is described as a strange looking forest animal, but in this story several body parts are added. I gave the groose rabbit ears to hear better with and eagle eyes to see better with.
2. Joey's problem was fully described. His problems were:
   a. Joey didn't listen. He started his work before Ms. Flips finished making the assignment.
   b. When Joey finished one assignment, he wouldn't go on to the next. Instead, he bothered students who were not yet finished.
   c. Joey lied to his teacher when she asked him if he was finished.
   d. He would not hand in completed work.
   e. He would not write down his homework assignments in his note-book. (Any of this sound familiar?)
3. The wise old owl intervenes.
4. The owl establishes his credentials that give him the authority to advise Joey.
5. The wise old owl offers Joey a solution to his problems. The owl told Joey to always remember and never forget to do all of the things that got

him into deep trouble. Of course the groose, who does everything back-wards, reverses the owl's instructions and does everything right.

6. The ending is good and the wise old owl is pleased.

"The Groose Who Needed to Fix Some School Stuff" is a story that can be adapted to many school problems. Impulsive behavior is a prime tar-get for a groose story. Some children throw fits, argue excessively, use rude language, and pout. Other children won't raise their hands before they speak, or are easily distracted by noise and activity. Groose stories can offer gentle help for these children.

Let's consider another type of story. As good as the groose stories are, I also like the little pig stories. The little pig stories also include the wise old owl and the solutions he offers. We will start with the little pig who wanted to be a horse. This story is about self-esteem, confidence, and ego strength. It is also about being rude, condescending, and disrespectful to those who are smaller, weaker, and different.

The Pig Who Wanted to Be a Horse

Once upon a time on a farm in a country far, far away lived a very unhappy little pig. The unhappy little pig lived in a fenced area near the horse corral. The lit-tle pig could clearly see the horse corral from his pig pen, and in the horse cor-ral lived a beautiful, tall, strong horse.

The pig didn't like anything about where she lived, and she was very unhappy with her life as a pig. She didn't like who she was or how she was treated. Every day, she ate grain, soaked in water, and ate scraps from the farmer's table, and she didn't like that either. This was one sad, grumpy, unhappy pig. The little pig always admired the big beautiful, free, strong horse in the horse corral, and she wished she could be just like him. After much piggy thought, she decided that if she practiced being a horse hard enough, she would be a horse. All she had to do to was copy everything the horse did. So the little unhappy pig left the pig pen and went over to the horse's corral to start practicing being a horse. She noticed that the horse held his head very high, so the pig held her head high. It was hard and hurt her neck because a pig is made to look down at the ground to find food, but she kept it up any-way. Next, the little piggy tried to sway her back like the horse. Piggies have humpy backs, and it was very hard for her to sway her back. In fact, it really hurt. A horse prances around, so the little piggy pranced everywhere, too. The tail was a problem. A horse has a long hairy tail that he holds high and swishes around. A pig's tail looks like a cute, little, curvy corkscrew. Finally, the little piggy was able to straighten her tail out like a straight arrow and wiggle it a little bit, but boy, did it hurt! Ouch! The horse ate hay, so the little piggy ate some hay, too. The horse whinnied loudly as he pranced, so the little piggy lifted her head and said loudly, "Oink-ee, oink-ee, oink-ee." The hardest thing the little piggy had to practice was sleeping in the sun on three legs. When a horse sleeps, it will stand on three legs and slightly lift one leg to rest it. A horse's thick hair protects it from the hot sun while it sleeps. When the little pig tried to sleep in the sun, she got a terrible sunburn all over her pink skin, because she had very little hair to protect her. Then, on top of everything else, she tipped over and fell on her side because she couldn't keep her balance on three legs. Her sides were terribly bruised. Poor pig!

The whole time this was happening, the selfish, prideful horse never noticed the little pig and didn't say a word to her. The horse was a rude dude. The horse showed piggy no respect and totally ignored her.

The wise old barnyard owl was sitting under the eaves of the barn roof watching everything that was happening in the barnyard. The owl flew down beside the little pig and asked, "What are you doing, little pig?" The little pig told the owl that she was practicing being a horse, so she could be a horse someday.

The old owl said, "How are you feeling, little pig?"

Little pig reported that she wasn't feeling well. Her throat hurt from loud oinking. Her back was killing her because she swayed it like the horse. Her neck hurt. Her tummy hurt and felt sick because of all of the horse hay she had eaten. Her tail hurt so bad she couldn't even wiggle it. Her legs were sore from constant prancing. Her skin was sunburned from sleeping in the sun, and her sides were sore because she kept falling over when she slept in the sun on three legs. The little piggy was one big mess.

The old owl said, "Little piggy, do you know who I am?"

The little pig said, "You are the wise old barnyard owl."

The owl said, "That's right, and what did your mother tell you about me?"

She said, "My mom told me that I had to do what you told me to do because you are very wise."

The wise old owl said, "Little piggy, I am going to tell you what I want you to do, but you won't like it." The owl continued, "Little piggy, I want you to go back to your pig pen and live like a pig for one week. I will fly down and check on you in one week." The little pig sadly went back home to live like a pig.

One week later, the wise old owl flew down to the pig pen to check on little piggy. The old owl said, "Well, little pig how do you like being a pig?"

The little pig said, "I think I really like being a pig. My back doesn't hurt. My tail doesn't hurt. My tummy doesn't hurt, and my throat isn't sore anymore. I really like playing pig games with my cousin, and I love being with my hoggy mom and dad. You know, Mr. Owl, the thing I like best of all about being a pig is my daily roll-around in our mud hole. After a mud roll, I can take a nap on my side in the sun, because I have lots of cool mud all over my hairless pink skin. I think I like being a pig."

The wise old owl said, "That's great, little piggy, and here is what I want you to always remember and never forget. It is best to live like a pig, because you are one."

The little piggy always loved herself from then on. She had lots of self-confidence and was very proud of herself. Oh, there was the time that the little piggy wanted to be a rooster, but she quickly remembered what the wise old owl said, and besides, she could never fly up to the roof of the barn and crow loudly. She also realized that even if she got up to the top of the roof, she would slide off and break her nose because she had little slick hooves, just perfect for walking around in the mud, not standing on a roof. The little piggy was never unhappy again.

The old owl was very proud of the little piggy and flew away with a smile on his beak and a tear in his big owl eye.

How to Tell a Little Piggy Story

The formula for telling a piggy story is the same as you would use to tell a groose story. The formula is:

1. Describe the situation, i.e., the farm, the pig pen, the horse corral, the horse and pig food.
2. Describe the problem. The little pig didn't like herself, was very unhappy, and thought she could solve her problem by being just like the proud, selfish, disrespectful horse.
3. The wise old owl intervenes.
4. The wise old owl establishes his credentials.
5. The wise old owl offers a solution. The owl asks the little piggy to go back to the pig pen and live like a pig for a week.
6. The solution works. The wise old owl is proud of the little piggy and flies away happy.

When I tell stories to young children (ages eight to eleven), I like to discuss the teaching message with the child. I first ask the child what they learned from the story. If they don't get it, I tell the child the teaching points with a short discussion. This works very well. The lessons in this story are:

1. It's always better to be yourself, love yourself, and respect yourself, just like the little pig.
2. Never, never be like the proud, selfish, rude, and disrespectful horse. The little pig honored the horse by wanting to be just like him, but the selfish, proud horse just ignored the little pig. The proud, rude horse thought he was better than the pig, but he wasn't. He was just different.

The little piggy story can be adapted to a wide variety of typical problems children have. Children who throw bawling, hitting, screaming fits at home or the grocery store can benefit from a piggy story. For example, the little pig can want to be just like the howling, fighting, biting barnyard dog. The wise owl tells the little pig to go back to the pig pen and be a pig. Pigs don't throw fits like mean dogs do. Children who are rude, argumentative, and use abusive language can profit from a piggy story. For example the little pig can want to be like the grumpy, rude, argumentative rooster who argues with mother hens, baby chicks, the farmer's wife, cows, and the irritating wind. The rooster wants to be boss of everybody. The wise old owl has other plans for the little pig. Problems with teachers, homework, tests, and social problems can be addressed through a piggy story, as well.

Children often have great difficulty expressing their feelings or telling their parents what is wrong. If a parent asks a child to tell what's wrong, the typical answer is, "I don't know." The ironic thing is that the child is probably right. He really doesn't know what's wrong. Parents, on the other hand, are pretty good about reading their children. Trust your instincts and choose a story found in this chapter, or make up a story that addresses the fear, depression, anger, or self-esteem issues that you are sensing. Remember, if you read your child wrong, there is no harm done, but if you are on target, your story will have a positive impact in your child's life.

The Sparrow–Eagle Story

Once upon a time in a land far, far away lived an eagle family. Mr. and Mrs. Eagle had four growing children. They all lived in a very large nest high up on a mountain wall. One day, while their parents were away from the nest hunting for food, the young eagles decided to play like they could fly, just like their mom and dad. They flapped their wings and had the best time pretending they were flying. Jimmy, the most adventurous of all of his brothers and sisters, thought that it would be even more fun if he stood on the edge of the nest and pretended to fly. Jimmy hopped up on the edge of the nest, dug his toes into the nest's twigs, and started flapping. His brother and sisters were so afraid for him. They begged Jimmy to get back into the nest, but Jimmy just flapped harder and harder. Sally said she would tell their mom if he didn't come down from the edge, but Jimmy just kept on flapping. Jimmy was enjoying scaring his brother and sisters, and he really loved the attention he was getting.

Jimmy flapped even harder, and that is when it happened! Jimmy started lifting into the air, lost his grip on the nest's edge, and fluttered into space. Since Jimmy was too young to know how to fly, he started fluttering and spinning down, down, down. Jimmy fluttered and spun all the way to the valley floor and hit with a big thud. He was scared and stunned, but he was alive.

Soon a flock of little sparrows landed nearby. The sparrows were pecking and eating seeds from the valley floor when one of the little squeaking sparrows noticed Jimmy. The little sparrow hopped over to Jimmy and looked curiously at this very large, strange-looking new bird. Jimmy said, in a fearful voice, "Who...who are you?"

The little sparrow said, "I'm a sparrow, but who are you?"

Jimmy replied, "I guess I'm a sparrow, too."

The sparrow flock adopted Jimmy and taught him how to eat like a sparrow, think like a sparrow, and fly like a sparrow. They were very nice to Jimmy. Sparrows are funny little birds. They hop a lot and eat little tiny seeds in the grass. Sparrows are nervous birds, and they don't stay in one place very long. They can be eating seeds in one place, and then all of a sudden, for no real reason, they will all fly to a nearby tree. Then, they fly back down to the same place they were before to eat some more seeds. Sparrows never fly much higher than tree tops and telephone pole wires because they are afraid of heights. They always fly and eat and do everything together as a flock. They are almost defenseless against anyone who wants to hurt them. Cats, owls, hawks, and little boys with BB guns sometimes hurt sparrows. It's not easy being a sparrow! They are nervous, scared birds.

A big, beautiful Bald Eagle, the kind with a big white head, was flying high in the sky and saw Jimmy, the sparrow-eagle, on the ground eating seeds with the sparrow flock. The Bald Eagle circled and glided its way down to Jimmy. The Bald Eagle sat beside Jimmy and said, "What are you doing, eagle?"

Jimmy the sparrow-eagle said he was eating seeds because he was really hungry.

The big beautiful Bald Eagle said, "Your curvy, sharp beak is made to eat rabbits, not peck up tiny seeds. No wonder you are hungry."

Jimmy said, "I have always wondered why it was so hard to get my beak around these little seeds."

Suddenly, the entire flock flew away to some nearby tree, and Jimmy went, too. Then they all flew back down to the same place to eat some seeds.

The Bald Eagle said, "Why did you fly away like you were afraid of something?"

Jimmy the sparrow-eagle said, "Because I am afraid all the time. All of us are afraid that something will hurt us!"

The Bald Eagle said, "You are made to fly high in the sky, way above any danger. Look, I will teach you how to fly high, catch a rabbit, and we will eat it and won't have to hunt again for three days."

Jimmy asked, "How do you catch a rabbit?"

The Bald Eagle explained that they would fly up high where the clouds were, and, with the sharp eyes of an eagle, look for a rabbit. He went on to explain, "When we see a rabbit, we will fold our wings and dive at one hundred miles per hour, scoop the rabbit up, fly back to my nest high in the mountains, and eat like kings."

Jimmy the sparrow-eagle said, "I would get a beak bleed if I flew that high, and if we fold our wings and dive at one hundred miles per hour, when we hit the ground, we will be a grease spot with lots of feathers flying around."

The Bald Eagle laughed and laughed and replied, "We are not going to hit the ground going one hundred miles per hour because we will spread our big eight-foot wings and slow way down before we snatch the rabbit. Come on sparrow-eagle, let's fly up high and I will show you how to catch a big juicy rabbit."

Off they flew, way up high, to look for a rabbit. Jimmy the sparrow-eagle was surprised that he didn't get dizzy and that he could see things so well on the ground. Soon, they spotted a rabbit, and the Bald Eagle folded his wings and started his fast dive with Jimmy right behind. They were right on the top of the rabbit in a flash, and the Bald Eagle spread his big, eight-foot wings and slowed his speed down. He put his big feet out and scooped up the rabbit with his big toes, and they flew back to the Bald Eagle's nest. His nest was high on the mountain wall, safely above all harm. It was a long journey, and the nest was high up and hard-to-find, but no one and nothing would bother them there. They ate like kings, and Jimmy the sparrow-eagle was so happy.

From that day on, and forever more, Jimmy the sparrow-eagle flew like an eagle, hunted like an eagle, ate like an eagle, and thought like an eagle. Jimmy was never afraid again. Jimmy was an eagle!

The Teaching Message of the Sparrow-Eagle Story

There are three major points in this story that I recommend that you discuss with your child. The teaching points are:

1.   Always help those who need help. The sparrows helped a young imma-ture eagle. The Bald Eagle taught the sparrow-eagle how to eat, hunt, fly, and think like an eagle.
2.   Don't take careless, impulsive, and thoughtless risks. Standing on the edge of the nest and flapping his wings was unnecessarily dangerous for Jimmy.
3.   Every boy and girl has natural gifts and talents. It is the parents' job to identify the outstanding qualities of their children and to encourage their development. The Bald Eagle recognized that the sparrow-eagle was not living up to his true and natural ability. The Bald Eagle made it possible for the sparrow-eagle to live like a real eagle.

Parents cannot overemphasize to children that helping others is a good thing. Children are, by nature, selfish and possessive, and they have to learn another way to live and interact with others. Parents are natural teachers for their children. It doesn't hurt if parents model this teaching theme by being aware of the needs of others and lending a helping hand to those who need it. Telling and modeling are great ways to teach chil-dren to be helpers.

Some children are born reserved and cautious, but there are an equal number of risk-taking children. I personally encourage parents to encourage their children to push the edges and take reasonable risks. The key word is reasonable. This is a great teaching point, and there is no one better to teach this lesson than a caring parent. After telling or reading the eagle story, take some time to discuss what a reasonable risk is, and contrast it with an unrea-sonable risk. Wing flapping in the nest might result in dislodging some nest twigs, feather clutter, sore joints, and a feather in the eye, but there is no dan-ger of death or permanent separation from the family. Similarly, it's okay to jump off a box or the side of the bed, but it would be an unreasonable risk to jump off the edge of the roof, hoping to land in the swimming pool.

The most powerful point of this story is the development of natural, God-given potential found in every child. All children have built-in gifts and talents. A gift is a natural ability to do something well. For example, some children have a natural gift for leadership and social interaction, and other children have a natural gift for mechanics, construction, and creativity. It is the wise parent who recognizes these natural gifts and makes it possible for a child to use and develop them. A talent is a learned skill that the child does exceedingly well. For example, some children take to math and learn mathematical skills easily. Other children learn crafting, art, and architecture easily. The Bald Eagle knew that the sparrow-eagle had the natural ability to fly high and see small animals on the valley floor. The Bald Eagle gave the sparrow-eagle an opportunity to learn how to hunt like an eagle, eat like an eagle, live where eagles live, and think like an eagle. The Bald Eagle also taught Jimmy how to live above danger, feel secure, and have confidence in his natural eagle ability. I really like this point and believe it should be discussed fully after reading or telling the eagle story.

One Last Groose Story

It is important to always remember and never forget that all behavior of children is goal-directed. It may not seem like your child has any goal or purpose behind his actions, but he does. For some children, this goal is to get and keep his parents' attention. If he can't get positive attention, negative attention will do just fine. As long as his mom and dad are scolding the child, they are involved. This is a story about an attention-getting groose by the name of Elmer.

The Groose Who Loved Attention

Once upon a time in a land far away lived a groose named Elmer. In those days, a groose looked very different from anything you have ever seen before. Let me describe a groose to you. A groose has gorilla ears, eyes like a bird, teeth like a lion, a nose like a donkey, a long neck like a giraffe, two humps like a camel, a tail like a monkey, hind legs like a deer, front legs like an elephant, zebra stripes on one side and leopard spots on the other side. With hind legs like a deer and front legs and flat feet like an elephant, the groose could run fast, very slowly. Although the groose looked strange and different from all of the other forest creatures, the strangest thing about the groose was that he did everything backward. If the teacher said to stand up, the groose would sit down. If the teacher said to be quiet, the groose would begin talking very loudly. If the teacher said to put the toys in the toy box gently, the groose would throw them into the box harshly. If the teacher said no running, the groose would run backward all around the room. All grooses do everything backward. They can't help it! No matter how much they want to change, they just do everything backward.

Elmer loved attention. Elmer wanted friends and wanted to be loved. Elmer got lots of attention, but it was always the wrong kind of attention. His teacher scolded him, got mad at him, and punished him because he did everything backward. The boys and girls made fun of him, teased him, and didn't include him in their games. Elmer got lots and lots of attention, but it was always bad attention for doing everything backward. Elmer didn't know what to do. Elmer's feelings were even backward. He didn't know for sure if he was happy or sad. He was happy to get all that attention, but he was sad that his teachers were mad at him and sad that the other forest animals teased him and made fun of him.

The wise old barnyard owl had been watching Elmer for quite a long time. One day Elmer decided to do something about his backward problem, so he ran backward, slowly as fast as he could, to where the wise old owl lived. Elmer asked the wise old owl if he could help him get the right kind of attention. The owl said, "I am the wise old barnyard owl, and I can help you because I am very wise. But," said the owl, "you must promise not to do anything I tell you."

Because the groose does everything backward, Elmer promised to do everything the wise old owl said.

The wise old owl smiled and said, "Your problem is simple. Your cooperator is busted. That's all that's wrong with you. Your cooperator is busted, and it needs to be rewound. Your cooperator runs backward. You have to practice and practice doing everything backward until your cooperator is rewound to the start. So here is what you do:

1. Run home backward.
2. Eat dessert first, before you eat your meal.
3. Never walk, always run.
4. Make many loud noises, scream, and shout until your teacher or mother tells you to stop.
5. Always blame the other boys and girls for getting you into trouble.

6. Always push and shove the other children.
7. Always throw toys and break everything.
8. Stay awake all night and never sleep.
9. Never, never listen to what your teachers or your mother tells you to do.
10. Always throw a bawling, squalling, hitting, yelling fit when your mother or teacher tells you no to anything you want.

Of course, you know what happened! When Elmer tried to run backward, he walked frontward; when he tried to talk really loud, he spoke softly; when he tried to throw toys, he placed them gently down; when he tried to blame the other children for his problems, he couldn't; when he tried to lie, he told the truth, because—you guessed it—a groose does everything backward. When he tried to do things backward, he did them frontward, the right way.

And it worked! He rewound his cooperator to the start and from that day forward Elmer did everything forward and frontward and right. His teachers loved him and gave him lots and lots of good attention for doing what they told him. All of the boys and girls gave him the right kind of attention by playing with him. He was the best loved and liked child in the school. Elmer's mother was very proud of him and gave him many, many rewards.

The barnyard owl just smiled and flew away with a tear in his big owl eye, thinking that some children just need to rewind their cooperator and start over. The wise old owl loves grooses, and he understands them better than anyone.

Last Thoughts

I have found that teaching stories are wonderful aids to the therapy I do with parents and children. I have given you examples of some of the stories I use and tell. I have also shared my thoughts on how I construct a story in hopes every parent will become comfortable with making up their own original stories. It's not that difficult to construct original stories for young children. They are not very critical and usually like and appreciate any story a parent comes up with. However, if you are uncomfortable constructing your own stories, it's okay to use my stories and/or stories found in children's story books. There are many story books available to you about anger, honesty, cooperation, death, depression, adoption, and divorce. The important thing is to identify the behavior, value, or issue you want to address and find a story that illustrates what you want to teach. After telling the story, discuss the teaching points with your child. Share with your child what you want them to learn from your teaching story.

Teenagers are in another world, so a different approach is required to get your point across to them. A story with a teaching point is difficult to resist, even for a teen, if the story is not told directly to the teenager. Teenagers can easily blow off direct advice from a parent, but a story can get through their defenses when good, healthy, sound advice fails.

The story should be about a real or fictitious person in the age range of your teen. The story is about a teen with a problem. Everything is bad and nothing is good for the teen. The story should be told to someone else with the teen as a listening audience.

Storytelling works. Try it, and I think you will be pleased. I feel confident that a story will help you raise a child you want to keep.

Go forth. Do good!

Chapter 12

The Scarlett O'Hara Technique

This technique is appropriate for children ages eight to seventeen.

The Scarlett O'Hara Technique was created to help kids who obsess, worry, fret, complain, ruminate, and criticize. The Scarlett O'Hara Technique teaches children to control their minds. It helps children to put their minds under better self-discipline and put worrisome, unwanted thoughts out of their mind. With a little help and a few parental nudges, a child can stop incessantly worrying.

Weeping Willa is twelve years old, and the most important thing in life is her social standing with her peer group. She worries about her clothes, saying the right thing, her hair, and facial blemishes. If a friend, or even a casual acquaintance, implies even the smallest criticism, disapproves of what she says or does, or gives her the cold shoulder, she will worry for weeks about what she did wrong. She endlessly replays conversations and actions that may have caused the problem. Willa obsesses and cries about her perceived place in her social strata. She also does a pretty good job of obsessing and crying about tests, papers, and homework. She is overly concerned about her standing with her teachers. Willa's mom and dad have reasoned with her and talked to her until they are blue in the face about not worrying about what other people think, but it hasn't helped. Willa admits she worries too much, but she believes that she can't help it; she accepts that she is just a worrier. What can a parent do to help Willa quit obsessing and dry her eyes? The Scarlett O'Hara Technique was designed for children like her.

Paul's problem is that he wants to live in a perfect world and be perfect in that world. Paul is ten years old, and he has set his personal standards so high that he seldom reaches them. He is perpetually disappointed in himself because he does not reach his unreachable standards. Perfect

Paul doesn't mind a bit about setting exceedingly high standards for others. Paul is an equal opportunity perfectionist. He lives life disappointed in others because they don't meet up to the standards he has set for them. Paul is extremely critical of others. He is not very well accepted at school because he is too negative. In Perfect Paul's life, everything has a place, and he thinks it is his responsibility to get everyone and everything organized. His room must be clean, his homework must be perfect, and his personal routine must not be altered. He eats dinner at 5:00 p.m. He does his homework from 6:00 p.m. until 7:00 p.m. He takes his shower at 8:00 p.m., and he goes to bed strictly at 8:30 p.m. If someone interrupts his routine, he is troubled and disturbed. Perfect Paul is an obsessive worrier.

Is Paul doomed to the pit of perfectionism? Can a concerned parent help him slow his worried mind and quit obsessing about his mistakes and the flaws of others? Yes, the Scarlett O'Hara Technique is designed to help Paul put his runaway mind under better control.

Lilly is fourteen and has a list for everything. If she loses one of her lists, she is a mess. She will spend three hours looking for her lost list, when it would only take her twenty minutes to rewrite the entire thing. Lilly the List-Maker loves rules. She keeps a notebook of school and home rules. Other students dislike Lilly because she tattles. If a fellow student breaks a rule, she feels compelled to report the rule violation. She also faithfully tattles on her eleven-year-old brother and eight-year-old sister. Lilly's mind is awhirl with worry about getting every item on her list done, and rule violators drive her nuts. She frets and worries, and her mom and dad are baffled as to how they can help her worry less. Nothing seems to slow her obsessing mind down. The Scarlett O'Hara Technique can help Lilly.

It is probably obvious to the reader that these examples represent extreme cases, and that these children will need a variety of help for their problems. You can probably see your child, to a lesser extent, in some of these examples. The first step in helping an obsessing, worrying child is to help him get his mind under better control, and to learn to dismiss unwanted or unhealthy thoughts. The child has to become the boss of his own mind. The Scarlett O'Hara technique is a mind-training method that helps children achieve mental control over obsessive worries.

The Scarlett O'Hara Technique

I named my technique after Scarlett O'Hara, the heroine of the classic book and movie, *Gone with the Wind*. In the story, Scarlett is a Civil War survivor who has many responsibilities as a result of the war. When Scarlett was highly troubled about tasks and problems, when she was about ready to sink under the troubled waters of having too much to do and too many problems to think about, she would wisely say, "I will think about that tomorrow. Tomorrow is another day." Scarlett knew when enough was enough, so she forced the troublesome thoughts out of her mind and did something else. I like that idea. Crowd the obsessive thoughts out of mind for now, and think about them later. Now that's real mental control!

The healthy goal for a worried, obsessive child is to tell her mind to think about a problem later instead of now. Obviously, a child's mind wants to think about it now, not later. How can children train their minds to postpone insistent worrying to a later time that is under their control? The Scarlett O'Hara Technique will give the worried child the ability to do this. Problems may seem very intense at the moment, but if thinking about them is postponed until the evening, the worrisome problems usually seem less intense, and sometimes, they cease to be problems at all. Delay is healthy.

The Scarlett O'Hara Technique comes in two parts. Both parts must be completed for the technique to work. Part one is about postponement. Part two is about worrying later. If all day long a child has been saying, "I'll think about that worry later," the child must honor that promise and think about everything he tried to put off all day long. A limited amount of time is allotted for the worry session. The worry time has a start time and definite finish time. For children who are twelve or younger, fifteen minutes is the length of time allotted for worry. Children thirteen and older are instructed to worry for thirty minutes. That's all the time per day allowed for worry. I think most children will find that fifteen to thirty minutes is more than enough time to worry about everything they tried to put off worrying about that day. Focused worry goes fast! Remember, your child is to only worry about what he promised his mind he would worry about later. New worries or very old worries are forbidden. The child just worries about what he tried to put off on that same day.

During worry-time, everything a child tried to put off is written down. For fifteen to thirty minutes, a child worries on paper. The brain must take an extra step to write words on paper, and worries become more concrete and more fully understood. If a child is twelve years or younger, a parent must be present to help and supervise. Writing the worries down helps the child experience a cleansed feeling. His emotions will feel scrubbed and squeaky clean.

Let's go over the five Scarlett O'Hara steps.

Step One: Explain

Explain to the child that she worries too much and too often. Elaborate by telling your child that her brain becomes frozen and locked down, and all she can think about is the current worry. If your child is driving-age, tell her that her brain is like a car that gets stuck in one gear when she obsesses, worries, complains, and frets about problems. Explain that she needs to unfreeze her brain and go on to something else. She needs to shift gears and move on. Tell your child you are going to teach her to use the Scarlett O'Hara Technique to accomplish this.

Step Two: Identify

In your explanation, identify and fully discuss with your child specifically what worries you want to work on. For example, in your discussion, you can point out that she worries too much about clothes, hair, friends, tests, grades, food, germs, or safety. Be specific. Tell your child that you are going to help her not worry so much about these things.

Step Three: Postpone

Explain that you are going to do something that seems too simple to work. If your child is twelve years or younger, tell her that when she begin to worry, she should say out loud, "I don't need to worry about that now. I'll worry about it later." As often as you catch a child worrying, require them to say aloud, "I don't need to worry about that now. I'll worry about that later." If your child is a big worrier, she may have to say this postponement statement twenty-five times from the time she arrives at home from school until her worry time in the evening. If you have a teenager, your job is to remind him to say his postponement statement to himself, either aloud or silently. You still will have to remind your teen when he is obsessing because he rarely will assume the responsibility to do it on his own.

You and your child should make a running list of every topic that he tried to postpone. You will use the list later.

Parents often question the value of the postponement statement. There are two reasons that this simple statement helps a child to stop obsessing on a problem. First, think of the statement in terms of a pushup. If a child will do one pushup a day and no more, someday he will do two pushups. If a child continues to do two pushups a day and no more, someday he will be able to do four pushups. Then, it will be eight, later, sixteen and so on, but it all started with one pushup. Saying, "I don't need to worry about that now. I'll worry about it later," is like doing one mental pushup. The child is putting a break on his runaway mind. Secondly, when a child says the postponement sentence, it acts as a distraction to the mind. One cannot have two equal thoughts at the same moment. The postponement statement monetarily interrupts the obsessive thought pattern. The postponement statement unlocks the brain for a moment, which will allow the brain to shift to some other thought pattern. Children will naturally and gradually get better and better at crowding out useless and purposeless obsessive thoughts. It really works.

Step Four: Fulfill the Promise

During the course of the day and evening, you may have asked your child to use the postponement statements one to twenty or more times. In the statement, your child promised her mind that she would think about the worry later. Since she promised, later has to come eventually. This is part two of the Scarlett O'Hara Technique. The child must sit down, with pencil in hand, at some point during the evening and worry about everything she tried to postpone. Take the list of postponed worry topics and ask your child to write a few worry thoughts about each topic. For example, if your child was worrying about having and wearing the coolest clothes, you would ask her to write one or more worry thoughts about clothes. It might sound like this, "I'm worried that Michelle will think my shoes are dorky. I am worried that Michelle will tell all of her friends, and they will laugh and make fun of me. " If the worry is about grades, the child may write, "I am worried that Jason will get the best grade in class."

Young children may need help with wording their worries, but teens will probably know what's bothering them. Your child may have only three problems on his list, but he may have worried about those three problems a lot. It most likely will not take a child fifteen minutes or a teen thirty minutes to write down all of his worries. Once all the worries are on paper, ask your child to write them down again. Repetition is very good at step four. His pencil or pen must stay busy for fifteen or thirty minutes.

A child may resist this step. Teens are especially prone to resist this part of the Scarlett O'Hara Technique. Don't give in to resistance or objections. Step four is vital to the success of the technique. Tell your child that writing down his worries is not optional, and it is not a choice he gets to make. If he rebels and says no, then use the 30-Second Technique, or the Now or Later Technique, to obtain compliance. (See chapters 5 and 6.) Without step four, the technique will fail. The postponement statement does not have enough power alone to fully stop obsessive worries. The combination of step three (postponement) and step four (the worry session) has plenty of power.

I am sure that by now you recognize that step four is the ordeal part of the Scarlett O'Hara Technique. Making a child write down worries when he is not in the mood to worry is a disguised ordeal. The child can escape the worry-writing ordeal, but he will have to cooperate by not obsessively worrying.

You should, over the next three weeks, see a significant reduction in the worry statements your child makes. He will begin to catch obsessive worries and not engage in them because he doesn't want to write about them in the evening. When you think he has improved enough to meet your standards, announce that since he doesn't worry so much anymore, he can give the Scarlett O'Hara Technique a rest for awhile. If you see obsessive worry creeping back, say to your child, "I've noticed that you are beginning to worry again, so I will be watching you for the next four days. If it doesn't stop, we will need to go back to the Scarlett O'Hara Technique." Once your child has experienced significant improvement in self-control, that statement is usually sufficient to put him back under good self-control again.

Step Five: Discard

After each fifteen-to-thirty-minute worry-writing session, ask your child to read over his worries once, tear the paper up, and throw those worries away where they belong: in the trash can.

That covers the essentials of the Scarlett O'Hara Technique. Next I want to share with you two teaching stories to illustrate how to use this technique. Let's take a tough one as an example, and then one that is more common in the average home.

Fretting Frank

Frank was an eleven-year-old boy who fretted about any new food. He worried that a new, untried food might make his stomach sick and that he might vomit. Frank complained endlessly about any new food put on the table, even if he was told he didn't have to eat it. He was horrible in restaurants, so his family rarely went out. Frank ate very little and had a very restricted diet.

Frank's mom explained to him that he worried too much about getting sick if he was even in the vicinity of a new food. She explained that he was afraid that a new food would somehow mysteriously contaminate him if he even sat in the presence of a new food on the table. She explained that he was worrying himself sick! She said that she was going to help him stop worrying by using a new method called the Scarlett O'Hara Technique.

His mother next identified what she would be looking for when they ate. If Frank said, "Don't put that on the table," "I can't stand it," "Please don't make me eat that; it will make me sick," "I don't want to look at it," "Take it away," or "Why did you cook that?" she was going to ask him to say aloud, "I don't need to worry about that now. I'll worry about it later." She informed Frank that by saying the statement aloud, he would gradually be able to postpone worrying about new, untried foods now, and worry about them later. Mother explained that eventually, he would stop worrying about new foods.

Next, she told Frank that since he would be promising his mind that he would think about it later, he had to fulfill his promise. She informed Frank that she would arrange an evening session, and he would worry about new foods for fifteen long minutes. Fifteen minutes should be plenty of time to worry about new food.

Freddy's mother carried out the plan perfectly. She served a new food every evening. Freddy was not required to eat it, but if he said any of the above statements about the new food, or acted worried through body language, she required him to say aloud, "I don't need to worry about that now. I'll worry about it later." She made him write every worry and complaint over and over in his fifteen-minute worry session. Frank hated it. He tore up his list when time was up and threw it away. In sixteen days, Frank had completely stopped his worrying and complaining at the dinner table. Freddy escaped the worry session ordeal by inhibiting his incessant worrying and complaints at the dinner table.

Since Frank voluntarily quit verbally complaining and worrying about stomach sickness and new foods, his mother and I were able to set up a very attractive rewards program for trying new foods. The first step was to put a small serving of a new food on his plate, and if he didn't freak out, he would get a very attractive personal reward. Frank liked this program, and we eventually got him to take small bites of various new foods. Today, Frank eats like a hog.

We couldn't use the reward program until Frank could put some brakes on his runaway obsessing mind. The Scarlett O'Hara Technique served its purpose very well.

Weeping Willa

Weeping Willa's problem often happens to late pre-teen and young teenagers. Willa was socially fragile and worried constantly about acceptance among her peers. She also worried herself silly about tests, reports, and school grades. When Willa worried, the tears would flow freely.

Willa's mom explained the problem she was concerned about and that she was going to help Willa stop excessively worrying about what her friends and classmates thought about her clothes, words, and actions, and about tests, papers, and school grades. She explained what she would be looking for, and what excessive worry meant. She said, "Willa, what I mean by excessive worry is the way that you think about the same worry or problem over and over and over. It's okay to wonder aloud if your pants will be liked by the other girls. Most teens think like that, and it's okay to say it once or twice. But when you cry your eyes out about it, it's too much. That's excessive." She explained excessive worry about tests, papers, and grades using similar words and rationale. She explained that they would use a new method called the Scarlett O'Hara Technique to help Willa with her excessive worries.

Next, Willa's mom identified what she would be looking for to help Willa determine when to use the Scarlett O'Hara technique. She said that Willa could verbalize her worry two times, but that was all. If she mentioned her worry a third time, her mom would employ the Scarlett O'Hara Technique. She identified crying as a sign of excessive worry. A brief tear down the cheek was okay, but uncontrolled sobbing was not, so she would use the technique at that point.

Willa's mom then went over the postponement step. She told Willa that every time she thought Willa was obsessively worrying, she would interrupt her and ask her to say the postponement statement, "I don't need to worry about that now. I'll worry about it later." In Willa's case, her mother decided to have Willa say the postponement statement aloud.

It is your choice. If you do not think your teenage child will say it silently, or if you think your teen is not saying the postponement statement silently, then require her to say the postponement statement aloud. Remember, you are the parent. You are the boss, so enforce the technique in the way you think is best.

Willa's mother kept a running list of notes about what Willa's excessive worries. She would put these notes to good use later.

Willa's mom told her that since she had promised her mind she would worry about her problems later, she would have to fulfill the promise. She explained all about the thirty-minute worry session. She explained that Willa needed to get her worries out of her mind, so she would be required to write about everything she tried to postpone that day. Of course, by the time evening came, Willa wouldn't remember half or maybe any of what she excessively worried or cried about that day, and that would be where her mother's list would come in handy.

Willa's mom sat with her and helped her with her worries. Willa was able to generate worry words that fleshed out the topics she tried to postpone that day. Her mom would not permit Willa to worry about new topics or to go back to issues of the distant past. They strictly focused on what Willa had promised her mind she would think about later that day. Willa hated these writing sessions, so it was clear that writing had become an uncomfortable ordeal. Her mom made her write her worries again and again for the entire thirty minutes! How could she escape the writing ordeal? She knew she could escape by shutting down her runaway obsessing mind, and that is exactly what Willa did.

Lastly, Willa was instructed to discard her worries. Willa read through her several pages of writing, gladly tore them up, and threw them in the trash. This step is an important one. A part of the brain, the emotional brain, responds well to pictures and symbols. Symbolically, Willa was throwing these worries away from her. They went into the trash where they belonged. This throwing away action was a strong message to the emotional brain to discard the habit of excessive worry.

The results of the Scarlett O'Hara Technique were very satisfying to both Willa and her mother. Willa became far less prone to worry and obsess about social standing and school requirements. Her mother heaped lavish praise on her for her newfound self-control. Because Willa put some rigid limits on her negative obsessing, she could hear and believe her mother's supportive compliments about Willa's looks and school performance. Willa's self-confidence grew a lot.

Conclusion

Some children obsess and worry too much about common life problems. Parents know it's not good for a child to worry so much and usually try to use common intervention techniques, such as heart-to-heart talks, warnings, scolding, lectures, and voice-control (yelling and screaming). Occasionally these commonly-used techniques work, but usually they don't. The Scarlett O'Hara Technique is designed to change how the brain cognitively processes problems children typically worry about.

A number of rather extreme cases were introduced to provide examples of how debilitating obsessive thinking can become. There is always a negative price to pay for excessive worry. The cost may be physical. Headaches, insomnia, stomachaches, and fatigue are not uncommon results of obsessive thinking. The cost of worry may be emotional deficits. Many worriers and negative thinkers are left to deal with anxiety, fear, discouragement, anger, or depression. Intellectual problems are not uncommon. An obsessive child may have trouble using rational problem solving skills to help him resolve a problem. There is always a high cost to the individual who worries obsessively. If the Scarlett O'Hara technique can help these extreme cases, it sure has a good chance to help your child as well with less extreme worries.

There are five simple steps to remember:

1. Explain
2. Identify
3. Postpone
4. Fulfill the Promise
5. Discard

The Scarlett O'Hara Technique provides a distraction from obsessive thoughts that, in turn, unlocks the brain to now move on to something else. Children who worry excessively have developed a long series of cognitive (thinking) bad habits. The ordeal (writing) part of the technique helps a child break this old habit of worry. By self-initiated effort and determination, the child imposes self-control on his runaway mind. He installs a set of brakes that he can apply anytime he chooses.

After using the Scarlett O'Hara technique, children feel empowered. This all happens as a result of escape learning. They eventually learn that they can escape the ordeal, but the only avenue of escape is to radically limit obsessive worry. Only when worry stops will the worry sessions stop. Clever, huh?

Go forth. Do good.

Chapter 13

The Poisoning the Well Technique

This technique is appropriate for children ages five to eighteen.

Our children are exposed to negative, immoral, dangerous, unhealthy, angry, offensive, and aggressive messages almost daily. These unhealthy, unwanted messages are delivered through television, music, movies, and even nursery rhymes! They may be very direct, such as justifying murder, or very indirect, as in the subtle suggestion that all adults are stupid schmucks. Some messages put down women, men, the police, and the government as evil, stupid, and no fun.

Some parents are so concerned about these immoral, unhealthy, and uncivilized messages that they go to extraordinary means and methods to protect their children from the influence of these potential message bombs. Some parents place their children in private Christian schools or home school their children for as long as possible in an effort to filter or screen at least some of these unhealthy influences. These and other protective methods can be helpful, but they are not enough. It's like using a teacup to bail water out of a sinking boat in a storm. It helps, but isn't nearly effective enough. Parents need to take affirmative action!

Rules That Don't Work

It is an old saying that a society cannot legislate morals, and it is well-known that children want to do what other children do. They are flock-programmed. If you make a rule that your child cannot watch television shows or movies that feature indecent, explicit sex, or the putting down of adults and authority figures, then that activity is given higher status in the child's eyes. I am not suggesting that you have a home with no rules, but I am suggesting that rigid rules are not enough, we can do more.

Most children cannot think abstractly or critically until their late teens. Children and teens have great difficulty with future planning. They are present-oriented, and are very inefficient with the kind of thinking that sees the harm in a risky activity or the negative consequences of an action one to five years into the future. Mostly, children just think that adults are too serious and love to make rules that suppress the fun of youth. A child is still making new brain cells until about age sixteen, so we adults need to teach them how to think critically and how to do future thinking. That's why Poisoning the Well is such a useful childrearing technique.

Children in each age group will be exposed to certain materials that may appeal to them, but that you believe to be unhealthy. For example, kids who are seven years old may like cartoons that promote violence, but may not be the least bit interested in explicit sex. However, girls may be interested in revealing clothes, piercing their body, and sexual manipulation, all of which may be based upon who and what they see in movies and television. Teens may watch teen television programs that suggest that all authority is bad and stupid. Police are dumb, employers are inept bumblers, and teens are bright, articulate, creative, witty, and innovative. Some of these shows depict parents as silly and uncaring. Then, there is music. Rap music often deserves its bad rap regarding the unhealthy, prejudicial, violent, and explicitly sexual messages the music raps out; country, pop, and rock songs can also convey some seriously disturbed messages. Even nursery rhymes like "Jack and Jill" and "Humpty Dumpty" can leave some negative messages in a child's mind.

Whatever you consider unhealthy or improper can be helped, bettered, or cured by using the Poisoning the Well Method.

Poisoning the Well

This powerful method can be summarized in three words—question, listen, question. There is power in listening. There is healing in listening. Everyone I know loves to be listened to. Children like us better, and are more compatible and compliant, when they believe that we care enough to listen to their thoughts. The poison is delivered by the questions you ask. The questions you ask will help a child to think about alternatives, consequences, the other side of the issue, and the big picture. Some parents might ask, "But aren't we just manipulating defenseless children?" The answer is, "Yes, we are." All of life is replete with obvious and subtle manipulations. If you tell a child to hold your hand while crossing a street or to play nice with her sister, or if you say, "I will give you $10 for every A you make in school," you are exerting manipulative influence on the child. You are manipulating the child *for the good of that child.* The choice is not whether to manipulate or not manipulate. The choice is really between responsible manipulation and irresponsible manipulation.

The question, listen, question technique can start very young. Let me give you a few examples from the life of my young granddaughter. Mariah was five when I started to teach her to think critically. I quoted Mariah this familiar nursery rhyme.

Humpty Dumpty sat on a wall.
Humpty Dumpty had a great fall.
All the king's horses and all the king's men
Could not put Humpty Dumpty together again.
Now isn't that a silly thought?

I asked Mariah what was silly about that thought. She didn't know. I asked her if horses should be asked to put the small broken pieces of an egg together. She said, "No, because horses' hooves were too big and flat." I asked Mariah if the king's men, who are soldiers and good at lopping heads off, should be asked to put the tiny pieces of an egg together again. She thought hard and said, "No, because their hands would be too big."

I asked Mariah who would be good to ask to put the pieces of a broken egg together again, and she said, "A doctor or you, Papa."

I asked if some little girl could ever be so broken that no one could put her together again.

Mariah's reply was, "Not if you ask the right people." She got the point.

I also asked Mariah why eggs shouldn't sit on a high wall. She replied, "The eggs have round bottoms and breakable skin, so they shouldn't sit on a wall." I asked her if there were things she should do to make sure she didn't get hurt.

Her reply was, "Look both ways when crossing the street, hold Mamma's hand in the parking lot, and never go anywhere with a stranger." Smart girl!

Question, listen, question works!

Bad Music

When Mariah was seven, I found her listening to a country western song about killing Earl. I didn't think it was appropriate for a child her age, so I poisoned the well. The song is about an abused woman who kills her husband. I asked Mariah, age seven, if there was anything wrong with the song. She said, "No." I asked her what bad thing Earl did to his wife. She said, "He hit her."

I asked if it was ever okay for a man to hit a woman, teenagers, or a little girl. Mariah said, "No." I said, "Is taking a life ever right?" She said, "No."

I asked her if there was another way to handle Earl. Mariah said she would call 911 and leave the house, or leave the house and call 911. I asked her if the police would protect the woman from Earl. Mariah said that she believed that they would.

After our conversation, when Mariah listened to the song, she would have another thinking pattern that would provide reasonable alternatives for her consideration. She now thinks that a man should never hit a woman, teen, or child. If he does, the right thing to do is leave and call 911 to ask for protection. The earlier you start using the question, listen, question method, the better the results.

Television Shows

I have watched with my children sitcoms that demean the police and portray parents as stupid. I would ask, "Have you met your friends' parents?"

Their answer was always affirmative, so my next question was, "Do you see any of your friends' parents acting or talking that way?" Their answer was, "No." I would follow up by asking them to tell me how their friends' parents did act.

Other questions might be, "Have you ever been mistreated by a policeman?" "Have any of your friends ever been mistreated or wronged by a policeman?" "Describe for me what you have personally seen a policeman do wrong while on duty." "Are parents really as dumb as they show us on television?" "Are all policeman brutal, bad, drunk jerks?" The child has a chance to balance the improper message gleaned from TV with real truths when you question, listen, question.

In the course of watching television or movies with my children, there would, at times, be an unexpected, spontaneous sex scene. Some of my questions in those situations were, "Is this woman using her body to get what she wants from this man?" or "When a woman says 'no' or 'don't,' should a man continue to pressure her for sex?" I might ask, "How do you think his children would feel if they knew he was having sex with a woman who is not their mother?" Remember to ask the question, encourage the child to sincerely respond, and accept the answers without rejection or negative comment. Older children or teenagers may give the wrong answer as a form of rebellion. That's okay, because your job is to give a second, third, or fourth way of seeing and thinking about a situation. Even if a teenager has given you a defensive answer, he had to have thought about the alternatives before answering.

Remember, poisoning the well takes time. The whole purpose of the Poisoning the Well Technique is to help your child to think critically, entertain reality, and deal with what is. They must be able to see both the good and the bad of a thing before a rational or reasonable decision can be made by the child to participate in an activity.

Poisoning the Teenage Well

The question, listen, question method works well for teenagers. They frequently believe that anyone over the age of eighteen is an idiot. Teens are not very open to direct advice from adults in general, and they are even less impressed with parental advice. They tend to think in the now and are reluctant to examine the long-term consequences of their actions.

What is a parent to do if a teen is infatuated with the wrong girl or boy, is bored with school, thinks school is useless, and thinks that drugs and alcohol rule? Poisoning the well can help. The following are examples of the Poisoning the Well Technique used in these kinds of situations. Use these examples to stimulate your own creative use of the method.

The Wrong Girl

It is not out of the question for your son, Matthew, to fall in teen love with a girl that just doesn't fit in with your family values. It would be very wise of Matthew if he would take a realistic look at how Katie treats her parents. This is a good test of how Katie will treat Matt and how she will fit into your family. Remember: question, listen, question. Accept any answer without criticism or elaboration. These example questions should make Matt think and ultimately poison his well.

1. "Does Katie have a father that lives in the home with her?"
   "No, they are divorced."

2. "Does Katie respect her father?"
   "I don't know."
3. "Does Katie seem to be comfortable when around her father?"
   "I have never met her father."
4. "Does Katie's father treat her well or poorly?"
   "She never talks about him."
5. "Does Katie privately criticize her father?"
   "No."
6. "Does Katie like her mother?"
   "Yes."
7. "Do Katie and her mother fight a lot?"
   "Not a lot."
8. "Is Katie happy at home?"
   "No."
9. "Is Katie critical of her mother?"
   "Sometimes."

Now Matt has a different perspective. He will observe Katie in a different way. Matt will be aware of Katie's relationships with her father and mother. Matt's well has been poisoned, but he doesn't know it yet. He will have to drink from the well for a while before the water makes him sick. If you are wrong in your evaluation that Katie is the wrong girl, then no harm has been done. Love her and value her. If you are right, Matt will soon move on to another girl who may be a better fit, and he will probably be more attentive to his next girlfriend's relationship with her parents.

School Is Boring

Teenagers may be sucked into the unhealthy belief that school is boring and that nothing taught there will ever be helpful in real life. Let's say Jenna believes that her English teacher is boring and that she will never use the stuff she teaches. These questions could prove to be helpful in disabusing her of these notions. They could very well poison her well, and change a very faulty belief system.

1. "Is your English teacher dumb or smart?"
   "Smart, I guess."
2. "Does your teacher seem to be well prepared for class?"
   "Yeah, she's okay, I guess."

3. "Does your teacher seem to like teaching?"
   "I don't know."
4. "Is your teacher fair to all students?"
   "Pretty much."
5. "Does your English teacher, joke, laugh, and have fun with the students?"
   "No."
6. "What kind of car does your English teacher drive?"
   "A Ford."
7. "Does your teacher live in a nice house?"
   "I don't know."
8. "Is your teacher married?"
   "Yes."
9. "Does she have children?"
   "She has two kids."
10. "Does your teacher seem to be liked by other teachers?"
    "I guess."
11. "Does everyone in your class think she's boring and that what she teaches is useless?"
    "I don't know."

Remember to accept any and all answers to your questions. No matter what Jenna's answers are, her teacher has taken on more personable, human qualities. Jenna will see her teacher with new eyes. The well has been poisoned. Give it time to work.

Drugs and Alcohol

Some teens embrace drug and alcohol use and search for plausible reasons to defend it. Brian is a teen who irrationally defends drug and alcohol use when confronted. Asking these questions just might poison Brian's well.
1. "Do drugs make the mind think better?"
   "I don't know."
2. "Are people smarter when high on drugs?"
   "No."
3. "Are drunk people smarter than sober people?"
   "No."
4. "Are drunk friends funnier that sober friends?"

"Yes."

5. "Do you know how long the jail term is for possession of drugs?"

"No."

6. "What is the legal penalty for underage drinking?"

"I don't know."

7. "Do drug users succeed better in life than non-drug users?"

"Maybe."

8. "Are alcohol users more popular than non-alcohol users?"

"I'm tired of these questions!"

Brian's well just got poisoned. You have caused him to think about the other side of drug and alcohol use. My opinion is that Brian will find it more difficult to unthinkingly justify drug and alcohol use.

Music

Many adults are offended by the lyrics of today's music. Frequently, the lyrics center on abusive cops, controlling mothers, absent fathers, and girls who cheat and manipulate boys. A dominant theme in much rap music, for example, conveys the concept that the rapper is misunderstood, abused, lied to, lonely, sad, depressed, suicidal, or homicidal. I think the theme that dominates much of rap music is, "I'm a victim of abuse and control, and I will strike back in some vengeful manner." The rapper's message often seems to be a plea to understand his personal pain, and a statement of intent to exact retribution or revenge on those who cause the pain.

Parents often find themselves in conflict with their teenager over whether they should or should not listen to this type music. Often a firm position against this music simply increases its value in the child's eyes. Thus, the music becomes a forbidden fruit that must, at all costs, be obtained and valued. Teenagers often identify with the rapper or singer, and the parent automatically falls into the role of the stupid, senseless, old-fashioned abuser. Parents become the enemy, and the performer becomes the hero.

The question most parents who oppose the type of music described above ask is, "So, what can I do to get them to stop listening to it?"

It's truly a catch-22, or a "damned if I do and damned if I don't" situation. If a parent forbids the music, the teen loves it more and seeks every available opportunity to listen to it. If the parent says nothing, the teen is free to listen to as much as they want. I believe the Poisoning the Well

Technique will help solve this problem. However, it will take courage and a strong stomach to carry the technique out to its conclusion. If done, however, the results are surprisingly successful.

A fourteen-year-old boy was expelled from school for fighting and using abusive language toward a teacher. His parents brought him to me for counseling. As family counseling progressed, both parents expressed concern about their son's fascination with rap music that was vulgar, abusive to parents, and that promoted rebellion against authority. The lyrics of one of these rap songs were printed on the liner notes. What follows is a fictitious example, but it is close enough to give you an idea of how to poison the well:

"Nothing good, nothing right

motherfucker parents screwed my mind,

all gone, brain gone,

brain gone, gone, gone!"

I read the lyrics to him and said I really didn't understand the meaning of this part of the song. I asked him to explain the meaning to me. He was somewhat uncertain himself as to the meaning of this verse. Finally David offered that the lyricist was depressed and upset about the way he had been treated. I asked more questions, such as, "Is he going to kill himself?" "Do most parents ruin their son's mind?" "Do you personally know any parent who has ruined their son's mind?" "Do any of your friends ever call their mothers motherfuckers?" "Have you ever called your father a motherfucker?"

We went over portions of the rap lyrics for the next four weeks. On the fifth session, David said, "I don't want to talk about this anymore, because I don't listen to this kind of rapper anymore." His well had been poisoned.

An Abused Daughter

A mother and father sought counseling because their eighteen-year-old daughter, Jessica, was in an abusive relationship with a man, Chris. She was living with him, and he smacked her around frequently. He picked fights with her parents and made any visit to the parents' house a long, miserable confrontation. They wanted Jessica out of the relationship and sought advice concerning what they could do to help her get out. They had already confronted Chris, and they had begged Jessica to leave him. Their daughter blamed herself for Chris's anger. She thought that if she were only quieter, got dinner ready on time, or gave him enough sex, he wouldn't get so angry. Her parents were desperate.

We used a slightly different approach for this situation, but it is essentially uses the same concept.

I taught Jessica's parents the principle of the Poisoning the Well Technique. They were asked to be overly supportive of Chris and to make excuses for his abusive behavior. I asked them to drop in unexpectedly for visits. During these visits, Chris would go to the bedroom. The parents were to be polite and inquire about his health and work (although he almost never worked). They invited both to come over for dinners and to celebrate special events. Chris wouldn't come, but Jessica would. Jessica would make excuses for him, and her parents would say things like, "I am sure Chris would like to come, but he is probably just too tired and too busy." They would encourage her to try harder to please him and meet his every need, desire, and demand. They made elaborate, unreasonable, excuses for Chris. Jessica's mom would call her daughter daily, and Jessica complained more and more about Chris's abusive behavior. Her mom wanted to say, "Now you're catching on! He is a jerk!"

Instead, she would say, "You know, Chris just doesn't know better because his father was an alcoholic, and he saw him beat his mother." Jessica never confessed that Chris beat her, but she would say, "Sometimes Chris gets rough with me."

Her mom would gulp and say, "I know he wants to have a good relationship with you and us; but his family was not close, so he doesn't know how to do it. I know it will be tough, but if you will do more to please him I'm sure he will be nicer to you."

Of course, the harder Jessica tried to please him, the more abusive Chris became. I know this approach seems wrong because it seems as if it encourages abuse, but remember, Jessica's parents had already been unsuccessful using reasoning and criticism.

Finally, Jessica threw the bum out and moved back home. I never met Jessica, but her parents reported that Jessica slowly healed and met a nice young man who treated her well and supported her family values. She married him, and they have two healthy children. The Poisoning the Well Technique may have saved Jessica's life.

Jungle Joe

Jungle Joe was the rebellious fourteen-year-old son of divorced parents. His father had withdrawn, and his mother couldn't handle him. Jungle Joe ran over his mother, abused his brother, terrorized his teachers, and greatly annoyed his principal. He was suspended from school on numerous occasions, which was okay with him because he didn't like school, anyway. Jungle Joe was pleased with his actions because they usually elicited a response from his teachers, counselors, and the principal to try to help him. He got attention and sometimes concessions as a result of his abuse. Jungle Joe increased his abusive efforts until one day, when he went much too far. Joe threatened to kill one of his teachers. Jungle Joe was arrested and charged with endangerment. The court sentenced him to counseling for anger management, which is how I met him.

Again, this is an example of an unusual use of well-poisoning. The approach depends upon the use of a paradox. It employs reverse psychology, but it is essentially the poisoning of the well method.

I had read Joe's records, so I came fully prepared for our first session. I asked Joe why he had come to see me, and he said he was supposed to work on his anger. I asked Jungle Joe what he wanted to get out of seeing me, and he told me that he would like to control his anger. That's when I started poisoning the well. I said, "Why would you want to do something like that? You have been getting your way by abusing others for years. Why would you want to give up something that has worked so well for you?" I paused and listened.

Joe reaffirmed his goal by telling me that his anger had brought nothing but trouble for him. I looked surprised and said, "I'm not buying a word you're saying. You're too good at it to want to give it up." I said, "How about if I help you to be angry more cleverly, with less chance of getting into trouble?"

He said, loudly, "Are you crazy?"

I replied sincerely, "The last time I checked I wasn't crazy." His well had just gotten a dose of poison.

Week after week, I added more poison. Joe's mother was a frustrated, loving mother who often gave in to Joe's demands out of sheer exhaustion. She would often believe his promises to correct his misbehavior. She was a sucker for a half apology mumbled to her as he passed through the kitchen.

One day, Joe was telling me about the improvement in his home behavior, and I told him that I was concerned about hearing that he was improving at home regarding his cooperation with his mother. I said he was dangerously close to giving up a method that had worked really well for him for years. I asked him to think carefully about what he was saying and doing.

Jungle Joe looked confused and asked, "What are you talking about?"

I asked, "Why would you want to give up conning your mother? You have avoided trouble for years by conning your mother into thinking that you would correct your misdeeds, and she has always believed your lies. Why would you want to give up something that works?" I waited for an answer. Three minutes passed without a word from Joe.

I asked, "Are you thinking?"

He nodded. I waited.

Finally, Jungle Joe said, "I know what you're doing."

I replied, "What is that?"

Joe told me that he had known for a long time that I said crazy things to get him to think about what he was doing. He said that he really was changing, and he didn't want to play this crazy game anymore. Joe's well was poisoned.

Therapy progressed nicely after that. Joe passed the eighth grade and got off of probation without further law-breaking.

It is not infrequent that children will know what you are doing but will continue playing the therapy game because they know it is helping them. When they don't need to play the game further, they often confess they know what you are doing and refuse to play further.

Conclusion

Raising children can be a very challenging experience in which traditional childrearing techniques prove to be ineffective. As they get older, children may react strongly against arbitrary family rules. The Poisoning the Well Technique can be very helpful with both young and older children. It's a technique that is hard to resist or rebel against.

Go forth. Do good. Poison well!

Chapter 14

Raising the ADHD Child

Albert, age eight, is in school, but he might as well be on Mars because he is getting next to nothing from his school experience. He sits on the edge of his seat and squirms and fidgets. He blurts out answers to questions without raising his hand. His teacher has told him hundreds of times to raise his hand before speaking, and he has been punished for violating this rule, but to no avail. He can't get started on his desk work because he plays with a paperclip and then pretends his fingers are pirates fighting. The teacher scolds Albert for not starting his work, and Albert cries. Albert wants to know what he has done wrong. He stares at his assignment like it is written in a foreign language. Albert breaks his pencil lead on purpose, and then, without permission, gets up to sharpen it. The teacher scolds Albert, and Albert gets furious. He throws his pencil, and it skips and bounces into Jennifer's cheek. Jennifer screams, and Albert is sent to the principal's office, and ultimately home. His mom asks Albert why he was suspended, and Albert, with great innocence, claims that he didn't do anything wrong and he doesn't know why he was sent home.

Then, the drama starts at home. Albert is sent to his room to clean the clothes and toys off of the floor. Thirty minutes later, his mom checks on him, only to find him playing with cars and army men, while not one toy or piece of clothing has been picked up. His mom is angry beyond words. She doesn't know what to do or how to get through to Albert, so she screams at him and gives him a whack on the bottom. Albert screams back that he was going to do it and that his mother is mean and stupid. He runs out the front door and doesn't come back until just before dark. By then, his mom is frantic! When he returns, Albert acts like he has done nothing wrong and the room-cleaning incident never happened.

Is Albert just a naughty, undisciplined child who has an unreasonable, rigid teacher and an incompetent out-of-control mother? No, Albert has a brain chemical problem called Attention Deficit Hyperactivity Disorder (ADHD).

This chapter is not a definitive explanation of ADHD, nor is it a chapter that absolutely, once and for all solves all the problems associated with a diagnosis of ADHD. This chapter has two simple goals:

1. I want each parent to have an increased awareness of the major symptoms of ADHD, so that the parent can make an informed decision regarding the need for a referral to an ADHD specialist.
2. I want to present eight sanity-savers that can help a parent improve the academic and behavioral problems of an ADHD child with possible Learning Disabilities.

What Is ADHD?

ADHD is not another word for a naughty child. ADHD is a biochemical/organic problem that is just as real as diabetes or any other bodily disease. When insulin is low, the diabetic has brain and physical symptoms. When norepinephrine and dopamine levels are low, the ADHD child, in like manner, has brain symptoms.

Currently, the best minds on the subject agree that ADHD is caused by a neurochemical imbalance. The two chemicals believed to be out of balance are norepinephrine and dopamine. These neurochemicals, when balanced, make vital parts of the brain capable of focusing, tracking, attending, thinking before acting, and limiting motor activity. Good stuff, huh? Children with less-than-adequate norepinephrine or dopamine levels are easily distracted, so they don't pay attention, have huge energy bursts, are hyperactive and impulsive, and act before they think through the consequences.

For the ADHD child, there are two therapies that are widely recommended.

1. Stimulant medication, which helps the brain function as it was designed to function.
2. Cognitive/behavior therapy, which has been found to produce positive outcomes for the ADHD child. This is an active type of therapy that does not put the major therapeutic emphasis on antecedents or past developmental stages.

The most effective treatment for ADHD is derived from a combination of both medication and cognitive/behavioral therapy. It's a strong duo.

How Do You Know If Your Child Has ADHD?

First, I want to point out that you, as a parent, are not trained or qualified to make an official diagnosis of ADHD. It is a complicated disorder, and only trained professionals should make the final decision regarding the diagnosis of ADHD. You can, however, use the information found in this chapter to make an informed decision about referring your child to a specialist trained in the diagnosis and treatment of ADHD and Learning Disabilities. These specialists are child psychologists and child psychiatrists. A psychologist can make the diagnosis and offer cognitive/behavior therapy but cannot prescribe appropriate medication. The psychologist will refer the child to a physician for medication. The child psychiatrist can diagnosis ADHD and prescribe appropriate medication, but rarely does child/family treatment.

All professionals use the *Diagnostic and Statistical Manual of Mental Disorders* (DSM-IV) by the American Psychiatric Association as a guide in the diagnosis of ADHD. The following information has been extracted from the DSM-IV to help a parent understand the criteria used to make an ADHD diagnosis. After reading this information, you should be able to decide if you need to make an appointment with an ADHD specialist. If your child has already received an official diagnosis from a qualified specialist, you may want to skip this part and go to the home treatment section of this chapter, called Sanity Savers.

Because ADHD and Learning Disabilities are not the same, a general look at the criteria used to diagnose LD is included at the conclusion of the discussion on ADHD. Often ADHD and LD coexist. It is important to remember that ADHD children can learn, but they cannot concentrate long enough or sit still long enough to make good progress in school without treatment. The learning disabled child has small brain abnormalities that interfere with processing academic material. A fun diagnostic technique is suggested in this chapter that will give parents enough information to make a decision regarding the wisdom of referring their child to a learning disabilities specialist. Most school systems have one or more learning specialists available who can officially diagnosis a learning disability. Let's get started!

Diagnostic Criteria from DSM-IV

The Diagnostic and Statistical Manual-IV requires that before a diagnosis of ADHD is given, there must be a pervasive pattern of inattention and/or hyperactivity-impulsivity that is more severe than is typically observed in individuals at a comparable level and age development. These problems must be of early origin; that is, there must be signs of inattention, hyperactivity, or impulsivity before the age of seven. These problems must markedly affect two or more life settings, such as home, school, work, or social functioning. There must be clear and convincing evidence that your child can't pay attention, can't stay focused, can't track, and is very easily distracted. Often inattention is accompanied by excessive energy, hyperactivity, and impulsivity. A hyperactive child is not necessarily one who chases his screaming sister down a hallway with knife in hand. Although that could be the case, usually what a parent sees is a lot of fidgeting, excessive body movement, can't sit still, and boundless energy. Impulsivity is characterized by speaking or acting improperly without first thinking about the effect those words or actions will have on others. ADHD impulsive children get into trouble over the silliest things. They just don't think before they speak or act. Parents take note of this: everything I just said must be much more pronounced and obvious than what is typically observed in most developing children with high energy. ADHD children are extreme in all of the areas mentioned above. To get a real and true diagnosis of ADHD, the problem patterns mentioned above must be observed and noted before a child is seven years old. ADHD doesn't start in junior high. You will notice these symptoms by the first or second grade. You must be able to clearly see these ADHD type symptoms at home, school, and with friends. Some ADHD children are noticeably hyperactive but some are not. Even children who appear to be mostly calm can have ADHD if they demonstrate clear evidence of gross inattention or distractibility. A child does not have to be hyperactive to receive a diagnosis of ADHD.

Let's take a closer look at the heart and soul of ADHD. ADHD children are inattentive, hyperactive, impulsive, or all three.

1. Inattentive-distractibility

    This is the foundation upon which the ADHD diagnosis is built. These children are easily distracted, careless, sloppy, unperceptive, and unobservant. Even if they identify what to focus on, they usually quickly lose their focus and cannot stick to a task. They get distracted from their tasks easily. At times the child with ADHD will be too focused, or hyper-focused. If they are highly interested in something, like a computer game, it is very difficult to get them to break away to do something else. It is not as if the child just doesn't want to attend to a task. They can't make themselves attend to something that is boring or that they consider too difficult. An ADHD child who loves football can memorize fifty football plays because he finds them interesting, but he cannot make himself do ten pages of social studies reading he finds boring. ADHD children are chemically programmed to be inattentive, and there is no way that math will ever successfully compete with football or computer games, unless the neurochemistry is balanced.

A word of caution: ADHD is not the only cause of inattention. Nervous, anxious, tense, uptight, and restless children may also have trouble focusing and staying on task. Depressed children also have trouble tracking and staying focused. A parent must be careful not to leap to the ADHD diagnosis without first considering anxiety and depression as a possible cause of inattention.

2. Hyperactivity

Parents often think of a hyperactive child as one who runs down the grocery aisles screaming and bumping into other shoppers. They may picture a child bouncing on the bed, slamming a pillow against the bed post with millions of feathers floating in the air. This, indeed, may be a hyperactive child, but more often, hyperactive children are wiggly, fidgety, or squirming children who are in constant motion. They cannot sit still, and one body part or another is moving at all times. They drum their fingers, tap their pencils, swing their legs, or bounce their feet. These kids also have the unique ability to talk nonstop about nothing. That's a hyperactive kid!

3. Impulsivity

ADHD children have great difficulty stopping to think before they act. They get around to offending almost everyone by a variety of thoughtless acts. They are well known to teachers as the children who always interrupt and blurt out answers before being called upon. They are very annoying to parents because they incessantly interrupt when their parents are visiting with friends or talking on the telephone. A young ADHD child may push another child down in order to be first in line, or he may knock a companion's building block tower over for no known reason. Older ADHD children tend to physically fight or use bully tactics. They have difficulty controlling what they say when mad, and they can be very sassy. They live in the now. Impulsive children are adept at focusing on the moment but lack the capacity to shift and focus on the future or on the consequences of their present actions. When a child is primarily focused on the now, impulsive acts make sense to her. This child rarely evaluates the long-term consequences of her moment-by-moment actions.

ADHD is diagnosed by a careful clinical history. There are no validated paper-and-pencil tests or medical procedures that can provide a fail-safe diagnosis for ADHD. The following list is taken from the DSM-IV. By looking at the list and evaluating your child against the DSM-IV diagnostic criteria, you can make a better decision about whether your child needs to be referred to a specialist. If you decide to refer your child to an expert in the field of ADHD, you will be a better historian and will be able to provide much more help to the clinician because of your familiarity with the DSM-IV criteria. You will know what the doctor is looking for and will be better equipped to provide relevant information.

Diagnostic Criteria for Attention-Deficit Hyperactivity Disorder

A. Either (1) or (2)

(1) Six (or more) of the following symptoms of inattention have persisted for at least six months to a degree that is maladaptive and inconsistent with developmental level:

Inattention

(a) often fails to give close attention to details or makes careless mistakes in schoolwork, work, or other activities

(b) often has difficulty sustaining attention in tasks or play activities

(c) often does not seem to listen when spoken to directly

(d) often does not follow through on instructions and fails to finish schoolwork, chores, duties in the workplace (not due to oppositional behavior or failure to understand instructions)

(e) often has difficulty organizing tasks and activities

(f) often avoids, dislikes, or is reluctant to engage in tasks that require sustained mental effort (such as schoolwork or homework)

(g) often loses things necessary for tasks or activities (e.g., toys, school assignments, pencils, books, or tools)

(h) is often easily distracted by extraneous stimuli

(i) is often forgetful in daily activities

(2) Six (or more) of the following symptoms of hyperactivity impulsivity have persisted for at least six months to a degree that is maladaptive and inconsistent with developmental level:

Hyperactivity

(a) often fidgets with hands or feet, or squirms in seat

(b) often leaves seat in classroom or in other situations in which remaining seated is expected

(c) often runs about or climbs excessively in situations in which it is inappropriate (in adolescents or adults, may be limited to subjective feelings of restlessness)

(d) often has difficulty playing or engaging in leisure activities quietly

(e) is often "on the go" or often acts as if "driven by a motor"

(f) often talks excessively

Impulsivity

(g) often blurts out answers before questions have been completed

(h) often has difficulty awaiting turn

(i) often interrupts or intrudes on others (e.g., butts, into conversations or games)

B. Some hyperactive-impulsive or inattentive symptoms that caused impairment were present before the age of seven years.

C. Some impairment from the symptoms is present in two or more settings (e.g., at school (or work) and at home.

D. There must be clear evidence of clinically significant impairment in social, academic, or occupational functioning.

Learning Disabilities

The various parts of the brain mature at different rates. Different sections of the brain must be correctly wired before a young child can learn his ABCs or count to ten, but some children with learning disabilities may consistently reverse letters and numbers because their brains are just not yet ready to read and do math. Educational learning specialists can help the brain to connect and wire itself correctly. Later in this chapter, I will discuss Stimulation Learning, which is a home exercise that can greatly help with the wiring process and with the learning of complex skills. If, after reading the Learning Disabilities section, you believe you have enough evidence to suspect LD, make an appointment with the school for an evaluation. You have a legal right to request from the school an evaluation under Public Law 94–142, Individuals with Disabilities Education Act (IDEA), at no charge to you. If the evaluation identifies specific learning disabilities, the school system will develop an Individual Education Plan (IEP) and, with your permission, will implement special services to fulfill the objectives of the IEP.

About 30–40 percent of the time, ADHD is accompanied by a Learning Disability. Remember, ADHD children have the ability to learn academic material. When neurochemistry is balanced, their brains function very well. Learning Disabled children have brain development glitches that interfere with the ability to fully and comprehensively learn. There are four types of these brain dysfunctions:

1. Input Disabilities
2. Integration Disabilities
3. Memory Disabilities
4. Output Disabilities

Below is a brief look at the essence of each of these dysfunctions.

1. Input Disabilities

We receive most sensory input from our eyes and ears for our brains to process. Smell and touch are also input sources for our brains, but the sheer volume of input from our eyes and ears is much greater. Children who suffer input problems may reverse numbers and letters. They may have trouble reading because they read the same line twice, put the middle letters of a word first, try to read from right to left, or skip lines when reading. Information is not correctly put into the brain; therefore, output is faulty. These children may be clumsy because they have depth-perception problems, and often spill liquid, knock things over, or fall out of chairs for no reason. They often cannot remember which way is left and which way is right. They may have difficulty sounding out words. These children can have difficulty distinguishing the subtle differences between similar sounding words like fun and run. When a child has input deficits, she may not start hearing an instruction being given to her until the second or third sentence of the directive. Parents of children with input disabilities often complain that when the children are playing, they never hear parental directives. Parents' voices are simply background noise, and the children innocently ignore their parents because of an ADHD/LD deficit.

2. Integration Disabilities

    After the brain receives input, it must do something with the information. For example, the brain must be well enough developed and properly wired to tell the muscles of the body how to do things like write words, hop, or tie shoelaces. Some children with integration problems can be extremely sensitive to touch on the skin. They don't like to be held or stroked. They complain that shirt labels hurt or that their underwear is too tight. In class, they fidget and rearrange their clothes. They can't listen because something is irritating their skin. They hate for their hair to be combed or brushed, because it hurts. They may have great difficulty with fine motor tasks like buttoning shirts or stacking pennies. They may not be able to stand on one foot and keep their balance. They may not be able to hop in place or master riding a two-wheel bike. Their writing may be painfully slow and very sloppy.

    Once information comes into the brain, something must be done with it. Information must be understood, processed, and integrated. A child with an integration disability may see and hear correctly (input), but get mixed up (failure to integrate) when trying to output accurately. She may clearly see the teacher write on the board, "32 + 8 = ?," but on her paper, she writes "23 + 8 =?" She may want to say, "You either shape up or ship out," but when it comes out, she may say, "You better ship up or shape out," and never know she reversed the saying. The child with integration problems rarely catches on to a joke, and she may fail to get the obvious moral to a story.

    Children with integration disabilities may be extremely disorganized. Their backpacks are a mess, and they lose stuff and put important papers in the wrong place. They may go to the trouble of doing their homework, but forget to turn it in. They absolutely cannot get things organized in the morning as they prepare to leave for school. Children with integration deficits also have trouble organizing their thoughts. They may tell the middle of the story first, and they are well-known for rambling as they try to tell something of importance. They drive some mothers crazy.

3. Memory Disabilities

The brain not only must accurately receive information and integrate it, but the information must also be stored for later retrieval. There are two forms of memory. Short-term memory is the ability to retain information long enough to accomplish a required task. Remembering telephone numbers is a great example. Once you've looked a number up, you remember it long enough to dial the number, and then you forget it. Some information is stored in long-term memory. Information that we use repetitively, such as our names and where we live, are remembered forever. Children with memory disabilities typically have trouble with short-term memory. While most children remember something with only a few practice repetitions, children with a memory disability will require many, many repetitions in order to retain the information. These children can almost never remember and carry out three instructions. They can, however, remember one directive at a time and carry it out. Children with memory disabilities may start to tell about something that happened in school, but forget the point or lose track of what they were saying. They may, with numerous repetitions, memorize their spelling words, but then forget 50 percent of them the next day. The information they put in their brain doesn't stick. A mother may say to her child that his room must be clean before he can go to his friend's birthday party at 1:00 p.m., but at 11:30 a.m., when his mom checks, the room hasn't been touched. When confronted, the child may claim he was never told to clean up or simply say, "I forgot."

4. Output Disabilities

This one comes in two forms: language deficits and motor deficits. Let's look at an example of a language deficit. Jim's dad asks him a direct question such as, "Tell me three good things you did in school today." His dad may only get a very long, blank stare. Nothing comes out. On the other hand, if his dad just hangs out with Jim, Jim is likely to tell him a lot about what happened in school that day. When children come to my office, I usually ask them to tell me why they are there or what their parents wanted them to talk about. Some children quietly say, "My temper," but others will sit there for five minutes and say nothing. I frequently interject, "Are you thinking?" and they often say, "No."

When considering motor output disability, look at the child's ability to climb, jump, ride a bike, or hit and catch a baseball. Children with motor output disability are often awkward and do very poorly in sports. Their brains cannot accurately tell the body muscle groups what to do. Very poor handwriting is a frequent sign of motor disability. The writing fingers, hand, and arm get tired quickly, and writing becomes illegible. It is difficult for this child to copy anything off of the board, and they may do it extremely slowly.

Do not despair if your child has a learning disability. They can work with a learning disability expert with great results. Remember, the problem is a brain maturity and brain wiring dysfunction. Once the brain is connected and wired properly, the learning disability usually improves. In the next section, I will share with you a practical, parent-friendly method to examine your child for the possibility of a learning disorder.

The Quarter Game

I have, for many years, used the Quarter Game in my office to help me identify the potential for learning disabilities and ADHD diagnoses. This exercise can serve you well in your efforts to decide if your child needs to be referred to a professional learning disabilities expert. Quickly read through the quarter game but slow down when you come to the "analyzing the data" part. The analyzing the data section helps you make sense of the quarter game.

1. Get a quarter and tell your child that you are going to play a game with him or, if the child is nine to ten years old, tell him that the two of you are going to do some interesting things with a quarter. This game is very useful for children of all ages, particularly those between the ages of six and ten, but children eleven years and older may see the game as dumb and not fully cooperate. Write down your child's responses to the game, and if he fails a part of the game, refer to the information below to see which learning disability applies to that function.

2. Ask your child to memorize four terms, and you will come back to them later to see if he can remember them in order. The terms are: quarter, apple, Mr. Johnson, and tunnel. Keep going over the words until they

are memorized. If the words are memorized in three to four tries, all is well. If it takes five to fifteen trials, consider memory disability. In about ten minutes come back to the four words and ask your child to say them to you in order.

3. Note the dominant hand. Is the child right-handed or left-handed? Tell him that you are going to toss the quarter to him and that he is to catch it with the dominant hand. Look for eye-hand coordination. If it goes into the dominant hand and rolls out, that's okay, but if it hits him in the chest or misses the hand altogether, consider input disability.

4. Put the quarter on the child's head toward the crown or back part of the head. Ask him to balance it there for fifteen seconds. Next, tell him to listen to all of the instructions and to do them one at a time. With your fingers, touch the bottom of his chin and look for any reaction like flinching. Tell your child that you are going to lift his chin until the quarter falls from his head, but he is not to look where it falls. (Impulsive children can't help but look.) Spot the quarter and tell him to look over his right or left shoulder and find it on the floor. Then, tell him to leave his right foot in place, step on the quarter with his left foot, and pick it up with his right hand. If he can follow all of the instructions, all is well. If he fails to do some or all of your instructions, if he can't keep the quarter balanced on his head, or if he flinches at your touch, he may potentially have input, integration, and output problems.

5. Put the quarter in your child's right hand. Put both arms down to his sides and ask him to squeeze the quarter rapidly again and again. Look at his left hand as he squeezes the quarter repeatedly in his right hand. Note if the fingers move or twitch on his left hand. Repeat with the left hand. If his fingers move or twitch, make a note that he may have input, integration, and output problems.

6. Place the quarter on the floor about ten to twelve feet away from your child. Ask him to walk heel-to-toe in a straight line to the quarter. When he gets to the quarter, have him pick it up with his left hand. Make a note if he loses his balance or if he can't consistently put his heel against his toe and walk a straight line. You can remind him once to remember to toe-heel all the way to the quarter. If he fails this coordination text, note potential input or output disabilities.

7. Put the quarter on the floor and ask your child to stand on one foot and balance on one foot for five to ten seconds, then repeat with the other

foot. Make a note of his ability to balance. Next, ask him to step on the quarter with his right foot and hop up and down on the quarter. Ask him to hit the quarter as many times as possible. Count the hits aloud. Repeat with the left foot. He may not be able to hit the quarter at all, or hit it only once or twice. Note evidence of poor coordination.

Also make a note about whether he is right-footed or left-footed. He should be able to hit the quarter more often with his dominant foot. At this point, you will know if he catches with his right hand and if he is right- or left-footed. If he is unable to do the hopping successfully, make a note of poor coordination and potential input and output problems.

8. Next, ask your child to tell you the four words he memorized. If he gets three out of four, all is well, but if not, note potential memory problems.

9. Give him four instructions to carry out in order. Say them only once. You can make up your own, but in my office, I give these instructions: "Take the quarter and give it to your mother. Take a business card from the holder on the little table and give it to me. Pick up a toy from the toy chest and place it in that chair. Lastly, draw a circle with an X in it on this pad." Note the number of instructions he remembers and the order in which he does the instructions. If he gets three in order, he has done well. If he remembers to do all four, but not in order, he has done pretty well. If he remembers only one or two of the four, note potential input, integration, and memory problem.

10. Ask your child to make a peep hole with his dominant hand by touching his thumb and forefinger together. Let's assume it's his right hand. Hold up the quarter in your fingers and ask him to "spy" the quarter through his peep hole. Note if he puts his right hand up to his right eye or left eye. If he puts his right hand to his left eye, note potential input and output problems.

11. Ask your child to put the quarter between the palms of his hands and hold his hands above his head. His hands should look like "praying hands." Ask him to fold his fingers together (demonstrate for him by interlocking your own fingers), and place his folded hands in his lap. Make a note of which thumb is on top. If he is right hand dominant, his right thumb should be over his left thumb. Also make a note of whether he dropped the quarter or if it is still in the palms of his hands. By this time, you should have a clear picture of his right or left dominance. If he is left-thumbed and right-handed, note potential input and output problems.

12. Next, ask him to sit on the edge of a chair or couch and cross his legs like a grown-up. (Demonstrate for him.) Ask him to alternate right over left and left over right a total of four times. Then, ask him to cross his legs in the way that feels best. Note if he is right-handed and favors his right foot, but likes to cross his left leg over his right leg. By now, you will know if his nervous system has fully separated into right or left dominance. Some children with learning disabilities are right-handed, left-legged, right-thumbed, left-eyed, and right-footed. Note that he may have a potential input and output problem if he's right-handed, but left-legged.

13. If your child is right-handed, put the quarter in his left hand and ask him to write the alphabet on a piece of paper. Look for reversals, missing letters, or out of place letters. Observe the speed with which he writes the alphabet. Note if he is very slow to write the letters. Note if he mixes capital letters with lowercase letters. If he is painfully slow, reverses letters, or gets letters out of place and he is in second grade or higher, note that he may have potential input and output problems.

14. Repeat the above instruction with numbers, one to ten. Look for reversed numbers and a very slow response.

15. Dictate a sentence for your child to write. If your child is six or seven, dictate "The dog ran." If he is older, dictate, "The dog ran across the street." He should be able to spell all of these words. Note spelling and word order. Note whether he had to ask for a repeat. Note if he is very slow writing the sentence. Look for letter reversals. If he can't remember the sentence, or if he misspells more than one word, note it. If he made any of these errors, note potential input and output disabilities.

16. Lastly, directly ask your child which one of the quarter activities he liked best. If he stares and fails to come up with an answer or his answer is delayed by one minute or more, note potential output disability.

17. Give him the quarter. He earned it!

Analyzing the Data

1. If there is strong evidence of mixed right/left-dominance, a referral for further evaluation should be considered. If he is left-eyed and left-thumbed, but everything else is right side, a referral is not indicated. If your child is right-handed, right-footed, but he is also left-thumbed, left-legged, and left-eyed, his left hand moved when he squeezed the

quarter with his right hand, and he failed four of the following nine exercises, a referral to a learning disabilities expert is indicated.

2. Mark pass or fail for each of the nine exercises:

   A. Memorizing four words: If he needed many repetitions, mark as failed.

   Recalling four words: If he recalled only one of the four, mark as failed.

   B. If he could not follow your directions when you put the quarter on his head and he dropped it to the floor, mark as failed.

   C. Evaluate remembering four directions in order. He failed directions if he could only remember two of the four directions.

   D. If he could not walk a straight line toe-to-heel, mark as failed for coordination.

   E. If he could not hop on the quarter and hit it at least two times, mark as failed for coordination. If he could not balance on one foot for five seconds, mark as failed for balance.

   F. When writing the alphabet, if there were reversals, letters left out, or if he was painfully slow, mark as failed for letters.

   G. If he reversed any numbers, mark as failed numbers.

   H. If he could not write a dictated sentence correctly, mark as failed dictation.

   I. If he could not answer a direct question or if he paused for more than one minute before answering, mark as failed for questioning.

Evaluation Conclusion

The quarter game is not a test for learning disabilities or impulsivity. The quarter game has no research studies to support its conclusions. I have, however, used it in my office for forty years and have found the game to be very useful as a guideline to help me decide if a referral to a specialist is warranted. I would suggest that you use the quarter game as a general assessment to determine if learning disabilities may be present in your son or daughter.

I have also found that the quarter game provides useful information that can be used to detect ADHD. The game requires focus and attention to carry out the tasks. If a child picks up a toy or wanders off, it suggests distractibility. If a child becomes quickly bored and resists instructions or is uninterested in continuing, it suggests ADHD symptoms. Non-ADHD children have fun and find the game interesting and stimulating. The game often brings out strong signs of impulsivity, which flags ADHD as a possibility. For example, when you tell the child not to look where the quarter lands on the floor after it drops from the top of his head, the impulsive child cannot stop himself from looking over his shoulder to see where the quarter stopped. The impulsive child will insist on modifying the four instructions and doing it his way. ADHD children do not listen well. Their brain is flying at one hundred miles per hour, and they will start doing the instructions immediately, before they have heard all four instructions (impulsivity), or will only half listen after the second instruction. Because of inattention, they can't remember and execute all four. Some children get irritated or angry when directions are given, and this, too, is an ADHD symptom.

If your child has mixed right and left dominance problems, and he failed four of the nine quarter exercises, I would recommend that you ask the school district to perform a learning disabilities evaluation. Request a conference with a school learning disabilities specialist and take the notes you have recorded from your child's performance on the quarter game. Present your findings to the specialist. The specialist probably will not be familiar with the quarter game, so refer him to this chapter. Be patient and kind, but be persistent. Most specialists will be impressed with your concern and supportive data. Using the quarter game, you have good evidence to support your belief that your child may have certain learning disabilities, and a professional screening evaluation is justified. All will probably go well, but do not be discouraged or back off if school personnel resist your request.

If the learning specialist finds learning disabilities, he will recommend a training program to address your child's learning issues. If learning disabilities are not confirmed through testing and observation, then thank him for his professional courtesy, and be glad! Remember ADHD is not considered a learning disability under IDEAS. If the expert finds that your child qualifies for an ADHD diagnosis, the school must make accommodations for a child with ADHD. For example, an ADHD child may have reduced homework assignments or he may be given twenty extra minutes to finish a test. When a learning disability is diagnosed, a special plan must be formulated to address these issues, but when the diagnosis is ADHD without learning disabilities, the student is only given accommodations. However, sensible accommodations can be very helpful to an ADHD student's progress through school.

How to Get Your ADHD Child to Pay Attention to You

Children with legitimate diagnoses of ADHD usually present three problems to their parents. They usually have problems with both academic performance and behavior control in the school setting. They usually have problems with self-control at home. ADHD children often take huge liberties at home at the expense of their parents, even if they are well-behaved in the classroom. A third problem ADHD children present is in the social realm. They frequently act up in public places or at a friend's house. I will address these three categories of ADHD problems.

This is a chapter about ADHD, not a book on the subject. There are many good books about ADHD, and I recommend getting a few and absorbing them. There are two authors I particularly like to read. Any book by Russell A. Barkley, PhD or Larry B. Silver, MD will be useful in expanding your awareness about ADHD. Two books by these authors that I have found very helpful are:

1. Larry B. Silver, MD. *Attention-Deficit Hyperactivity Disorder*, 2nd edition, (American Psychiatric Press, Inc., 1999).
2. Russell A. Barkley, PhD. *Taking Charge of ADHD* (Guilford Press, 2000).

The control and repair methods suggested in this chapter are not promoted as the end-all and only way to treat ADHD at home. I have found them to be very useful in my practice, and I think they will prove to be very useful for you too. I have named these techniques Sanity Savers. Successfully raising a child with ADHD can make you feel a little crazy at times. Teachers with one or more ADHD kids in their classroom can be brought to the point of despair. Even your child will, at times, think he must be nuts. These Sanity Savers may be just what you need to help you, your child, and his teacher save your collective sanity!

There are eight Sanity Saver methods in this book for your consideration. Four of the eight sanity savers are elaborately discussed in previous chapters, so I will not review them again here. I would recommend that you go back and review the full explanation of Behavior Shaping, Now or Later, Pillow Talk, and More Not Less before you apply these techniques. Four of the Sanity Saver techniques (Stimulation Learning, The Parent Strike,

Time-Out, and Beat the Buzzer) are original to this chapter and will be discussed in detail below.

Lastly, let me review the guiding theme of this book. The most important thing you can teach your children is how to willingly live under parental authority. If you can successfully teach this concept, your ADHD child will grow up to be a man or woman who can live under self-control in a society of rules and order, and you will probably want to keep him or her! Because of their chemical imbalance, ADHD children are prone to live out of control, but the following methods will help support your efforts to get your child to willingly live under your authority and develop self-control.

Sanity Saver One: Behavior Shaping

The worst thing that can happen to an ADHD child is becoming discouraged and defeated. Enormous academic progress can be obtained in the classroom if the child does not feel like a broken or disposable product. We live in a very negative world, and most school systems operate on a system that emphasizes the errors made in the classroom. ADHD children make many mistakes that other children do not make. We cannot change the negativity of the world, but it doesn't have to be that way in your house. Home is where you are in charge. It's at home that your child will recharge low batteries and ready himself to return to a negative, critical world. Your influence on your child is incredible. For your child, it is your opinion that counts. Behavior Shaping is an easy-to-learn and simple-to-apply rewards program that ADHD children love. (See chapter 3.)

Sanity Saver Two: Stimulation Learning

If you have an ADHD child in your home, you have probably received a note from his teacher pointing out a behavioral or academic problem with an implied hope that you will do something that will help to resolve the classroom problem. Teachers have many problems to deal with in the modern classroom. Their ability to administer discipline is greatly restricted. They have high curriculum goals and often have to prepare students to pass the standardized tests required by their state. Classrooms are crowded, and teachers are required to make reasonable accommodations for the ADHD students in their classroom. They need as much help as a parent can reasonably provide. Stimulation Learning can provide that help. Stimulation Learning is also useful in obtaining better homework production from underachieving learners.

As mentioned earlier in this chapter, 30–40 percent of students with an ADHD diagnosis also experience various forms of learning disabilities. I have seen remarkable results with LD children who reverse letters and numbers, who have memory problems, and who have messy handwriting. Stimulation Learning has been a wonderful asset to students who have basic skill deficits in spelling, ABCs, addition, subtraction, and multiplication. First- and second-graders must master basic skills to be successful in the later grades, and Stimulation Learning has proven over and over to be helpful to students needing to master basic skills. Reading can be a nightmare for ADHD children. They often do not read to remember, but hurry through to finish. Reading can be very boring to an ADHD child, and they will guess at words just to get through the assignment. Stimulation Learning helps all children to focus and concentrate more efficiently.

Here is how Stimulation Learning works. It is clear that the brain needs a rich supply of blood and oxygen for it to operate efficiently. The brain of an ADHD child functions better when stimulated. The following is a teaching story based upon one of my young ADHD clients.

Jim was seven years old and couldn't spell "cat." His spelling was horrible. I gave him four words to spell: cat, man, coat, and please. He misspelled all four words. I printed all four words on a white piece of paper and asked him to stand in front of me so I could demonstrate how I wanted him to learn to spell these four words. I did a deep knee bend as I said the letter "C." I did another deep knee bend and said the letter "O," then another knee bend as I said the letter "A," another knee bend and the letter "T" and lastly, I did a knee bend as I said the full word, "Coat." Next we did it together. We both said "C" and a deep knee bend, then "O," etc., until the word was spelled. Then we did our last knee bend and said, "Coat." We repeated the same processes several times. Next, I made him go through the routine, but this time I had him shout, "C-O-A-T," interspersed with deep knee bends. I then had him whisper the same routine. Next, I instructed him to turn his back to me and spell "coat" while doing his deep knee bends. By this time, his pulse was up, and he was breathing deeply, sending blood and oxygen to his brain. We went through the entire list of words together. I often vary the routine by telling the child to put his right index finger on his nose and hold his left ear lobe with his left thumb and index finger. Then we spin fully around and say, "C," then again and say, "O," etc., until the word is spelled. ADHD kids love stimulation and variety. After only six minutes of Stimulation Learning, I gave him a test. He spelled all four words correctly! There is even better news to report. After a two-week gap in appointments, I gave him the same four words to spell. He correctly spelled all four words after a two-week lay off and no practice. This story has been repeated over and over with many children. Remember, variety helps keep up interest. I have used hopping, running in place, and jumping jacks to stimulate.

Children with ADHD and Learning Disabilities often have trouble remembering what they read. They may get distracted easily, not know how to sound out words, not know the meaning of key words, or read to get through the reading assignment as fast as possible. Here is what I have done hundreds of times with excellent results. I have a number of age-appropriate books in my office, and I will choose one to approximately match the child's age. For nine-year-old Clyde, I chose *The Lion King*. He read a page aloud, but couldn't pronounce four of the words. I wrote the four words on a white piece of paper, and we went through the deep knee bend routine and practiced the words for about three minutes. He re-read the page and pronounced all four words correctly, but could tell me very little of the meaning of the entire page. I told Clyde that he was having a little trouble remembering what he read, so his brain needed more stimulation. I asked Clyde to stand and do twenty deep knee bends and then re-read the page, but this time, I asked him to read to remember. He was able to accurately remember what he read, but when he read the next page, he could not tell me what he had just read. I told him that his brain needed a little more stimulation, so he should do another twenty deep knee bends, and then reread the page, reading to remember. He was able to accurately tell me the meaning of that page. I next said to Clyde, "I want you to read the next page, and don't forget to read to remember." He read the next page and was able to tell me its meaning without stimulation. Clyde's memory was miraculously healed because of the effect of stimulation. (But he hated those deep knee bends!)

There are two forces working simultaneously in the Clyde story. The first force is the brain stimulation, and the other force is the ordeal. Clyde needed the blood and oxygen for clear thinking, but he also caught on very quickly that if he didn't read and remember, he would have to do another set of twenty deep knee bends. His motivation to read for accuracy was greatly accelerated. He could only escape the ordeal if he read to remember.

For children who have trouble getting to work on their homework, I start them off with twenty deep knee bends. Every ten minutes, they do another set of deep knee bends. Motivation is increased, accuracy is increased, and speed is increased using Stimulation Learning. If you will be creative, imaginative, resourceful, and inventive, you will be able to find many ways to use Stimulation Learning. It is an adaptive technique that can be applied in a variety of ways. My examples are designed to tweak your interest, teach you how to use it, and encourage you, but they definitely are not the only ways to apply Stimulation Learning.

Always remember and never forget that ADHD children's brains need stimulation to do their best thinking. In school, teachers tell students to sit down, be quiet, and learn. ADHD children might do better if they stood up, ran around the room, screamed, and then sat down, got quiet, and learned. Stimulation is an aid for learning. Use this concept wisely and you will see good improvement in the academic performance of your child.

Always remember and never forget that Stimulation Learning encourages and promotes motivation, pleasure in doing things, and attention. In part, this is true because the principle of escape learning is involved in Stimulation Learning. It is true that the brain is stimulated, but it is also obvious to the child that he will have to continue to do deep knee bends, jumping jacks, or twirling around with a finger on his nose until he successfully learns the spelling list or math facts. Stimulation Learning is a great motivator for obtaining effort and purpose from your child. Use it well, and it could save your sanity, your child's teacher's sanity, and your child's sanity!

Sanity Saver Three: Now or Later

Punishment for an ADHD child usually must be very firm for it to work in a positive direction. ADHD children are often in trouble with someone. They make many mistakes that bring sharp punishment from various authority figures such as parents, teachers, neighbors, scout leaders, Sunday school teachers, and older children. They're punished so often that they sometimes become desensitized to punishment, and commonly used punishments fail to have the desired effect.

The Now or Later Technique (chapter 6), is a correction method that is truly effective, even with ADHD kids. The Now or Later Technique puts you in charge again because a child cannot control later. I would recommend that you actively look for an opportunity to use the Now or Later Technique. A child needs to have the full-blown program applied once, so that the easy follow-up technique can be used. Read the Now or Later chapter to get a more comprehensive overview of this powerful technique. Saving your sanity is worth the read!

Sanity Saver Four: Pillow Talk

ADHD children have difficulty breaking old, useless, inappropriate habits, and replacing them with more useful behaviors. Pillow Talk (chapter 5) can help a child with ADHD install mental brakes that can help them avoid impulsive behavior. Current research now suggests that the executive, problem-solving part of the brain is active at night while we sleep. Pillow Talk uses this understanding of how the brain works. Read the Pillow Talk chapter to get a comprehensive understanding of how to use this innovative technique.

Sanity Saver Five: More Not Less

Read the More Not Less chapter (chapter 8) to get a full appreciation for how this technique works. The More Not Less Technique works best for children between the ages of three and twelve. This technique is a disguised ordeal therapy. The entire outcome depends strictly on the teaching value of escape learning. ADHD children, especially those with learning disabilities, often are unorganized, forgetful, easily distracted, willful, and impulsive. This is fertile ground to develop a gaggle of bad habits. When scolding doesn't work, when take-aways don't work, when loss of privileges doesn't help, or a whack on the fanny doesn't do the trick, try the More Not Less Technique. It could save your sanity.

Sanity Saver Six: Time-Out

I am pretty neutral about time-outs. I like the method, and it is very popular. Time-out works well for some children, but not so well for others. My daughter literally hated isolation, but my son didn't mind much. If I sent him to his room, it became a pirate ship. If I isolated him by the wall, he played games with shadows on the wall. He was creative. Time-out worked for Amanda, who would promise to correct anything to get out of jail, but for Mark, time-out was useless. Use it if it works for you. Why do I list it as a sanity saver?

There is one situation in which I think time-out works every time. I cannot count the number of times parents have come to my office and said, "My kids never mind me in the car. They fight all the time!" Their kids bicker, push, shove, scream, and cry when in the car. Parents are very limited in what they can do to correct the situation. The More Not Less Technique can work here, but Time-Out can also do the trick.

Here is what I would recommend. Stage a practice drive. In this case, you actually have nowhere to go, but you pretend to be on your way to some-place important. In about five minutes, your children will start their bicker-ing and fighting over nothing. That's your cue to pull into the first parking lot and say, "Kids, because you are fighting, I'm going to have to put you in time-out." Make them get out of the car, and have one sit by the back wheel while the other sits by the front wheel. Make sure they have proper clothes if it is winter. If it is summer and the asphalt is blistering hot, stay in the car with the air conditioning on. Sit in stony silence until they are quiet. After a five-to-ten-minute time-out, put them in the car, or return to the car, and ask if they are ready to go on without fighting. Get started again and drive until the first signs of fighting start again, which is usually in about forty-five seconds. Pull into the first available parking lot and repeat the five-to-ten-minute time-out. Continue the pull over/time out routine until they can successfully ride for thirty minutes without bickering. Praise them for their self-control and return home. Later that day, load the kids up for another drive. Don't tell them that you are just practicing. Pretend to be on your way to an important event. If they bicker and fight, repeat the time-out routine until they can ride for thirty minutes without fighting. The next day, take another drive. One weekend of Time-Outs will usually break this dis-ruptive cycle. However, in the next two to three weeks, they invariably will once again slipup and start bickering. That is your cue to say, "If the fight-ing doesn't stop right now, we are going to have a time-out." That simple reminder that you mean business is usually enough. If they continue, pull over for a time-out. Nothing you have to do is more important than teach-ing your children to willingly live under your authority. If you're late, it's okay, because your priorities are in the correct order. Children first! This one, for sure, will save your sanity.

Sanity Saver Seven: Beat the Buzzer

ADHD children have many problems with organization and promptness. They become easily distracted and derailed from their assigned tasks. Mornings are very difficult for a child who has attention and distraction problems. Here is a typical scene.

Billy, twelve years old, is awakened by mom and told to start getting ready for school. It is breakfast time, but Billy hasn't come down to break-fast. His mom goes to his room, and there Billy is, still in his PJs, playing a video game. His mom is angry, of course, but Billy shrugs, and simply replies, "I forgot what time it was." It's a battle every morning to get Billy out the door to catch the school bus. There are many available training tech-niques that will address this problem. For example, his mom could let Billy experience the consequences of not getting ready for school. He, of course, will miss the bus, his mom will have to take him, and he'll be late. His mom could say, "I have an errand, and I will be leaving the house at 10:00 a.m. I will take you to school then." The consequence is that Billy is late with no parental excuse, so he will have to serve detention, and since he missed two hours of school, he will probably have extra homework to do as well. I like natural consequences, but I like Beat the Buzzer better.

The night before school, Billy's mom explains the new rules. She will set the portable kitchen timer for 7:40 a.m., and Billy must beat the buzzer by walking out of the door before it rings. If he doesn't beat the buzzer, he will lose thirty minutes of free time for every minute he goes past 7:40 a.m. This means that he will go to bed thirty minutes earlier for every minute he goes over his time. This is a wonderful tool. First of all, getting ready on time becomes an interesting game of competition. Secondly, kids hate to go to bed early. There are a few who play a hard game and will lose so much time that they will have to go to bed immediately upon arrival from school, and straight to bed it is, with no play and no distractions. Lying in bed, covered up with lights off and shades drawn is the punishment for not beating the buzzer. It is surprising how many children never have to serve any penalty. They just seem to find a way to beat the buzzer.

Sanity Saver Eight: The Parent Strike

A family can be described as a team. The job of each individual is to help the team. Another way of describing a family is as a system. If one piece of the system breaks down, it affects all parts of the system. The following is true no matter how you describe a family: "If one part suffers all parts suffer." If an ADHD child doesn't contribute to the family in a healthy way, all family members pay a high price for the child's lack of cooperation. There are four behaviors a family cannot tolerate. These are the four horsemen of the apocalypse!

1. Verbal insults—cursing, screaming, shouting insults; or severe putdown language like idiot, stupid, and crazy are examples of verbal abuse.
2. Physical attacks—hitting, slapping, pushing, violent threats, or breaking, throwing or hitting walls, doors, and tables are examples of physical abuse.
3. Stonewalling, stubborn defiance—walking away from mom or dad when given a direction or an icy stare while turning away in silence when asked to do something are examples of stonewalling.
4. Running away—threats of running away, running away, leaving and hiding out for hours, isolating in one's room for days are examples of running away.

Children of all ages may engage in one or more of the four horsemen of the apocalypse but ADHD teenagers are particularly prone to engage in these abuses. The parent strike works for all ages, but it tends to work very well with teenagers. Parents—especially mothers—tend to continue to provide parenting services even though abused by a child. It's very upsetting to a mother to see her child suffer or be denied essential parenting services even when being brats. The truth is that by the time an ADHD child has reached their teens, the usual, common parental disciplining methods often don't work anymore. Voice control, time-out, and take aways no longer have power over a rebellious teen. If a strong teenage boy or girl refuses to go to his room for a time-out, there is not much a mom can do about it. But all is not lost and the last chapter in the family book has not been written. There is still the parent strike!

Phil the Fit Thrower is fifteen years old and very defiant. His mother is a single mom and feels bankrupt to do anything about Phil's fits. If mom asks Phil to clean his pigsty room, Phil throws a fit. If mom wants help with preparing dinner, Phil throws a fit. If Phil wants $15 for the movies and mom doesn't have it, Phil throws a fit. When Phil throws a fit, he uses verbal abuse, physical abuse, or stonewalling. He will slam doors, break glasses, smash dishes, or he will punch a hole in the sheet rock. Phil will call his mother names like bitch and whore. Sometimes when she asks him to do a family chore, like carry out the trash, he will glare at her and walk away.

Here is what I told mother to do. I asked her to go to Phil and tell him that his behavior is abusive, and she will not tolerate his abuse any longer. She told him exactly what was abusive about his actions. Here is what she said, "Phil breaking my dishes, glasses, and pictures; punching walls; calling me a bitch and whore; and walking away from me when I ask you to do a family chore is abusive and so inappropriate. I have decided to go on strike until your apologize and tell me you will not do these things again. I will offer you no parenting services until your home behavior radically changes. This means I will not cook for you, do your laundry, fold and put away your clothes, give you lunch money, or provide transportation to or from school. The bus line is eight blocks away on 6th Street, so I would suggest you call this number and get the bus schedule of departures and arrivals. I will do nothing for you until you apologize and change your abusive behavior."

Phil was shocked, but in his heart he just knew she would give in and do all the things she had always done for him. With encouragement, mother stuck to her strike. For awhile Phil prepared his own food, rode the bus to school, and wore the same socks and underwear again and again. Mother "hung tough." It took three weeks but Phil caved in. He and mom had a healthy long talk about his behavior, and Phil apologized. He no longer abused his mother, and Phil learned a valuable lesson. For some unexplainable reason, Phil's school attendance and grades also improved.

Any hormonal teenager can, at times, go out of control. ADHD children, because of their impulsivity and tendency to live in the now, are more at risk for out of control behavior. Phil knew mother was right and he really did want to live under authority, but until mother could prove that she could control him, he knew no limits. The parent strike did save her sanity. It didn't hurt Phil's sanity either.

A Word about Medication

ADHD is a real problem that is biochemical in origin and fraught with many behavioral bad habits. The popular media has slandered stimulant medication, and many parents are very wary of medicating their children because of the bad press that medication has received. Scientific research, however, tells a rather different story about medication. Not only does it help most children attend, track, and focus better, there are no known damaging side effects to taking stimulants. Stimulant medication has been researched for fifty years, and as of this writing, no long-term negative consequences have been found.

There will occasionally be a research study that will identify a potential negative outcome of taking stimulant medication. As of the date of this writing, no negative outcome study has stood up to the test of replication. The risk of permanent harm has been found to be very, very low for stimulant medication. Scientific research continues to emerge regarding medication. Stay alert for new studies. This is a popular subject so most newspapers will report the results of such studies.

Many parents hope their child will outgrow their concentration problems without resorting to medication. Look at it this way. If your child breaks his leg in a bike accident and you pull it straight, splint it with two broomsticks, and duct tape the splints together, it is certain that the leg will mend itself. However, this child may walk with a limp and perform terribly in sports for the remainder of his life. Similarly, children with ADHD can learn to make-do and employ some offsetting accommodations, but they will very likely mentally limp for the rest of their lives. Of course, there is always the exception, but why take that chance? Medication does help and it does not harm.

Go forth. Do good.

Chapter 15

Final Thoughts

Throughout the writing of this book, I have often thanked the father who sat in my office and asked the question that set my mind ablaze. This curious father wanted me to explain, in plain English, why my therapy techniques worked. I knew they worked because I had used them thousands of times over a thirty-plus-year career. This father knew they worked because he had successfully applied many of them with his own children. I simply could not answer his question, but I wanted to.

Early in my career I developed a number of child correction techniques on my own. I have not seen them published anywhere. As I examined each psychological tool and compared one with another, to my surprise and delight, I discovered that there is a consistent theme that ties them all together. For example, the Marks Method and the Now or Later Technique seem to be quite different, but they both promote the same theme. The theme that is so important for life success, the one most important thing that a parent can teach a child is to willingly live under parental authority. If this life lesson can be successfully taught in a child's developmental years, he can grow up to be an adult who can live under self-control in a society of rules and order.

When children learn to willingly live under parental authority, they are capable of incredible adult achievements. For example:

1. They can postpone immediate reward and pleasure for higher, more fulfilling long-term goals.
2. They can go to college or vocation school, graduate, and achieve career goals.
3. They can join and succeed in the military, where cooperation with higher authority is a must.

4. They can work hard for promotion within any chosen profession.
5. They can get married, knowing they have the ability to form long-lasting relationships within a system that requires teamwork and cooperation.
6. They can live in compatibility and harmony with neighbors.
7. They can submit to the requirements of faith and religion.
8. Best of all, they have a good chance at raising children they'll want to keep.

More Thoughts about the Theme

Raising children you want to keep pivots on teaching children to willingly live under parental authority. Most parents will readily agree that parental authority is an indispensable part of childrearing, but they ignore the other part of the theme: willingness. Both parental authority and willingness on the children's part are key. Parents often jump to the authority part of child-rearing and ignore the willingness part. Other parents work 24/7 to foster good relationships with their children and may go so far as to spoil and indulge them. They systematically ignore the authority part of the equation.

Willingness

Teaching a child to willingly to live under authority starts with developing a stress-free, bonded, comfortable, relationship between parent and child. There are four general characteristics of a good parent child relationship.

1. Acceptance

   The more a parent can accept a child as they are, without a felt and pressing need to fix or change their child, the stronger the bond between parent and child becomes. This does not mean that a parent cannot correct the error of a child's ways. What this does mean is that a child does not have to correct or improve before a parent offers unconditional love and care. A child feels safe and connected if he is good enough now to get his parents' love.

2. Positive admiration

   We all live in a very negative world. We typically receive many more negative inputs than positive. For a relationship between parent and child to prosper and thrive, there must be far more positive exchanges than negative. Research suggests that for a relationship to reach a healthy level there must be five positive exchanges between parent and child for every one negative. This means that, for best results, a parent must give at least five praises for every one criticism. Unless you are a very unusual parent, this one will need a lot of work. The effort is rewarded with a great payoff. Kids like to hang out with a parent who praises, and they are definitely more compliant and cooperative with parental directives.

3. Fun

Children learn to be adults by playing and having fun. One of the fundamental characteristics of a quality relationship is the ability of the parent and child to frolic. Kids are naturals at having fun, but parents, who are busy with many things, often forget how important fun is. A strong relationship depends on having fun. Children are much more likely to willingly submit to parental authority if their relationship with their parent is laced with fun!

4. Forgiveness

Children are frequent rule-breakers and values-breakers and must be frequently forgiven. Forgiving a child's wrongs and indiscretions does not imply that a parent should embrace a system of indulgence. Discipline should be clear and firm, but when discipline has been fairly administered, then it's done and forgiveness is applied. Forgiveness is closure. Forgiveness is a period at the end of the sentence. Forgiveness prevents the harboring and internalization of parental resentment. Forgiveness should be thought of as a pardon. A pardon is something granted, not because of merit or because it is deserved, but because it is right. A pardon is the beginning of a do-over. A relationship can go on because a parent grants forgiveness. It's good for both parent and child.

Authority

Willingness to submit to parental authority is a mutation of a pleasant, bonded, stress-free relationship. Willingness is not enough without authority. Parents must also be willing to set fair and reasonable boundaries, and then enforce them with fair and reasonable methods of control.

Children are only willing to live under parental authority if they know they can trust their parents to treat them with dignity and respect. They are only willing to trust parents if they have experienced fair, reasonable, and just authority. Children can learn to trust and submit to a parent if the parent has been found to be trustworthy. Abusive, controlling, and harsh parents can obtain compliance from their children, but control comes with a high price. These children will submit to authority but not willingly. The cost to parents who use harsh correction methods is paid out in the child's teen years. In those typically difficult years, living under authority is over, with good reason. At the moment of a child's birth, every parent enters into an implied contract with his or her child. The parents' part of the contract is to form a close, bonded relationship and to set fair, firm, and reasonable rules for their child. The child's part of the implied deal is to learn to trust his parents and willingly live under their authority. If a parent does not nurture the relationship and uses mean-spirited, harsh control methods, then the contract is broken and all bets are off. Under harsh, abusive authority, a child learns to trust only himself and to survive by any means possible. This book is designed to help parents with the terms of their contract as they raise children they want to keep.

It may not seem like children want rules, boundaries, and consistent firmness, but they do. Children who live out of control live a frightening, insecure life. They know that they are not capable of running a complex family system. They intuitively know that they are not mature enough to be or capable of being the boss of their parents. If a parent does not establish firm, but reasonable authority, a child will try to take over and set rules that seem right to him. Out-of-control children constantly send out the message, "I will do what you tell me to do, but you will have to make me, and please, please make me."

Willingness and authority to a child is like electricity to a home. Without electricity, the most wonderful appliances simply do not function. Without reasonable authority, a child simply will not develop in the way God designed the system to operate.

Final Thoughts about Parents

Parents want to be in charge of their children. I have never had a parent say that the premise from which I work is lame or silly. So far, every parent is in agreement that the one best thing they can teach their child is to learn to willingly live under parental authority. They know that the principle is sound, but often, by the time parents get around to bringing their child to my office, they are bankrupt to effect any positive change in their family system. They want to, but don't know how.

There are two ways to teach children anything. A parent can either reward cooperative behavior or punish uncooperative behavior. Both systems work really well. Children will repeat anything that brings them reward and pleasure. Rewards programs are sensitive and only work if all of the laws of learning are followed. A considerable portion of this book is devoted to learning how to plan and execute an effective rewards program. I am particularly fond of the Behavior Shaping Method of rewards that I discuss in chapter 3. One of the greatest rewards a parent can give a child is praise and approval. It is so simple, yet so powerful. A parent merely has to identify one or more behaviors that a child doesn't do, and shape them into occurring on a regular basis by praising the child when they do occur. I will not review the entire method here, but I would encourage you to review chapter 3 to get a good grasp and understanding of the Behavior Shaping Method.

Punishment of uncooperative behavior is a time-honored way of teaching children to cease bad behavior and substitute cooperative behavior. Psychologists often shy away from the word punishment and substitute the phrase, "negative reinforcement." I like to call it ordeal therapy. Ordeal therapy happens when a parent creates an ordeal that is moral, legal, and ethical, from which a child can escape, but will require cooperation on the child's part. Most of my corrective methods presented in this book are based upon ordeal therapy. Parents often tell me that nothing works with their child. They have tried every punishment known to mankind, to no avail. Children are masters at taking away parental punishers. The best method a child can use is to say or act as if they don't care. A parent may say, "Go to your room." A child will say, act, or think, "I don't care." A parent may use take-aways, but all a child has to do to take away that punishment is to say, "I don't care." Methods like Pillow Talk, Marks Method, More Not Less, and Now or Later are comprised of several powerful mental health techniques, but there is a strong ordeal in each one of them. These tools, and other techniques I teach in the book, empower parents by restoring their authority with their child.

Parent Problems

Some parents find it difficult to carry out the suggested methods I offer because of a lack of time. These parents feel overwhelmed by daily demands and responsibilities. Most of the change techniques I teach in this book require a considerable up-front investment of time and energy. Some parents feel too tired and frustrated to make a big investment in the correction of behavioral problems.

Some parents complain that my therapy tools punish them more than they punish their child. They resent the time and effort it requires to successfully employ the techniques I suggest in the teaching chapters.

I must admit, without apology, that my therapy techniques are front-end-loaded, but the follow-up methods are simple and quick. The big investment of time and energy is invested in the first application of the technique, but the next application of the tool is quick and efficient. The alternative is to let things go on as they always have and see your child and your family flounder or get worse. The time investment involved with the use of ineffective correction techniques is much greater, over time, than you will ever put into using one of my proven techniques. Also, the emotional misery associated with raising an out-of-control child exacts a heavy cost to parents who love their children. My methods are extremely cost efficient over the long run.

When a parent brings a child into the world, there is a minimum eighteen-year commitment made. Parenting is not a simple task. It takes huge amounts of time and energy to successfully raise a child. I believe it is the job of every parent to find the most effective and efficient methods possible to raise a child, regardless of the time and effort it takes. The tools I offer actually ease the burden of this commitment.

Parents are Heroes

I am continually impressed with parents who take their job seriously. Many parents are eager consumers of my child discipline tools. The positive effects are dramatic and awesome. Many parents can see what isn't there yet. They have the foresight to see a young man or woman who can live under self-control and make his or her way in a complicated world. These parents do not count the cost of raising a child they want to keep. There is no cost too great to successfully raise a child. These parents are my heroes. They do not mourn the lost time or resent the effort it takes to equip a child to live in a complex society. The parent I admire is the one who is child-focused and family-oriented. My hero is a mom or dad who puts a child's needs before his or her own.

My heartfelt desire is that the psychological tools I have presented here will help you to raise a child you will be proud to keep.

Index

30-Second Technique 2, 27, 69–83, 179, 184, 200, 204, 244

A

abusive parents 4, 12
ADHD 72, 82, 167, 173, 263–289
    DSM-IV 265, 266, 268
    learning disabilities 269–278
    medication 289
    sanity savers 280–288
awareness technique 89, 90, 109, 174, 210

B

behavior shaping 60–67, 295
    lawful rules 63, 64
bonding 4, 43, 66, 133
building relationships 43–67
    four principles 45–59
    communication 53–59
    fun 52, 53
    respect and admiration 49–52
    tolerance 46–48

C

childrearing 15, 22, 33, 66, 67, 119, 131, 252, 262, 292
    fathers 131–164
        eight keys 135–153
        love is... 153–158

F

family therapy 29, 30, 44, 82
five basic needs 27–29
Follow-Up Technique 80, 81, 94, 117, 119, 121–124, 130, 169, 171, 176, 182, 284

H

how to get your parents to give you anything you want 183–193
    goals 184–188
    rewards 187, 188

M

Marks Method 27, 40, 195–211, 291, 295
    anger 196, 197
    control 197, 198
    depression 198, 199
    fear 195, 196
    steps 200–211
More Not Less Technique 2, 26, 165–182, 284, 285, 295
    common problems 172, 173
    parental concerns 174–181

N

negative reinforcement 2, 14, 30, 32, 40, 60, 71, 75, 99, 175, 295
nonverbal messages 44, 129

Now or Later Technique 2, 27, 40,
108, 115–130, 145, 174, 184,
200, 208, 209, 244, 284, 291,
295
passive/aggressive 115–118,
126, 128, 130

P

parental authority 1–6, 9–11, 15, 17,
20–23, 25–27, 29–31, 33, 35,
37, 39, 41, 43, 56, 59, 66, 116,
118, 130, 131, 145, 216, 280,
291–297
benefits 6–22
Pillow Talk Technique 26, 85–113,
279, 284, 295
always remember and never forget 56, 86, 88, 91–97, 103, 113,
118, 136, 137, 140, 142, 144,
145, 147, 148, 150, 152, 175,
184, 222, 227, 230, 235, 283
for adults 110–112
picture-drawing version 88,
97–101, 105–109
teaching stories 102, 103
Poisoning the Well Technique 143,
251–262
drugs and alcohol 257, 258
girlfriend/boyfriend 255, 256
music 253, 254, 258, 259
school 256, 257
teenagers 255–262
television/movies 254, 255
positive reinforcement 30, 32, 35,
37, 39, 175

R

reinforcement program 30, 36–39
rewards 3, 20, 21, 22, 31, 32, 35–38,
40–43, 56, 58, 61, 63, 64, 66,
91, 126, 185–188, 190, 206,
237, 246, 280, 295

S

Scarlett O'Hara Technique 239–249
steps 242–245
self-control 1, 5–9, 11, 14, 15,
18–21, 23, 29, 70, 71, 74, 80,
83, 96, 105, 108–110, 125, 126,
128, 129, 131, 149, 159, 181,
202, 206, 208, 209, 213, 214,
244, 248, 249, 279, 280, 285,
291, 296
self-esteem 14–16, 18, 21, 25, 34,
35, 43, 53, 214, 220, 228, 231

T

Tell a Story Technique 213–238
children 219–222
groose stories 221–228,
235–237
piggy stories 228–231
sparrow-eagle stories 231–235
teenagers 217–219

About the Author

Experience cannot be purchased, learned, or taught. Experience is earned by action. Dr. Jerry R. Day has earned his experience through thirty-seven years of clinical practice with children and their parents. In addition to many years of experience, Dr. Day has received invaluable training as a teacher, school counselor, college professor, and private practice clinician. He received his bachelor's and master's degrees from West Texas State University and his doctorate from Oklahoma State University. Dr. Day has enjoyed a thriving clinical practice in Tucson, Arizona, for thirty years. Jerry R. Day, Ed.D., is eminently qualified to teach parents how to raise kids they want to keep.